Praise for *None of Us Were Like This Before*

"An important and revealing book. While ⟨...⟩ by American soldiers when the investigat ⟨...⟩ didn't quit. His personal journey and journ ⟨...⟩ hidden chapter of the U.S. involvement in Iraq and Afghanistan."

  —Deborah Amos, Correspondent for National Public Radio and author of *Eclipse of the Sunnis: Power, Exile, and Upheaval in the Middle East*

"This book contributes enormously to the struggle to abolish torture in our time by showing how immoral and illegal policies taint institutions that, in every society and for every mission, need the trust and respect of the citizenry to be effective in fighting crime and terrorism."

  —Juan E. Mendez, UN Special Rapporteur on Torture and author of *Taking a Stand: The Evolution of Human Rights*

"A deeply personal story of a generation of American soldiers plunged into conflict after September 11. Joshua Phillips tells these brave Americans' stories with compassion and vivid detail. *None of Us Were Like This Before* reminds us why, on some bedrock issues of American values, there should never be any room for compromise."

  —Senator John F. Kerry

"*None of Us Were Like This Before* details the wrenching journey that American soldiers and officers faced trying to report and halt abuse and torture during the 'war on terror.' The stories contained in this book reveal how brave American service members tried to stop torture and abuse—often at the expense of their careers, and their lives. Their sacrifice, and the losses that they incurred, are absorbed by all of us as a nation."

  —Daniel Ellsberg, Former Defense and State Department official who revealed the Pentagon Papers

"A masterwork of narrative nonfiction."

  —Chris Lombardi, *Guernica*

"A model of conscientious reporting on a volatile subject ... His ethical and compassionate approach is an act of citizenship."

  —Barry Lopez, author of *Arctic Dreams* and *Crossing Open Ground*

"This shattering book is a journey into the heart of American darkness. What Joshua Phillips makes shockingly clear is that the misbehavior of some of our best soldiers in Iraq and Afghanistan came about because of a failure of military leadership and because political leaders lacked the courage to admit the word 'torture.' "

  —Richard Rodriguez, author of *Brown: The Last Discovery of America*

"The first and best heartbreaking tale not only of the abuses taking place within our military prisons ... This outstanding book should provoke urgently needed and highly meaningful conversations about who we are as well as what we thought our military and our political leaders should be. This book is an absolute an eye-opener for anyone who thinks war is 'over there' or that the use of torture has no impact on our society."

  —Kristina Brown and Paul Sullivan, Veterans for Common Sense

"A tour de force of investigative journalism, based on interviews with men who had tortured detainees in Iraq, Afghanistan and Guantanamo and with the victims of the same torture, a journey into darkness at noon in America ... a vivid account"

  —Eamonn McCann, *Belfast Telegraph*

"[W]hat makes *None of Us Were Like This Before* such an engaging read, and why there needs to be more attention on the issue of what happens to those who torture when they return, is that the stories are up close and personal ... For those who thought that torture and abuse were isolated to Guantánamo Bay, Afghanistan, and Iraq (not counting the CIA's black sites or extraordinary rendition), think again. It's coming home."
   —Matthew Alexander, *Huffington Post*

"The American public and the world have a right to know the truth about the crimes committed under the command and responsibility of the Bush administration... But we will probably need many more books written by investigative journalists like Joshua Phillips until the truth will be fully recovered, and justice will eventually be done."
   —Manfred Nowak, United Nations Special Rapporteur on Torture (2004–2010)

"Phillips shows that the recourse to blaming a 'few bad apples' should be recognised as a disgraceful, face-saving fiction."
   —David Simpson, *London Review of Books*

"There are many things in this book that are fascinating and generally unknown ... This book really shows how a situation can drive a unit that has no background at all in torture to start down a very dark road."
   —Darius Rejali, author of *Torture and Democracy*, naming *None of Us Were Like This Before* one of the best books on violence for *The Browser*.

"This is an important book ... What a story it is."
   —Faith Middleton, Faith Middleton's Book Show

"This is an important book showing the damage abuse does to the torturers as well as to their victims ... Phillips's message is that we most need the rules banning torture when we most want to break them."
   —Oliver Bullough, *Independent*

"A fascinating yet distressing account ... Far from neglecting the suffering of the victims, Phillips, through meticulous research, also brings home the full horror of the war crimes inflicted upon the citizens of the occupied nations."
   —Craig Hawes, *Gulf News*

"The causes and consequences of systematic abuse and torture are all explored by Joshua Phillips through a careful but searing narrative."
   —Dominic Alexander, *Counterfire*

"One of the long-standing arguments against the use of torture is that it dehumanises the torturers and in turn the country that allows the practice. In the Bush-Cheney era this was considered a naive or old-fashioned view. Joshua Phillips' book shows that America's leaders were wrong."
   —*National*

"I would recommend this very readable book for its eye-opening narrative and its ability to keep you involved until its painful ending, which highlights the fact that wars have victims on both sides."
   —Charikleia Tsatsaroni, *Engaging Peace*

NONE OF US WERE LIKE THIS BEFORE:
AMERICAN SOLDIERS AND TORTURE

Joshua E. S. Phillips

VERSO
London • New York

This paperback edition first published by Verso 2012
First published by Verso 2010
© Joshua E. S. Phillips 2010
Foreword © Jonathan Shay

1 3 5 7 9 10 8 6 4 2

Verso
UK: 6 Meard Street, London W1F 0EG
US: 20 Jay Street, Suite 1010, Brooklyn, NY 11201
www.versobooks.com

Verso is the imprint of New Left Books

ISBN-13: 978-1-84467-884-6

British Library Cataloguing in Publication Data
A catalogue record for this book is available from the British Library

Library of Congress Cataloging-in-Publication Data
A catalog record for this book is available from the Library of Congress

Typeset in Bembo by MJ Gavan, Truro, Cornwall
Printed in the US by Maple Vail

Contents

Foreword

By Jonathan Shay, MD, PhD

The torture and the degradation of captives (we now call them "detainees") strengthens the enemy and can cause trauma capable of disabling our own service members. This excellent book by Joshua Phillips documents this terrible truth.

Rather than being an effective military tool and a means to protect service members from enemy action, abuse (such as torture) and related atrocities are a mug's game, a lose–lose "value proposition" for the nation.

Positive leadership at all levels is essential to *prevent* abusive violence. Such leadership means vigilantly preventing abuse and atrocities, and pursuing prompt, vigorous, and truthful followup of any abuse reports coming up the chain of command. This is the biggest forgotten lesson of the Vietnam War, one which slipped our minds during Operation Enduring Freedom and Operation Iraqi Freedom (OEF-OIF). As a direct consequence, we suffered the greatest strategic defeat in our history—Abu Ghraib—a defeat that was entirely self-inflicted.[1]

The late Colonel Carl Bernard was a retired Army infantry officer, who fought in both Korea as an infantry lieutenant in Task Force Smith and also in Vietnam. During part of his time in Vietnam, he was a province senior advisor in the Mekong Delta. On May 10, 2001, he wrote this to me in an email:

> How little Americans knew about the "Peoples' War" that … the rest of us were in. Simply stated, we did not know how to fight such a conflict at its beginning, and we learned very little during its course, in significant part because of the constant transfer of personnel. I was damned unkind … in restricting the activities of the SEAL team in Vinh Binh [Barnard's province] … As I told them in some dudgeon, their activities were sustaining the Viet Cong's recruiting effort even better than the Air Force's activities.[2]

When the enemy can provoke us to respond atrociously, indiscriminately, or massively against the civilian population, we fail. Turning to torture means losing local cooperation and recruits fresh enemies who, in turn, target our own service members.

In the end, *every atrocity potentially disables the service member who commits it*. When I say this, I do not refer to the distant future when the soldier in question may well be a haunted, guilt-ridden veteran. My point to military forces today is that this service member can be traumatized and lost *today*. Sober and responsible troop leaders and trainers are concerned about the prevention of psychological and moral injury as a *readiness issue*.[3] These military leaders cannot be dismissively branded as "politically correct." An injured service member is lost to the force, whether the injury is physical or psychological.

I intentionally do not address here what most people would call the moral argument: the harm to innocents. As important as this is, there are other elements of torture's harm to those inflicting it that are often overlooked, but those have already been carefully assembled within this book. Abusive (non-military) violence in war is a potent source of domestic violence, post-combat criminal behavior, and disabling psychological injuries such as post-traumatic stress disorder (PTSD).[4] Abusive violence contributes to long-term damage to veterans, their families, and their communities.

A perennial weed in the folk culture, sprouting sometimes even at high levels of military command and civilian leadership, is the idea that we need to respond to our enemies with tactics that are at least equally, if not more, horrific than the ones they have used against us. One way I have heard this folk belief expressed is: "If we kill their parents and children, the enemy will get the message, and won't fuck with us." With interrogation, the equivalent folk belief is: If you are not getting what you believe your detainees have in the way of "actionable intelligence," it's because you have not applied enough violent coercive "pressure." Neither high military rank nor civilian authority confers immunity to this destructive illusion.

The overwhelming majority of people who volunteer for our armed forces are not psychopaths; they are good people who would be damaged were they to live with the knowledge that they had applied torture or committed murder. The distinction between lawful combatant (who may be legally and morally attacked) and protected person is the bright line between soldier and murderer. You do not "support our servicemen" by mocking the Law of Land Warfare[5] and calling it a joke. Francis Lieber's "Instructions for the Armies of the United States" (1863) expressed what I believe to be the continuing consensus of serious military professionals: "Men who take up arms against one another in public war do not cease on this account to be moral beings, responsible to one another and to God."[6] Even tough-guy gunslingers in the ground forces, and all those whose ideals include "supporting our troops," have good reason, based on national self-interest, to respect and support the "rules of war." Those who claim "there are no rules" fail to support the troops patriotically. Furthermore, those who hawkishly advocate torture (sometimes called "harsh interrogation techniques" or "coercive interrogation") should think again about the adverse impact of participation in torture on our military forces. The toxic legacy of torture during the "war on terror" is starkly articulated in this book.

The "purity of arms"—all arms and all Military Occupation Special-ties (MOS) and all actual tasks service members are assigned to do, regardless of their MOS—*is something we do for ourselves to win fights and remain whole.*

Jonathan Shay is a retired VA psychiatrist and is the author of Achilles in Vietnam: Combat Trauma and the Undoing of Character *and of* Odys-seus in America: Combat Trauma and the Trials of Homecoming, *which includes a joint foreword by US Senators John McCain and Max Cleland. Shay speaks frequently at the invitation of US and allied forces and has held a number of consultative and teaching posts, such as the Commandant of the Marine Corps Trust Study (1999–2000), Chair of Ethics, Leadership and Personnel Policy in the Office of the US Army Deputy Chief of Staff for Personnel (2004–2005), and the 2009 Omar Bradley Chair of Strategic Leadership at the US Army War College (spring semester 2010). He describes himself as "a missionary from the veterans I served: They don't want other young kids wrecked the way they were wrecked. So listen up!" He has been a MacArthur Fellow, beginning January 2008.*

Introduction

TWO STARK SENTENCES wedged in the center of a military document curtly summarized the demise of a twenty-four-year-old soldier: "SGT Gray was found dead in his barracks room at 1921 hrs on 29 August 2004. Subsequent investigation by CID (Exhibit 5) found that his death was accidental." An autopsy report provided a few more details about the deceased: "He spoke at length of many positive experiences in Iraq, such as rebuilding schools and eating with Iraqis. However, he also made reference to events that bothered him and that he could not speak … about."

Sergeant Adam Gray rarely spoke of those "events that bothered him." He shared these experiences with loved ones during one tearful evening, telling of one incident that involved an accidental shooting that claimed two Iraqi lives. But there were other events that distressed him and other soldiers from his unit as well. After military sweeps, they detained Iraqis in a makeshift jail in Iraq and occasionally roughed them up. Sometimes the roughing up took an extreme turn. Friends and family noticed that Adam seemed "troubled" by those events and witnessed his struggle against anger, substance abuse, and depression after his tour in Iraq. Military documents show that he even professed to have attempted suicide at his Army barracks room in Alaska. The documents also reveal that "Gray said that [his] problems were due to the way he felt about what happened during his deployment." But there is no indication that the military genuinely tried to understand the source of those problems from his tour in Iraq, namely what happened during his deployment.

Three weeks after that attempted suicide, Sergeant Adam Gray was found dead in the same room. The circumstances leading up to his death led Adam's friends and family to question whether it was accurately summarized as "accidental." Some also puzzled over how ordinary soldiers like Adam Gray—a tanker, not an interrogator—became involved in detainee abuse and torture.

Understanding how and why US forces have engaged in detainee abuse and torture is a difficult and uncomfortable inquiry. It forces us to examine who we are as a nation and what has compelled us to choose such a path. This issue does not involve only the soldiers who abused and tortured detainees, but also the government, military, and intelligence officials whose policies enabled it and sometimes ordered it, the doctors and psychologists who oversaw it, and the agencies that failed to investigate the abuses, among others. Among those "others" is us, the American public. Even though Americans have consistently opposed torture in recent years, as evidenced by polling data, the myths surrounding torture (e.g., its effectiveness for questioning terrorist suspects) have influenced its acceptance and use.[1]

This book contains several expository narratives to illustrate the causes and costs of US torture and detainee abuse during the war on terror. The central story is about members of an Army unit that turned to torture, and the toll it took on them all. That is the story of Sergeant Adam Gray and some of his fellow soldiers from Battalion 1-68. One story cannot wholly explain the disparate factors that led US forces to engage in detainee abuse and torture, nor can it fully address the total costs of that experience. But it does help illuminate many critical issues that have been overlooked in the discourse about US torture—some of which involve enormous human tragedies.

Overall, the Central Intelligence Agency has held far fewer detainees than the military; by most estimates, there have been roughly a hundred detainees held in CIA "black sites," compared with the tens of thousands of detainees that the US military has held in Iraq, Afghanistan, and Guantanamo Bay.[2] This book does not cover CIA operations such as "extraordinary renditions" or the black sites, in which US personnel (aided by allies) have abducted and sent terrorist suspects to secret foreign prisons. While investigative reporting in this area is critically important, those CIA programs are an enormous subject that deserves the attention of another book. Moreover, the CIA's programs and the agency's involvement in torture during the war on terror have been different than, and separate from, the experience of US military forces (the former being more directly managed by Bush administration officials, as evidenced by recently released legal memos and documents). However, military and intelligence forces have shared some similar associations with torture, and operations by CIA and military personnel sometimes overlapped on the battlefield.

As for torture carried out by US soldiers, President Bush and his supporters have narrowly referenced the Abu Ghraib detainee "abuse" scandal (never called torture), claiming it was an isolated incident and attributing it to the actions of "a few bad apples." By their account, these perpetrators were swiftly investigated and punished, and the problem of detainee abuse was thus eliminated. But this position was dishonest. Even if we were to accept this account, it doesn't explain what enabled those "few bad apples" to engage in torture.[3]

The other problem with this analysis is that it myopically focuses our attention on one high-profile case: Abu Ghraib. To be sure, the torture and abuse at Abu Ghraib was notorious and deserved much scrutiny. Yet it represented just one example. Reports by journalists and human rights organizations have shown that US detainee abuse and torture spread far beyond that single prison during the war on terror. This is consistent with the military's data. In 2006, the Department of Defense announced that it had opened investigations into 842 allegations of detainee abuse, 600 of which were criminal inquiries.[4] According to military investigators, there are possibly hundreds, if not thousands, of detainee abuse cases "that nobody is aware of … that have never seen the light of day." As for accountability, in the case of Abu Ghraib, eleven soldiers were convicted (nine of whom were sentenced to prison), while five officers received administrative punishment.[5]

The question "How did US forces turn to torture?" may even be too broad. To properly answer the question, one has to break it down further. That means asking: Why did US forces and officials think torture would be effective? Why did they think it would be permissible and necessary? How did they turn to certain techniques? Where did their ideas about the effectiveness of torture come from, and why were they so pervasive? And what other factors led US forces to engage in abuse and torture?

Recent films and books about US torture have referenced some social and psychological explanations to make sense of cruel behavior.[6] Yale University psychologist Stanley Milgram provided one paradigm in what was later termed "the Milgram experiment." In 1961, Milgram set up a "learning" scenario wherein an "experimenter" instructed participants to deliver a series of electric shocks of increasing voltage to a concealed but audible victim, even as the victim's screams grew in volume. Unbeknownst to the participants, there weren't any actual electric shocks and the screaming victims were merely pretending. Nonetheless, Milgram's experiment revealed how normal participants can be lured by an authority figure into carrying out sadistic acts.

Ten years later, in 1971, Stanford University professor Dr. Philip Zimbardo conducted another kind of social-psychological experiment. Zimbardo hired ordinary students to play the roles of guards and prisoners in a mock prison scenario. As in Milgram's experiment, Zimbardo set out to see if simple situations could move normal actors to do things they would not otherwise do. Within a week the guards brutally abused their captives, and Zimbardo had to abruptly call off the experiment. Zimbardo's "Stanford prison experiment" is often referenced to show how situations can move normal people to become depraved and abusive.

Both experiments are revealing, but neither can fully explain how and why US forces abused and tortured their prisoners. Milgram and Zimbardo set up specific conditions—volunteers, participants, instructors, equipment, and oversight—in order to generate behavior they could analyze for one case of violence within each of their lab experiments. The narrow scope of the Milgram and Zimbardo experiments makes it difficult to extrapolate from them to real-world examples of violence.[7] In other words, one cannot take the carefully constructed lab conditions as a given, and so it is crucial to understand the particular circumstances—such as pressures, orders, resources, and oversight—that led to US prisoner abuse during the war on terror.

Some have speculated that rage over the September 11 attacks could have fueled abuses. Gary Berntsen, a CIA agent who fought al Qaeda troops in Afghanistan in late 2001, voiced a feeling that seemed to be shared by many Americans after the attacks on the Pentagon and World Trade Center. "One word kept pounding in my head," Berntsen said. "Revenge."[8] Festering anger over September 11 could have contributed to a desire for violent retribution, leading to torture and abuse. But most soldiers who handled detainees served with honor and distinction, and never tortured. Moreover, troops who did engage in torture have cited many reasons and explanations beyond lingering anger over the September 11 attacks. For instance, some soldiers have said that their rage and frustration about combating Iraqi insurgent groups contributed to prisoner abuse. Others provide far more mundane reasons, including boredom.

Many critics (and apologists) of US torture have pointed to inexperienced interrogators and violent conditions to explain how abuse took root. But this doesn't explain why other inexperienced interrogators who worked in violent areas in Iraq, Afghanistan, and Guantanamo didn't abuse or torture detainees. There are also cases in which experienced interrogators have worked in far less dangerous environments and have turned to torture (e.g., Guantanamo).

A common explanation for the spread of detainee abuse during the US war on terror runs as follows: White House and Pentagon officials drafted memos sanctioning coercive techniques for interrogation in Guantanamo; many of these methods were used, turned abusive, and sometimes led to torture. Officials from Guantanamo, most notably Major General Geoffrey D. Miller, were transferred to Iraq and "Gitmoized" the military facilities there, namely Abu Ghraib.[9] This combination of events allowed the horrors of Abu Ghraib to take hold and spill out elsewhere in Iraq.

But this fails to explain how and why troops turned to torture in Afghanistan and elsewhere prior to this string of events.

As this book will make clear, some US forces tortured and abused detainees even before government officials drafted and disseminated memos permitting coercive interrogation and certain "harsh" techniques. (There were, however, early cases of US abuse and torture after the Bush administration lessened certain provisions of the Geneva Conventions by refusing to classify detainees as prisoners of war.) This poses a predicament for those whose theories of US torture stem from the so-called "torture memos," along with the personnel who drafted and dispatched them. Solely ascribing the rise of torture to the Bush administration memos that sanctioned harsh techniques is inadequate.

In the course of my reporting, I tried to find a straightforward interpretation for the development of US torture during the war on terror. But I failed to find a one-size-fits-all explanation for the myriad cases in Afghanistan, Iraq, and Guantanamo. As one human rights lawyer told me, "There isn't a grand theory of US torture that encapsulates and explains all the different abuses that have taken place in the war on terror." The more I learned about cases of detainee abuse, the more I have found myself agreeing with that sentiment.

There are several explanatory narratives for US prisoner abuse. Yet they share many common threads—some are woven together, some hang as loose strands. Collectively, these threads offer an account of US torture and abuse, and it is possible to discern in them patterns that have been replicated throughout the war on terror.

American soldiers, interrogators, generals, psychologists, senior Bush administration officials, and lawmakers shared many of the very same compulsions and beliefs that led US forces to assume that torture was effective, permissible, and necessary. There has likewise been a pattern in the costs incurred through the abuse of prisoners in Iraq, Afghanistan, and Guantanamo. The toxic dividends of torture are shared by victims and victimizers, and have shaped the legacy of US torture during the war on terror.

Chapter 1:
Searching for Answers

THE HORIZON UNFURLED along the westward road as distant figures slowly came into view.

Neglected orchards dotted the landscape. Ochre-colored mountains sliced across the smooth expanse. Dust devils flared across the horizon, tightened into long, thin funnels, whipped across the plains, and dissipated into light wisps of sand. Oil refineries chugged away, clouding the air with thick fumes. As the road curved and sloped uphill, a large prison complex, encircled by glistening coils of concertina wire, punctured the sky and interrupted the placid scenery that surrounded it.

An American soldier scanned the scenery.

"It reminds me of Iraq," said Adam Gray. He was now back home in Tehachapi, California. His stepfather, Roy Chavez, was driving him home while Adam sat beside him, gazing at the familiar landscape and quietly reminiscing.

After serving a year-long tour in Iraq, Adam went on leave to visit Roy and his mother, Cindy Chavez.

"It really shocked me when I picked him up at the airport. He wasn't in his uniform; he just had his regular clothes," said Roy. That he had changed clothes might have seemed like a small detail, but it surprised Roy, given how much pride Adam took in his military service. "I don't know if he was just sick and tired of it and [thought] 'I'm on leave, I don't want to deal with this anymore. I just want to have a good time, see my mom, just be a regular normal person.' "

Regaining that normalcy wasn't easy for Adam. The jagged bluffs that encircled his hometown area were remarkably similar to the scenery he had seen in the Middle East, and they plunged him back into a time and place that had irretrievably affected him.

Other members of Adam's Army unit also had great difficulty making the transition back to the US. The camaraderie that bound them was no longer intact; each went his separate way after their unit returned. They were no longer linked by a common purpose; their mission was over. "Accomplished," said some.

Yet it was unresolved for Adam and others in his unit, Battalion 1-68. They still carried unsettling memories and tried to slowly digest them as they readjusted to their old lives back in the States.

I first learned about Adam Gray in 2006, when I met some soldiers who had served with him. Jonathan Millantz, an Army medic who was assigned to Battalion 1-68, first told me about the life and death of Adam. Millantz sensed that Adam was haunted by what he had seen and done in Iraq. At first, Millantz would only talk cryptically about those events. But he often stressed that he empathized with his former war buddy and shared many of the traumas that plagued him during his own return to civilian life.

Other soldiers who served with Adam puzzled over what happened to him and mentioned that his mother was also struggling to make sense of his experience. And so, in mid-2006 I called Cindy Chavez in Tehachapi. Her husband, Roy, answered the phone. He welcomed my call, but was firm with me.

"I'm going to give the phone to Cindy, my wife," he said. "But I want you to promise me that you're going to be very careful with her, because she has already been through a lot."

I promised, and he passed the phone to Cindy. We talked extensively and traded phone calls for several months. After nearly a year of conversation, Cindy agreed to meet and discuss her story in person. In August 2007, I traveled from San Francisco to see her and Roy at their family home. My colleague Michael Montgomery, a producer with American Radio Works, came along to interview them.

Part of our drive followed the very same westward route that Roy and Adam took from Bakersfield to Tehachapi. As we scaled the Tehachapi Mountains—a chalky, rugged range that links Bakersfield to Mojave—I tried to imagine Adam's earlier homecoming. During our visit, dense wildfire smoke filled the valley with choking fumes. Soot coated the sunset with a rusty orange haze, turning the evening sky into a dramatic, apocalyptic backdrop. Such striking imagery, like the area's harsh and arid landscape, truly seemed evocative of Iraq's scenery. After five hours of driving, Michael and I pulled up to Roy and Cindy's house, where assorted wind chimes fluttered in the breeze. A Green Bay Packers flag, set beneath an American flag, waved above their driveway—Adam and his mother had originally hailed from Wisconsin. Cindy and Roy greeted us warmly and welcomed us into a cavernous living room with a deep-purple carpet, assorted antiques, and a big-screen TV tucked into the corner.

A pile of photos lay on top of a coffee table, chronicling Adam's life in Iraq and back home. Cindy had made two-by-four-inch laminated prints of Adam in his sergeant's uniform, set against the red and white stripes of an American flag background. It captured Adam's smooth, oval face, his buzz haircut, and his gentle features. The bottom caption read:

> In Loving Memory Of
> Adam James Gray
> "The Bomber"
> March 20, 1980–August 29, 2004
> Our Hero

She handed us two pictures to take home with us: "Just so you have a face to go with the name."

Cindy recalled how Adam had wanted to serve in the military ever since he was three years old. Growing up in Wisconsin, he and his family lived around the corner from a Navy recruiting station. Adam would often return home with military souvenirs, such as caps and pens. His mother saw him as a rollicking, spirited child with boundless energy. Friends and family nicknamed him "The Bomber." The nickname stuck. And Adam's ambition to join the military continued into his teenage years.

Even though Cindy saw a stream of damaged veterans return from Vietnam during the 1970s, she felt she could never discourage her son from pursuing his dreams. Adam jeopardized that future at eighteen when he and local high school friends got arrested for burglary. Cindy downplayed the incident, and said it was quickly settled, but it did leave a mark on his record. The arrest meant he could not enlist in the Navy.

Adam was devastated. But his mother was determined to help him, and together they pushed on looking for other ways Adam could join the military. In the end, Adam was finally able to join the Army.

Cindy saw her son and his friends from his platoon after they finished basic training. They spoke respectfully to others and wore neatly pressed uniforms. Cindy didn't even recognize her son after he had finished boot camp.

Who is this kid? she thought.

"Before he went to boot camp, he was a bit of a thug," said Roy. After his training "He grew … he grew into a man." Adam was fit, pressed, and polite. "The Bomber" had finally become an enlisted soldier.

Adam was always drawn to tanks and planes, and eagerly pursued further training for an armored cavalry unit. Shortly after basic training he was dispatched to Fort Carson, Colorado, home of the "Iron Brigade." There he learned how to operate M1 Abrams tanks and joined Battalion 1-68, a tank unit with the 4th Infantry Division, 3rd Brigade Combat Team.

Members of Battalion 1-68 remembered Adam enjoying his time in Fort Carson and making close friends on the base. Most of them noticed that he craved to learn as much as possible about tank warfare and seemed excited about joining a four-person tanking crew with the battalion. Adam had finally achieved what he had longed for since he was a young boy. But he was a warrior without a war.

Adam looked forward to taking some time off after he completed his training at Fort Carson. In September 2001, he went on leave and joined his family at Lake Elizabeth, California, near Los Angeles. He spent his evenings chatting with his mother and friends, soaking in a hot tub, and partying into the night.

At six in the morning on September 11, Roy called upstairs to Cindy.

"I just heard something about the Twin Towers or something," he said. "Something is going on."

She ran downstairs and switched on the television. It wasn't clear what she was watching. Was it a movie? she wondered. Cindy focused her eyes on the screen and concentrated on what the TV announcers were saying. It soon became clear to her that it wasn't fiction. She ran to fetch her son.

"Adam, get up! Something's happening."

By the time he woke up and walked over to the television, the second plane had hit the South Tower. The three of them stared at the screen and absorbed what was unfolding across the country.

"Mom, it's fucking al Qaeda!" said Adam.

"I don't know who you're talking about."

"It's bin Laden."

She still didn't know what he was referring to, nor did she know what to expect. But Adam knew it meant war. He would now finally be able to apply his skills in a meaningful mission.

"I need to get on a plane. I need to get back there," he said, referring to Fort Carson. "We're going to deploy, I know it."

Gray reported to Fort Carson soon after, and there was a nervous, excitable energy on the base. Were they going to Afghanistan? Would they fight the Taliban? Were they going to help take out bin Laden and the al Qaeda camps? No one had answers, and Adam and his unit played hurry up and wait.

It finally came out that they would not be deployed to Afghanistan. At first, he and his fellow soldiers felt deflated. Everyone was hungry for payback, and it was tough to watch other soldiers march into action. But the call finally came on January 20, 2003: as part of the 4th Infantry Division, Adam and Battalion 1-68 received orders to deploy to the Middle East.[1]

President George W. Bush, British Prime Minister Tony Blair, and their allies alleged that Iraq had developed and secretly hidden weapons of mass destruction (WMDs)—nuclear, biological, chemical weapons—designed to inflict mass damage and casualties. They demanded that Saddam Hussein come clean by revealing and destroying Iraq's WMDs. But none appeared.

Bush pressed on during his 2003 State of the Union address, declaring that the country could not wait. The president insisted that Saddam was disregarding the UN by concealing WMDs from the prying eyes of their weapons inspectors, and that an ominous "mushroom cloud" of devastation loomed if these weapons were left unchecked.[2] Bush and Blair argued that Saddam was as dangerous as he was intractable, and that the threat from his regime was imminent.

On March 20, Gray celebrated his twenty-third birthday. Just one day earlier in 2003, American forces and their allies pushed through the Iraqi border in the first days of their military campaign. Adam and Battalion 1-68 were on the front lines of battle in Iraq. He was at last a soldier in action.

★   ★   ★

After serving a year-long tour in Iraq Adam returned home to visit his family and friends in Tehachapi during March 2004. Cindy clearly remembered the day Adam pulled up to their house in Tehachapi after Roy picked him up from the airport. Adam seemed to have the same weathered disposition as her nephew, who also served in the Iraq war, and Cindy recalled having the same sense about his return.

He was glad to be home; he was safe.

Friends and family warmly welcomed Adam home. But they found it was sometimes hard to engage him in conversation. Adam's mind seemed to be elsewhere. "He would get this glazed look over him and we'd be in the discussion and his eyes would literally get glassy and he would just disconnect," remembered Cindy. Adam was in Tehachapi, but he seemed to be locked onto memories of Iraq. "And you know he was back there because there was something maybe in the background —maybe a song or the TV or something—and he would just stare straight ahead."

You could almost hear the bombs and the noise, thought Cindy.

It seemed something had been growing inside him since he got back from Iraq. "This stuff was building up," Cindy said. "He had to go do something before it exploded." She phoned local veteran groups and asked their advice about how best to approach her son. She spoke to Vietnam vets and those who fought in Desert Storm (the first US war with Iraq in 1991).

"Don't push him," they would tell her. "He'll talk about it if he wants to. Just don't push him, because you don't want to trigger anything … Don't go up behind him without him knowing. Always speak before you go up behind him. Don't shock him, because you may not come out of it. He doesn't mean anything by it; it's just a reaction."

Cindy took their advice. She would tell Adam she was going out to pick up milk or run errands and wouldn't come back for five hours in order to give him some space. She and Roy had learned that from noon to four o'clock in the afternoon "you didn't talk with him … you just didn't." Cindy said he would "just get weird. I don't know if he had to just reflect with himself or what, but he could get angry."

"When he came home he was a different boy," Roy said. "He was aggressive. His mood swings were horrible."

Roy saw how his stepson seemed to be deeply affected by his time in Iraq, yet trying to disengage from it while he was on leave. He saw that Adam often remained reticent, latched onto solitude, and mostly sat in his room for hours. At times, Roy saw Adam's anxiety boiling over.

"You could sometimes hear him screaming in his sleep and not being able to talk about anything," said Roy.

"He would have his dark moments," Cindy remembered. "He'd play his guitar, and he would get into music and just disconnect, but not really disconnect because he always had that kind of glazed look on his face."

Sometimes he would tell his mother, "I shouldn't be here."

"Why shouldn't you be here?" she would ask. If not here, then where? she wondered.

"I should be back there with my guys."

In a way, she wasn't surprised by his state of mind. She had grown up during the 1970s and remembered the empty stares and tensed bodies of returning Vietnam veterans. But it was unsettling to see her son and other returning Iraq war veterans exhibit the same behavior.

"Just looking at him—it was very weird, very surreal," she said. "He was way different, that's for sure ..."

I gently pressed Cindy to further describe how her son had changed. She paused as her mind recreated that visit three years ago.

"He looked troubled. I think that's the only word I could say. Troubled for what he saw, troubled for maybe what he had to do," she said.

Why was he troubled? I asked.

"That I don't know, Josh. That's what I want you to find out."

Adam seldom discussed events in Iraq with anyone. At one point, he promised to open up to his family.

"One day I'll tell you guys," he said.

After a long night of drinking, he finally did. He told his mother about some of his experiences, including how his unit went on patrols in Iraq's volatile Sunni triangle. They surveyed for improvised explosive devices (known as IEDs) and those who planted them, and occasionally took machine gunfire. One evening, Adam's tank was on patrol and fired on a small group of insurgent suspects, killing two of the three Iraqis they targeted. They later noticed the Iraqis weren't insurgents after all, but a small family that included a little girl.

"Ma, we couldn't see," he told his mother, choking back tears. "It was just the night vision, and all it does is give you a shadow."

Maybe, she figured, it distressed him so deeply because he had such a strong affinity for the Iraqi children he saw. But he was upset about other experiences as well. Adam told his mother how he and fellow soldiers kept order in a small jail in Balad, Iraq, by instructing their prisoners not to speak to one another. And he described what they would do to detainees who disobeyed them.

"Inevitably one will start speaking," Adam explained to Cindy. "So then we tie their hands up and then tie them to the highest rung on the [jail] bars. And then they'd have to hang there for a couple of days and they're not allowed to sleep, drink, eat."

Adam told her how they kept detainees up all night long by blasting loud music next to their ears, and how troops tried to frighten detainees when questioning them. For example, Adam described how he brought hooded detainees into a room, placed them in chairs, and removed their blindfolds. It took a while for the detainees' vision to clear, and when they were able to focus they would see that the walls and floor were splashed with blood.

Adam assured his mother that "it wasn't any human blood—it was chicken blood. But they didn't know that, because they were blind-folded. And then we'd take the blindfold off and they'd start screaming."

They screamed uncontrollably, he told her. Other detainees would hear their friends shrieking in horror. "And they'd tell us anything because they were so sleep-deprived and hungry and everything else," he explained to his mother. "That's when [we] started getting them to spill their guts."

During that night of heavy drinking, Adam revealed why they felt compelled to abuse their detainees, and he detailed the techniques they used. Cindy patiently listened to her son's justifications for mistreating Iraq detainees, and yet she felt that Adam was still troubled by what he had done. She told him to stop describing the torture they used—she couldn't bear to hear any more. It sounded "so incredibly inhumane."

"I'd rather be shot in the head than have to torture somebody like that," she said. Yes, she understood it was war. And yes, they faced life-and-death decisions. But as a mother, she still felt sympathy for the Iraqi prisoners.

"They're people, they're human beings," she said. "It doesn't make any difference who you are, just because they live in a different environ-ment. Those mothers still love their children."

The evening of beer and confessions wore down, and mother and son finished discussing disturbing wartime memories. After that evening, Cindy partly understood what troubled her son. But she didn't want that evening to be his lasting memory of being back home. With limited time to cheer up her son during his short leave in Tehachapi, she offered to take him to Las Vegas. He had always wanted to go there.

"No, mom, I don't think I could handle the noise."

But she pressed on, and threw parties for Adam. In fact, she crammed all the year's holidays into his March visit. They went to a local nursery to buy a tree for Christmas, festooned their house with festive lights, and baked holiday cookies. Then they celebrated New Year's Eve and quickly slipped in Valentine's Day. And finally, they commemorated his twenty-fourth birthday on March 20.

Adam left Tehachapi shortly thereafter. During his time off he was able to decompress, unload some of his memories, and be cheered by loved ones. Cindy captured some of the happier moments in photographs. She shuffled through a pile of pictures before her on the coffee table, and softly teared up.

"The very last picture that I got of him was at that birthday party," she said. "He never came home."

After his month-long leave in Tehachapi, Adam headed to Alaska to undergo training for armored combat vehicles known as Strykers. According to Adam, the training was delayed because of a hold-up with the Strykers' production. He quickly found himself stuck in Fairbanks with little activity, few friends, and no battle comrades. He told his mother that he felt lonely and frustrated by the lack of action, and had trouble relating to the soldiers at Fort Wainwright.

"Ma, there's not one of these sons of bitches up here that has ever been out of the country," he told her. "They've never been to Iraq. They've never been to anywhere. Alaska is the farthest away that they've ever been from their homes."

The soldiers at Fort Wainwright sensed his resentment and his lingering feelings about Iraq.

Get over it, they told him. And that only incensed him further.

Some soldiers taunted him about his moodiness and bitterness. Adam seethed with anger, and he finally snapped. He pinned down a soldier who had goaded him and held a knife to his throat.

"If you were over there, you'd be dead right now," Adam told him.

Soon Adam was called before a board of officers and received a dressing-down. One of them called him a "waste of flesh," Cindy recalled, and he could only stand at attention and absorb their reprimands.

"I think at that point it crushed Adam's spirit because he took those men as gods," Cindy said. He told her he would rather be in Iraq full-time than be in Fairbanks. At least he had a purpose there.

He even considered quitting the service and returning home.

"Adam, when you come back here, then what are you going to do?" his mother asked him. "What's your plan of attack? I mean, you could be a prison guard, you could be a police officer."

"Nothing like that," he said

There were limited options for him in Tehachapi, and few jobs remotely close to what he had hoped to do in the military. "You're going to be very unhappy," Cindy warned him.

She reminded him that he always wanted to be in the military, and even wanted to be a tanker since he was a small boy. "That's what you wanted to do your whole life."

He paused and reflected on what she said.

Adam seemed resigned to his situation. In the end, he decided to stay put in Alaska and bide his time until he was called up for battle again.

Cindy and Adam talked during the evening of August 29, 2004, when he was in his barracks in Fairbanks. He seemed upbeat and talked about preparing for a getaway with an Army friend during his off days. Cindy could rest that evening without worrying about his mood or career problems. He seemed to be working through his issues.

The following morning, at around eight, she got a call from her ex-husband, Adam's father, Jeff Gray. He lived in Wisconsin, where they were originally from. Adam's parents were separated by thousands of miles but remained friends and kept in touch about their son's welfare.

"Cindy, why would there be a soldier coming here?" Jeff asked Cindy.

"Oh, for Christ's sake," she said. She assumed that Adam and his friends went off drinking the night before and got into trouble. "He's probably coming to find out who wants to bail the kid out."

They laughed about it, knowing their son's pugnacious spirit. "Okay, I don't have this kind of money," she told Jeff, fearing how much bail they'd have to pay to spring Adam from a night in jail. "Maybe you could do it. And you're closer to him; you could fly up there."

In the end, she relented and agreed to come up with the cash. Jeff promised to call her back with an update after he met the officers at his door.

Cindy waited a long time for the phone to ring. When it finally did, she snatched up the receiver.

"Okay, how much do I owe you?"

Her offer was met with a halting silence. And then he told her.

"Adam's dead."

"What?"

Jeff repeated the words to her.

"Oh, bullshit. That's not even funny. I just talked to him last night."

But Jeff wasn't kidding, and Cindy froze in stunned disbelief. No, they've got the wrong kid, she told herself. After all, Adam seemed to be in high spirits the night before. He was just heading off to bed so that he and his friend could get up early for their trip.

That might have been the case, said Jeff, but the officers who had just visited him said they were sending someone from Edwards Air Force Base to Cindy and Roy's house in Tehachapi to relay the news about their son.

Cindy waited by the door and held her breath as she peered through the window and watched the cars drift by. One finally pulled into her driveway. Two uniformed officers got out and walked towards the house.

"Then I knew it wasn't a lie," she said.

I visited Cindy in August 2007 just a few days before the anniversary of her son's death. It had been three years since officers walked to her door. Her memories were still fresh, her emotions still raw.

She remembered that a chaplain accompanied the military entourage, and how they greeted her. They could tell she was distraught and sensed she had already learned the news about her son.

"Well, by now, I'm sure you heard …" they began. "We're very sorry."

Cindy understood they had a difficult job, but she felt their delivery was cold and rehearsed.

"Then they get up and leave," she recalled. "You're in absolute, absolute devastation and shock. You don't really know what they just said."

Shortly thereafter, a casualty advisor showed up with a thick stack of documents that Cindy had to fill out. It took until late in the evening. "And you don't sleep because you're just entering into the worst nightmare of your life," she said.

Gradually, she summoned the strength to ask how to deal with her son's remains and assemble a memorial for him. They held a service in

Wisconsin, and later a second one in California. A handful of servicemen came by, some from Adam's unit, and paid their respects. Much of that period remains a blur to Cindy.

Adam's fellow unit members were also stunned by the news of his death. They remembered his high energy and his enthusiasm for the Army, and would never expect that his life would end so tragically back in the States. There was disbelief, followed by questions about what had happened. Roy sought out answers at Adam's funeral to clarify what exactly had occurred at Fort Wainwright. Until that time, they only had murky details about Adam's death.

"We were under the impression it was a self-inflicted gunshot [or] accidental death," said Roy. "I had to be prepared to find out as much as I could before [Cindy] did."

Roy approached Richard Boone, one of Adam's friends from Fort Wainwright. Boone, too, was a sergeant, and a loyal soldier. He wanted to be faithful to his friend's family by helping answer their questions, but there was an open investigation into Adam's death, so Boone told Roy that he couldn't discuss what went on in Alaska. Roy pressed on.

"I'm not here to crucify anyone," he told Boone. "See that lady?" said Roy, pointing to Cindy. "I gotta get through this with her. I need to be prepared. I just need to know what happened."

It turned out that Cindy and Roy had mistakenly believed that Adam had shot himself. It was difficult for Boone to describe what had happened: Adam was found in bed with a plastic bag twisted over his head, and beside him sat a can of Dust-Off (compressed gas used for cleaning electronics).

Roy took a deep breath. Oh crap. We're in for a long haul, he said to himself. He saw Adam's father, grandmother, and friends, and he felt he couldn't—and shouldn't—divulge what he learned, fearing it would only traumatize them further.

"I wish I didn't know," said Roy. "It was like the devil dropped something on me. I knew his mom. She was going to want to know who was responsible and why. To watch her ask questions when I could have answered them …" Roy's eyes watered and his voice trailed off as he remembered that time.

The Iraq war exacted a heavy toll on its veterans. Many turned to substance abuse, and suicides gradually mounted.[3] The numbers of soldiers diagnosed with post-traumatic stress disorder (PTSD) steadily climbed.[4]

And, as with Vietnam veterans, soldiers who return with PTSD can also transfer some of their distress onto their families.[5] Cindy and Roy Chavez were no different.

"We're human beings, and we find ways to numb ourselves," said Roy. He later told me how he and Cindy tried to blunt their pain with alcohol after Adam died. But Cindy's intake turned toxic. According to Roy, she landed in the hospital for twenty-seven days because of "a broken heart and alcohol."

"It was a scary time. A scary time," said Roy. "You sit there and go, 'Oh the war's going to take another person—my wife. And I'm going to be all alone.' "

Cindy ultimately recovered from her stay in the hospital, and her sharp decline from depression and alcohol became a stiff wake-up call for her and Roy. Afterwards, they agreed to swear off drinking from that point on. Cindy even pursued grief counseling in Tehachapi and felt it helped her better cope with the extreme pain she felt. But she couldn't put aside her questions about the circumstances of her son's death.

"It became her quest to find out," said Roy.

"You just want to know why is your child dead," Cindy said. "I know there's more to this story, I just don't know how to get it. And I'm not going to give up until I find out. I'm afraid as the years go by it will all disappear."

One of Adam's Army buddies from Iraq, Tony Sandoval, was also searching for answers to his friend's death. He faithfully called Cindy, and the friendship he had shared with Adam soon extended to his mother.

"I hope I can be instrumental in finding out what happened, because he was a brother of mine and such a good friend," said Sandoval. "She'll be a lifelong friend," he said, referring to Cindy. "She knows that my mind holds a treasure for her in memories of him."

Cindy met some of the other soldiers who served with Adam, and through them she learned what many veterans were coping with. The military prescribed Paxil and Valium for them (anti-depression and anti-anxiety medications, respectively), but Cindy felt they never received enough treatment for what they endured in Iraq. She noticed Adam's friends were frequently getting drunk and getting into fights. They had difficulty focusing on their work and maintaining lasting relationships.

"This is not just about Adam. This is about all of these kids that are in serious trouble," Cindy said. "I want to be a voice to say that these kids are not getting their medical treatments."

Cindy felt that such "serious trouble" wasn't just a result of the difficulties that veterans had faced coming home.

"I just know that something happened in Iraq," she said. "I want to know exactly what screwed all these kids up in Iraq."

During the time that Cindy first sought answers, she and Roy received from Fort Wainwright a videotape of the memorial service that the Army put together for Adam in 2004. There were grainy images of a military gathering in a packed auditorium.

"We gather here today to remember Sergeant Adam Gray and bring closure to his death," began an officer. Minutes later, the same officer described how many on the base thought Adam had committed suicide. Roy and Cindy were taken aback.

What gave him the right to say that? they asked.

Was it, in fact, a suicide? True, he had acute PTSD, but his family believed his condition had been stabilizing. Or did he inadvertently kill himself using improvised recreational drugs? The military assumed it was the latter. Investigators said Adam accidentally killed himself when he inhaled the fumes from the Dust-Off. Others, including Cindy, weren't so sure. She felt it didn't add up.

"It was a blow. How can you talk to your kid one night and the next day they tell you your boy is dead?" said Roy, explaining the continued confusion over Adam's death. "It doesn't make sense."

Tony Sandoval agreed. He also puzzled over the military's response.

"Now if somebody should come back and say, 'It's true, it's positive, he committed suicide,' then there's still another big fight," said Sandoval. "Why? Why did he have to do that? Nobody was there to help him. It doesn't just happen. How come somebody didn't notice this?"

Six months after uniformed officers came to their house with news about Adam, Cindy was finally able to start probing what had happened to her son. She first went through the personal effects from his barracks room in Fort Wainwright. Then she tried to make sense of the paperwork that the military sent her. Cindy figured there were more Army documents about Adam and tussled with the military for months just to get basic information.

Eventually she contacted her congressman, Bill Thomas, to apply further pressure on the Army. Thanks to their combined pressure, Cindy finally received a pile of paperwork from the military. Thumbing through the pages, she saw that investigators had classified Adam's room as a crime scene and labeled his belongings in a "Record of Personal Effects." There were also reports about discovering Adam's body and his physical pathology, his medication, a death certificate, and finally a psychological autopsy.

During one of my visits to Tehachapi, Cindy allowed me to examine the files. The pages of the autopsy revealed that Adam "had experienced poor sleep, decreased appetite, stomachaches, headaches, and hyper-vigilance" since returning from Iraq.

"Gray was upset by thoughts of not being a good NCO," the report said. "Gray said that those problems were due to the way he felt about what happened to him during his deployment. Gray said that he could not sleep without alcohol, and that the last time he did sleep without alcohol, he woke up screaming with the sheets soaked with his sweat."

Such symptoms weren't uncommon for veterans who suffered from PTSD. But perhaps the most arresting part of the report was this: "Gray had risk factors for suicide. He had made a suicide gesture three weeks before his death."

On August 8, 2004, a friend of Adam's and his girlfriend entered his barracks room around 9:30 p.m. There they found him hanging by a belt that was fastened to the top bunk bed. Adam was breathing but unconscious. His friends hoisted him up to loosen the belt tied around his neck, then quickly called 911. Adam might have died that evening had they not stumbled into his room and roused him.

According to the report, Adam "suffered from post-traumatic stress disorder from his experiences in Iraq, and he had a substance abuse problem. Both conditions increase his suicide risk. His status as recently being released from a psychiatric hospital increases his statistical risk of suicide."

And yet the forensic opinion ended with the statement that Adam Gray's "death is best classified as an accident."

Cindy felt that the investigation was incomplete; basic information about the barracks' guard rotations that would have checked in on Adam during the night, the record of his phone calls, and his financial information appeared to be missing. Apart from the lack of investigative follow-up work, there also seemed to be basic unanswered questions about Adam. If he "had risk factors for suicide"—and even attempted suicide three weeks before his death—why hadn't the military taken more aggressive measures to monitor and treat him? Why didn't the military try to deal with the particular "problems … due to the way he felt about what happened to him during his deployment"?

Was the Army covering something up? she wondered. Why didn't they seek answers to such seemingly obvious questions?

Cindy tried to contact the doctor who treated Adam in Alaska to see if he could help explain what had happened to her son. But her calls went unanswered. Then she tried to locate former unit members from Alaska. She finally got a reply from Richard Boone's wife, Lisa, in the form of a handwritten letter. She was contrite about Cindy's loss and tried to offer some insight into Adam's state of mind during the time she and her husband knew him in Alaska.

"Adam stated something to the effect that he had a hard time dealing with what he had done," she wrote.

By way of explanation, she recalled that Adam came over to their house during the summer for a night of heavy drinking.

"That night those boys tied a good one on. I'm talking two cases of beer between them both," wrote Lisa. As the night progressed, Adam's friends drifted off to bed. He decided to stay up longer, drinking and smoking on a recliner.

"He was tired, and had way too much to drink, began rubbing his forehead and saying, 'I just wish I could show them what I had to do,' " continued Lisa. "At that point I took the beer away and everyone decided to go to bed."

Her letter then made a vague reference to Adam's troubled thoughts: "Anyway … it was the comment he made about the things he did that I was getting to." Despite the vagueness, Adam Gray's family and friends agreed that they needed to further understand "the things he did" in order to make sense of his decline.

Throughout the time I reported on Adam Gray and Battalion 1-68, I told Cindy that I was concerned about relaying any new details that would add to her pain.

"I'm not worried," she insisted. "This chapter has been opened for three years … I've already been through the worst. I just want answers. But I want the truth. I want to find somebody on this planet to find me that information."

Cindy had already been through the worst. Nothing could undo the loss of a beloved son.

"They're born with part of your soul," said Cindy. "And once they're gone, that's a whole part of you that's gone."

She could no longer sit through any movies that depicted violence. Anything on television that had to do with Iraq was impossible for her to watch. But she had also gained an enormous amount of empathy. Her heart sank whenever she glanced at a newspaper that pictured a young soldier who had just been killed in combat. She knew there was a mother out there attached to one of those souls about to go through the worst journey of her life.

"Every time I turn on the news and they have that ten-second segment, my heart breaks for the person that's on the end of that phone call," Cindy said. "If I can make any difference in the world with that, that would be an ultimate goal."

Cindy's journey, or quest, demanded great courage, since it meant confronting many disquieting facts. "I want to know exactly what screwed all these kids up in Iraq," she often said.

There are multiple explanations, too varied to cover fully in this book. But answering what happened to Adam James Gray, and by extension others who were "troubled" by their experiences in Iraq, involves looking at individual circumstances as well as common experiences during the war on terror.

Adam and those on his tank seemed upset by the shooting that accidentally claimed the lives of an Iraqi family. But he and others in his unit were also affected by the abuse and torture they inflicted on their prisoners.

To better understand what happened to Adam Gray, and US personnel who shared similar experiences, one needs to answer the following questions: How did American forces turn to torture? And how has the use of torture during the war on terror affected detainees, troops, and our counterterrorism efforts?

Those questions don't belong just to Cindy Chavez and her quest to understand what happened to her son. The US military and policymakers want to hear the answers, also; so, too, do the torture victims, other mothers, and the American public.

Chapter 2:
The Story Begins in Afghanistan

COMBINE THE WORDS "US" or "American" with "detainee abuse" or "torture," and the response will likely contain "Abu Ghraib" or "Guantanamo."

But the American use of torture during the war on terror did not begin with Abu Ghraib, nor did it begin in Guantanamo. It's easy to lose track of that fact, given the powerful images associated with both of those facilities: the Abu Ghraib pictures of sexual sadism, and photos of hunched Guantanamo detainees clad in orange jumpsuits and darkened goggles, surrounded by coils of concertina wire.

"The White House always put forward that Abu Ghraib was an exception, just some rotten apples," said John Sifton, a former senior researcher on terrorism and counterterrorism at Human Rights Watch. "But US personnel in Afghanistan were involved in killings and torture of prisoners well before the Iraq war even started. The story begins in Afghanistan."[1]

No flashy photos show these abuses, at least none that has emerged into the news media with the same force as the images from Abu Ghraib. It takes an attentive reader to identify these cases and track their chronology. And it takes a dispassionate approach to parse out when and where government officials willfully contributed to coercive interrogation, when officers and soldiers acted with relative autonomy (or without explicit instructions), and how commanders and officials were complicit in overlooking abuse.

Human rights organizations recorded cases of detainee abuse shortly after US boots hit the ground in Afghanistan in 2001. Some instances occurred in the heat of battle or when troops were "roughing up" detainees upon capture. To be fair, some roughing-up is a by-product of detainee arrests that is fairly typical of combat situations, and is by no means exclusive to the US military. But consistently roughing up suspects when they are captive in a detention facility is a different matter. During the early phase of US combat operations in Afghanistan, some of these abuses were relatively mild. Others were quite severe. Some even turned lethal.

Perhaps the most famous early cases of US prisoner abuse involved two detainees known as Habibullah and Dilawar. The events surrounding their deaths occurred in Afghanistan in December 2002. Three years later, the *New York Times* first detailed their experiences and the early abuses at the Bagram Air Base.[2] Over time, Habibullah and Dilawar's stories have gradually gained more public exposure in print and in film (e.g., in the Oscar-winning documentary *Taxi to the Dark Side*). But these events deserve to be revisited because of their timing and what they reveal about the early development of US abuses.

Journalists had already interviewed many of the guards who abused detainees in Bagram. Yet I never heard them provide an explanation that seemed adequate; most of their reasoning seemed incomplete at best and self-serving at worst. And so, in 2007 I traveled to Afghanistan to interview former Bagram and Guantanamo detainees who could describe events from an Afghan perspective.

Years after the US-led coalition toppled the Taliban in 2001, violence engulfed southern and eastern Afghanistan, making travel to provinces like Khost increasingly difficult. Car travel, conceivable in the years just following the US invasion, was now strongly discouraged. By mid-2007, the road connecting Kabul to Khost was rife with banditry and talibs, making it especially perilous. Non-Afghan travelers typically sought out limited air transport to Khost, which meant flying into Forward Operating Base Salerno—the very base where Dilawar and his companions from Khost first arrived.

Wahid Amani, my translator, fixer, and friend, accompanied me there to retrace some of the steps of those who were released from US captivity. Wahid was a twenty-seven-year-old journalist from Wardak province who worked as a freelance journalist for several years, and then as a reporter and trainer with the Institute for War and Peace Reporting (IWPR). We worked together for IWPR, and he occasionally assisted foreign journalists with their projects. But he grew uneasy about taking assignments in provinces like Khost, where violence had become prevalent.

Wahid didn't mention our journey to his family or fiancée. It was risky, and he didn't want to worry them. Just a few weeks before we set out, the Taliban kidnapped an Italian journalist from *La Repubblica*, Daniele Mastrogiacomo, in Helmand province, where Wahid and I worked for the IWPR. The Afghan government feared it would lose Italian support if Mastrogiacomo was killed, and negotiated his release by trading him for five Taliban prisoners (including the kidnapper's brother and other Taliban commanders).[3] But the affair ended badly when the Taliban beheaded Mastrogiacomo's driver, and then his translator. And their fate resonated among Afghan reporters, fixers, and translators— especially those who helped foreign journalists.[4]

Helmand continued to be a major Taliban stronghold. It was also known as "Little America" because of the US development projects established there during the 1950s–1970s. It seemed like a perfect irony to travel from "Little America" to Khost, also known as "Little Moscow"— provinces whose Cold War monikers recalled the legacy of past policies.[5]

I grew a thick beard during my stay in Afghanistan in order to blend in. From Lashkar Gah, Helmand's provincial capital, I cloaked myself in a *patu* (a long blanketlike scarf), wore a sparkly round hat typically donned by Pashtuns (Afghanistan's largest ethnic group), and long, sweeping clothes whenever I traveled outside our armed compound. My wardrobe and routine were no different in Khost. There, as in Helmand, I was largely confined to an armed compound, and beyond the gates I dressed in local garb, avoided eye contact and speaking in public, and tried to mimic the locals' gait. Many Afghans still recognized that I was a Westerner, but journalists and aid workers often take such measures to curb conspicuous attention.

Before we arrived in Khost, a local reporter, Kamal Sadat, assured us he would do everything in his power to ensure our safety.

"You will be our guests in Khost," he said. "Just come whenever you can. I will be waiting for you."

Clean-shaven, wearing a flowing white kurta shirt, Sadat greeted us at Salerno's last checkpoint, just before the main road leading to Khost City. Sadat was a medical student practicing journalism to earn some extra money (he was the fifth young doctor-reporter I met in Afghanistan). He had worked for the BBC's Pashto service, then became a correspondent for Voice of America and Reuters.

"I talk to everyone: the government, the coalition forces, the Taliban. Everyone," said Sadat, explaining his evenhanded reporting. At one point, he too became a local news story when he was arrested and detained by the Americans. Like other Khost detainees, he was bound and hooded by US forces, shipped to Salerno and then on to Bagram. Soldiers held Sadat's family at gunpoint and rifled through his reporter's notebooks.[6] His arrest provoked a public outcry, and US forces soon released him, explaining they had mistakenly captured the wrong suspect. The US military apologized to Sadat, and he maintains that he wasn't mistreated (except for the property damaged in his home during the arrest) and said he holds no resentment toward his captors.

During our ride from Salerno to Khost City, he asked me many questions about my visit. There were a lot of Taliban in the province, and the area was often gripped by violence. Weeks before we arrived, Khost suffered a string of suicide bomber attacks that claimed fourteen lives.[7] Sadat was especially curious why an American journalist would visit such a hostile region in order to report on detainee abuse.

"I have very good relations with the American base," he said. "The American soldiers will be unhappy when your book comes out, no?"

Sadat seemed worried that even the slightest involvement with my reporting would sour his relations with the local US military forces in Khost. I had a feeling that Wahid was also unsure about the value of our research. Afghanistan has seen many long and bloody wars that have wrought untold misery. Why focus on one tragedy in Afghanistan, no matter how appalling?

Sadat weaved his car through Khost's bustling, dusty streets, seeking shelter for his new guests and a meeting place for our local contacts. The Governor's Guesthouse, where meetings and official functions took place, offered the best accommodations in town, though it lacked certain amenities—no regular running water, the electrical power switched on only after sunset, and one unsanitary bathroom shared by two floors of guests. Tall concrete barriers lay on alternating sides of the entrance road to prevent oncoming cars from gaining enough momentum to crash a suicide car bomb into the building. Guards languidly settled themselves in the sort of plastic chairs commonly seen on suburban American lawns, and shifted positions only when a new visitor arrived, checking bags, frisking, prodding them with questions, and so forth.

A lush flower garden in the main courtyard, just past the perimeter, perfumed the air with assorted roses and wild jasmine. A row of small stone stools and faucets lined the entrance for guests to perform ablutions before prayer. Staff and occupants warmly greeted new arrivals by simultaneously slapping one another on opposite shoulders. Such contrasts are ubiquitous in Afghanistan—a severe country, punctuated by harsh landscapes and perennial violence, yet home to welcoming and generous people.

One of the Guesthouse residents was the governor's security attaché, a stocky Tajik Afghan whom Wahid and I nicknamed "Tank" on account of his build. Tank stood out because he didn't wear a thick beard and local clothes. Instead, he sported a neatly trimmed mustache, black slacks, and a white short-sleeved shirt. He flashed a glamorous smile, walked forcefully with an open, holstered sidearm, and rapidly dispatched soldiers and security personnel. Tank had personally shielded Khost's governor against four assassination attempts. The last one occurred at a hospital, when a man dressed like a doctor exploded his suicide bomb just four yards away. You need a keen eye to pick out suicide bombers, said Tank, who explained that he could quickly recognize suspects because they often sweat nervously and dress in bulky clothing or seem to be carrying suspiciously heavy gear. And how do you stop them? Tank said he tried to shoot them in the leg instead of the head (which is difficult to aim at) or the chest (where the bomb is typically strapped).

"It is very difficult, and if you miss you hit people behind him," he said.

A large sign with "Civilian Military Operations Center" emblazoned in English in large black letters occupied the main wall upstairs. Khost's Governor's Guesthouse was once the location for US military offices, and our rooms were plastered with military maps: the "Afghanistan Town and Airfield Plans (AIR)," produced by the DGIA (the UK's Defence Geographic and Imagery Intelligence Agency), and a massive gray "unclassified" map of Khost province "produced by the 25th Engineering Detachment, 25th Infantry Division (Light)." Our accommodations seemed to afford the best security in the city, and yet these relics of a foreign military presence hardly made it an ideal place to meet former detainees.

Many of the Afghans connected to the Dilawar case were wary about describing their experiences; some feared meeting with an American, perhaps suspecting I was connected to the US military. Wahid and I first met Shapoor, Dilawar's older brother, who raised and sold livestock in Khost province. He was initially leery about helping us, but once he understood that we genuinely wanted to learn what had happened to his brother, he changed his mind and helped arrange interviews with the taxi driver who witnessed how the Afghan forces handled Dilawar during his initial arrest. Days later, Shapoor informed us that the taxi driver "had to go to a family funeral."

"I think he will not come—I am sure he is too afraid."

We asked if we could meet Dilawar's closest friend, Bacha Khan.

"He will not meet you. He is too afraid."

How about meeting the rest of the family? Maybe your parents?

"Every time they hear his name, it is as though he has just died," explained Shapoor. "As soon as they hear 'Dilawar,' they begin crying and don't stop for twenty days."

"This upsets us so much because we support the government," he said, referring to the US-backed government of President Hamid Karzai.

Shapoor combed his hair with his henna-painted fingernails and tugged his *pakol* hat around his head. He inhaled deep lungfuls of cigarette smoke and described how he tried to rescue his younger brother and allay his parents' fears.

We met others who knew Dilawar and were with him at various times during his journey, including former detainees from Bagram. Parkhudin was one of Dilawar's passengers. He had been with Dilawar from the start, when their journey first began on Khost's dirt road to Salerno, and he eventually wound up in Guantanamo after being held by US forces in Afghanistan. After he was released from US captivity, he returned home and was soon jailed for robbery. The only way to interview Parkhudin was to meet with him in an Afghan jail.

One afternoon, Sadat drove us to Khost's local prison, an old fortress-like facility that offered a panoramic view of the city. Parkhudin hobbled into a crumbling prison office wearing a blue-striped pajama-like uniform, his wrists bound by handcuffs. Friendly prison guards dressed in olive green uniforms served us tea and milk candies. They filed in and out of the office past washed-out photos of President Karzai.

Parkhudin had been with Dilawar from the start, when their journey first began on Khost's dirt road to Salerno.

On December 1, 2002, a family of ten gathered near Yakubi, a small town in eastern Afghanistan. They were preparing to celebrate Eid, the Islamic holiday that marks the end of fasting for Ramadan. Eid is the Muslim version of Thanksgiving or Passover—a dinner to give thanks and celebrate the virtues of peace and forgiveness.

The mother of the family had summoned her son Dilawar, a twenty-two-year-old who, like many Afghans, went by one name—a name that means "brave" in Dari (the predominant language of Afghanistan). Dilawar's mother asked him to collect his sisters so they could join the rest of the family for dinner. His sisters were married and lived in other villages, so Dilawar needed to fill up the tank of his white Corolla before setting out. One good taxi fare would be enough. He headed for the provincial capital, Khost, about fifteen miles past the American base, Forward Operating Base Salerno, nicknamed "Rocket City"—a favorite target of the Taliban.

It was a long, bumpy ride to Khost, a small bustling city set amidst gray-and-white-flecked mountain valleys. Fighting regularly plagued the region: in the 1980s, during the eight-year Russian siege of Afghanistan, Khost was a robust pocket of resistance; during the Taliban's tenure, Osama bin Laden used a CIA-built facility to train al Qaeda recruits; in August 1998, President Bill Clinton bombed the Khost camp with cruise missiles. After September 11, 2001, the Taliban battled advancing US forces from these hills and often crossed the nearby Pakistan border to seek cover. The road that connects Yakubi to the provincial capital slices through Khost's northeastern valleys, so local Afghans had to brave routine violence to travel on it. In Khost City, Dilawar found three customers who were headed to the Yakubi district. It was a perfect arrangement for Dilawar: his customers' fare would provide plenty of money for fuel and also take him closer to where his sisters lived.

His customers crammed into the Corolla. Like Dilawar, they had recently returned to Khost province after many years of fighting had forced them out of the country. One of them, Parkhudin, had worked in Dubai when the Taliban ruled Afghanistan. He scratched out a modest living cleaning fish, fixing nets, and working in factories. After the US invasion, Parkhudin joined the "campaign forces" that aided American troops in the fight against the Taliban.[8]

Parkhudin and his friend Zakim Khan, a local farmer, were looking for a ride to Yakubi, where Khan's sister lived; she was preparing a meal for them to celebrate Eid. Abdul Rahim, a young baker, was the third passenger in Dilawar's taxi.

The trip from Khost to Yakubi would take just under an hour. Dilawar and his passengers headed out of town, past the lush green swaths of farms and fields that encircled the city, beyond the edge of

Salerno's perimeter that pierced the horizon, and continued on the dusty road toward the stark valleys.

The road became bumpier as they drew closer to Yakubi, and their car vibrated on the poorly graveled surface. After driving fifteen minutes past Salerno, they dropped into a narrow canyon and went by a remote cemetery festooned with tattered green flags that marked the graves of Arab warriors who helped support the mujahideen or supported the Taliban.[9] An uninterrupted desert vista stretched before them, dotted only with sparse clumps of grass.

A small patrol of armed Afghans suddenly emerged and spilled onto the road. They shouted orders and stopped Dilawar's car, then brusquely yanked him and his passengers out. Another taxi appeared. It was on its way to Khost, and the driver slowed down to steer clear of the armed men and avoid inspection. The soldiers searched Dilawar's car and found an electric stabilizer and some walkie-talkies that Parkhudin had brought with him.

Four Afghans in a white Toyota with electrical gear and communications equipment, heading east (toward Pakistan) to a treacherous district in Khost—it was enough to arouse suspicion. Parkhudin admitted that the walkie-talkies were his and that he used them to communicate with the "campaign forces" when he helped combat the Taliban. But he didn't have a uniform or proof of his connection to those forces. The soldiers brought Parkhudin to their commander, who searched him and found phone numbers for Dubai and Pakistan in his pocket.

Could he be al Qaeda? Why else would he have foreign numbers? And why was the driver transporting an electrical device? What was it for? Was he using it to fire rockets? Those questions were all it took.

The soldiers loaded the four Afghans into their vehicle and sped away. No one explained to them where they were being taken and what lay ahead. Their trip lasted only a few minutes, as they were first taken into American custody in Salerno. Burly American soldiers hauled them out of the vehicle and instructed them to lie down beside a chain link fence.

Dilawar trembled, and his eyes fell downcast. Strangers now surrounded him—young American soldiers with M16s slung across their shoulders, their eyes concealed by opaque plastic glasses—and he was in an unfamiliar place, wedged between his former passengers.

One hour had passed since the time of their capture.

The soldiers approached and ordered the Afghan prisoners to stand upright. They fastened the detainees' wrists behind their backs with stiff white plastic flex-cuffs and pulled heavy dark hoods over their heads. The Afghans were then ordered to lie flat on the ground, and their ankles were cinched together with the same plastic ties.

Hours went by. Parkhudin remembered that they were left in this position on the ground outside; they couldn't extend their limbs in a relaxed position because their wrists and ankles remained bound. Vehicles rolled past, jets screeched, and helicopters thundered above them day and night, making sleep difficult. Bored soldiers would occasionally throw small rocks at them and laugh.

Eventually, they were told they were being shipped elsewhere. Soldiers helped raise them off the ground, and their joints ached from hours of atrophy. The four prisoners were tethered together and walked forward on a gravel road, unsure where they were being shepherded. Blinded by their hoods, they could rely only on their muffled senses to grasp what would happen next. They could feel heavy rotor wash beat down on them from a transport helicopter. They were loaded into an enclosed space, then felt vibrations and the sensation of being airborne. They were being ferried from Salerno to the Bagram Air Base.

Since the day they were apprehended, time had blurred from one sleepless day to the next. But after their flight, it quickly sped up. They arrived in Bagram in what felt like less than an hour, and were loaded onto a bus and escorted to a building where they were finally unhooded. It was now December 5, four days since their arrest. None of the new detainees knew it at the time, but it was one day after a Bagram detainee known as Habibullah had died.

Their eyes burned, and they squinted against the light in their new surroundings. Once their vision cleared they saw a brightly lit hall where soldiers shuffled among prisoners, organizing them into a single-file line. Then they were ordered to strip.

"We were very ashamed, but we could not do anything," said Parkhudin.

After a brisk medical check by Army medics, the prisoners were ordered to put on orange uniforms and herded into a cell made of chain link fence. "They were giving us water to drink and bringing us food, and there was a big drumlike pot we used as bathroom," said Parkhudin. "But we were not allowed to talk to each other."

They were jammed in with ten or fifteen others. Qader Khandan and Said Abaceen, two detainees from Khost whom I met during my trip there, went through the same sequence months earlier. At first, Khandan was forced to engage in acts designed more to humiliate than cause discomfort. Khandan said he was given a toothbrush and water and ordered to wash the floor while his hands were bound. Then soldiers dirtied the floor and made him start over.

Like Dilawar and his passengers, Khandan was neither permitted to look at soldiers nor allowed to speak. Infractions were met with a routine response.

"Punishment," Khandan said in English, invoking a term that was commonly used by US soldiers throughout his detention. And "punishment" for Khandan meant "forced standing"—a stress position that involved prolonged, painful standing—for two hours, he said.[10]

The first time prisoners deviated from the rules, they were forced to stare into a bright light for two or three hours. First it stung. Then it became blinding. And finally, their heads pounded from the pain.

"It was not only me," said Said Abaceen, who was in Bagram in early 2003. "I think all the prisoners there were speaking to each other and [forced] to look into the light, one night or for ten hours." Abaceen later learned that his eyes had sustained permanent damage and he has to wear sunglasses on sunny days to lessen the pain.

One by one, detainees were led from the holding cell to small individual cells. According to prisoners' descriptions, these cells were not high enough for standing upright nor long enough for lying down.

"It was a place designed so that you cannot sleep and cannot relax," said Khandan.

The ordeal had already rattled Dilawar. Parkhudin had known the taxi driver only since he hired him in Khost, but to him, Dilawar seemed terribly afraid: "He was not like a brave guy—he was not used to this kind of problem."

Fellow inmates often heard Dilawar crying to his captors, "I'm not with these people. I'm a driver and I don't know who they are … I just don't know. I didn't know these people."

Soon a regimen of interrogations would begin.

Dilawar came from a family of seven brothers and three sisters, and was always considered quiet and shy. When he was seventeen years old, his family married him off to a local girl from Khost, and soon afterward they had a daughter, Rashida.

His parents were native Afghans, but like his other siblings, Dilawar was born in Pakistan. They fled their homeland during the mujahideen wars that erupted after the Soviets invaded in 1979. Like many Afghan refugees in Pakistan, they lived day to day, laboring for migrant wages.

No one in Dilawar's family was sympathetic to the Taliban. But after the Taliban gained control of Afghanistan in 1996, the violence declined for a while. That respite offered Dilawar's family an opportunity to return to Khost and claim a plot of land where they could grow corn and grain.

Shapoor, the oldest sibling, used the wages he saved from working in Dubai to start up a business buying and selling goats and cows. Dilawar was responsible for shepherding the goats, taking them out to the mountains for grazing and returning with them at night. Eventually the family built a simple seven-room house with stone walls in Khost's Yakubi district.

Yet the family regularly encountered problems with the Taliban. In Khost, talibs routinely harassed locals who were caught in the streets instead of attending the mosque during prayer time. One day, a small group of talibs stopped Shapoor's car, yanked him out, and beat him up for disobeying a law under the Taliban regime: listening to music.

Dilawar was Shapoor's favorite sibling, and Shapoor worried whether his little brother could survive the tough environment of Afghanistan under the Taliban, where religious laws were enforced with violent severity. As a teenager, Dilawar could grow only wisps of facial hair, and his family urged him to stay home since he couldn't fulfill the beard-length requirements imposed under the Taliban.

Dilawar didn't have the frame or stamina for hard labor. After his shepherding work, he would move stones from the mountains with the family tractor, selling them to locals for house construction. But Shapoor noticed how Dilawar struggled with his job, and how it wore out his slight body.

The money Shapoor had saved from working at hotels and driving taxis in Dubai was enough to buy Dilawar a Toyota Corolla. Shapoor hadn't provided his brother with a wedding gift, but knew that this present would be more meaningful, since he would no longer have to haul heavy rocks with a clumsy tractor. Dilawar was overcome by his brother's generosity. He finally had the means to pursue work that was less physically taxing.

On the day Dilawar was abducted, Shapoor was about thirty minutes outside of Khost, where he had gone to sell sheep and goats, when a taxi driver edged alongside him and rolled down his window. It was the taxi driver who had been traveling on the same road where Dilawar and his passengers had been pulled over. He told Shapoor that they had all been arrested and that the Toyota's windows had been smashed. Shapoor feared what had happened to his young brother.

Back in Bagram, the detainees were roused late at night for questioning. Soldiers poured ice-cold water on them and ventilated the prison to allow the freezing night air to gust over their wet bodies.

Then the guards came with chains.

By now the prisoners were accustomed to having their wrists bound. But the soldiers were lifting them by their arms, hoisting them upward by chains attached to the ceiling. The weight of their bodies, pulling downward as their arms were stretched upward, made breathing difficult. The soldiers still wouldn't permit them to relax, and often made noise to frighten them or keep them awake. Detainees remained hooded, causing further disorientation.

"We did not know if it was day or night," said Parkhudin. "The lights were always on."

There were bathroom breaks twice a day for a few short minutes. During interrogations, the men were lowered, unchained, and ushered to small rooms for questioning. Their limbs creaked as their bodies returned to a normal position.

"We could not walk because our feet and hands were hurt," said Parkhudin.

Then the questions began.

Why did you have the numbers from Dubai? What about the walkie-talkies? What were you doing with the electrical stabilizer? Did you use it to launch rockets?

Interrogators occasionally presented photographs and questioned prisoners about the subjects contained in them, such as Osama bin Laden and Taliban leaders. Troops applied various kinds of pressure if prisoners said they couldn't identify people in the photos, if they didn't have answers, or if they seemed evasive in any way. Qader Khandan said he was forced to do push-ups while a soldier stood on his back. Other detainees said they were beaten. Some were ordered to hold their bodies in stress positions for hours, their arms and legs trembling from exhaustion, their ankles swelling, pain shooting through their extremities. Then interrogation sessions ended, and they were once again hung from chains.

It became a routine. Some prisoners claimed they were chained ten days and ten nights, their toes just scraping the floor, lowered just for interrogation sessions and short bathroom breaks. Again, no talking was permitted. More infractions meant more beatings on their arms, legs, and feet. While suspended, prisoners were vulnerable and could not shield themselves from the blows.

Parkhudin couldn't see Dilawar, but could hear him being beaten. He seemed especially distressed, more so perhaps than the others.

"I could hear what he was yelling and that he was crying, asking for his mother, asking, 'Where are you my God?' " Parkhudin recalled.

Soldiers laughed when they heard Dilawar's anguished cries. Fellow detainees thought soldiers were taunting Dilawar "just to make fun," said Parkhudin.

When Shapoor relayed news of Dilawar's capture to his family in Yakubi, they were desperate to help, but uncertain about what to do.

"We were running around trying find ways to release him," said Dilawar's younger brother, Mohammad Rafik. "We went to the government officials, the village elders. Everyone."

As the oldest child, Shapoor was charged with trying to determine where Dilawar was being held. He was granted permission to use all family resources to secure his release.

He went first to the governor's office and learned that Dilawar had been taken to Forward Operating Base Salerno. The Taliban had recently attacked the base with rockets; local officials may have speculated that Dilawar and his passengers were arrested as suspects. Khost's detainees were first sent to Salerno, then forwarded to the Bagram Air Base, where they were processed and questioned. Shapoor didn't understand the process; he just wanted to secure his brother's release.

He traveled to the outskirts of Khost City and implored the guards at Salerno's checkpoint to help him locate his brother.

"They said they knew some people in the base that could help me," said Shapoor. "They were always asking me for money."

Shapoor remembered that he had seen one of the guards in the governor's office when he was first searching for a contact for the Americans. But he needed more than anguished pleas to help Dilawar.

"I did not want to lose him," said Shapoor. "He was the one I loved most in my family."

Desperate, Shapoor used the family's savings, adding it to his own money, to dole out bribes: first to local government officials, then to Afghan military guards at Salerno. Each of them promised they'd help locate Dilawar; some assured him they would even go to Kabul to try to gain his release. But they rarely relayed news about him.

Each morning Shapoor set out at seven o'clock to make rounds, bribing guards and officials and pursuing any leads, and then returned home by nightfall. When he arrived back home the family pelted him with questions.

"How many people did you see? How much did you pay them?" they asked. "Is there any hope?"

He tried to assure them that Dilawar would be released the next day, maybe the day after. "Just telling them lies so that they would not be very sad, giving them a hope that he would be released," said Shapoor.

But it went on for weeks, and the family's savings eventually dwindled to nothing. All told, Shapoor estimates he spent 800,000 Pakistani rupees (about $13,323) in bribes for Dilawar's release. In a rash move, Shapoor even offered his daughters to one of the main Afghan guards who promised he would help Dilawar.

"When I was out of money, I told the guard that if you will help me release my brother I will give you my two daughters," he said, explaining that they could be married off to his sons or grandsons.

The guard recoiled. "You just have to wait—he will be released," he said. "You have to be patient."

It was the same refrain Shapoor heard from everyone. Once again the guard assured him that he would personally travel to the American base to locate Dilawar.

"But no one helped me."

Khandan was hung by his wrists for days and lowered for two or three hours a day for interrogation. Soldiers lowered him so he could relieve himself and then, he said, they would strike him and roll him down a flight of stairs. Khandan soon feared the bathroom and reasoned it would be safer to consume less food and water. After three days he stopped eating and drinking. Eventually a soldier pleaded with him to stop fasting and assured him that he would be able to use the bathroom safely.

Many of his fellow detainees could no longer control their bowels, and the prison began to smell of human waste. Khandan saw flecks of dried blood on the floor whenever guards removed his hood to give him water. It seemed that some prisoners had sustained grave injuries from their detention in Bagram. One of them was Habibullah—sometimes referred to as Mullah Habibullah—the brother of a Taliban commander from Afghanistan's Oruzgan province.[11]

During his detention, Khandan heard guards tussling with Habibullah. Other prisoners heard Habibullah exchanging shouts with the guards, and then they heard soft thuds—what seemed like body blows. Next they heard what seemed like sputtering sounds coming from Habibullah. And then silence.

Habibullah died from his injuries on December 4, 2002.

The interrogations did not stop, and the soldiers resumed their routines. Prisoners once again heard the standard battery of questions in the interrogation room: How long have you known Osama bin Laden? How many times did you meet him? Where are the Taliban commanders? Who did you work for? How long have you supported al Qaeda?

Over time, prisoners grew increasingly weary and less articulate.

There were also misunderstandings during interrogations because Bagram's Afghan translators had difficulty understanding the prisoners from Khost.

"All the translators had problems with us because of our accent," said Parkhudin.[12]

Some troops believed detainees were purposely confusing interrogators and evading questions by feigning miscommunication.[13]

Once again Dilawar pleaded with his captors.

"I'm just a taxi driver," he said. "The only reason that they arrested me was because of the stabilizer they found in my car. That is why they brought me here."

"He was crying," recalled Khandan. "It was all because of the pain, and he was saying 'Oh, my mother. Oh my God. Oh, I'm about to die.' "

But no one heeded his words.

And soon Dilawar, too, succumbed to his injuries.

Word about Dilawar's death gradually percolated into Afghan governmental channels. Afghan officials puzzled over how to convey the news to his family and how to return his body to Khost. Eventually a government worker who knew about Dilawar contacted his uncles.

"My family, my uncles, they didn't let me know," said Shapoor. "They just went to Kabul by themselves and brought the body."

Dilawar's body traveled from Bagram, between family houses, until it reached Yakubi. At last, his uncles broke the news to his father, and the family crumpled in sorrow.

Dilawar's prized Toyota sat in front of the family house, and his mother wept whenever she saw it. Bits of shattered glass still encrusted the edges of the windows. Shapoor eventually sold it for $1,000 and used the money for Dilawar's funeral ceremony.

Since then, said Shapoor, whenever Dilawar's parents heard his name "they would get very weak, and I had to take them to see a doctor."

His mother even developed a respiratory condition from the grief, said Shapoor. Dilawar's five-year-old daughter, Rashida, understood her father had been captured and killed, but no one could make sense of it. No one understood what anyone would want with Dilawar, the most unassuming member of the family. All they had were documents that established he had been in US custody.

Nearly a year after their arrest, US authorities cleared Parkhudin and Zakim Khan of all charges, allowing them to return home. Shortly after they arrived in Khost, they traveled to visit Dilawar's parents.

Dilawar's mother pleaded to hear what happened to her son. The released detainees could tell that Dilawar's death had already exacted a devastating toll on his family, and they didn't want to add to their grief. They simply couldn't bring themselves to convey the truth about Dilawar's suffering to his parents. Parkhudin insisted "there was no punishment at all … the Americans did not beat him and they did not beat us." Maybe Dilawar was sick, said Parkhudin to his parents, and perhaps he had a health problem that led to his death.

"I told them that Bagram was a comfortable place, and the Americans were very nice people."

At the Khost prison, where Wahid and I interviewed Parkhudin, two bearded Afghan guards with narrow faces and chiseled cheeks sat on opposite sides of the room and listened to Parkhudin unpack his experiences. It took him several hours to describe the ways in which American guards and interrogators ratcheted up pressure with pain and humiliation, and what he told Dilawar's family about how the US military treated them. After he finished his story, the guards grimaced and looked puzzled; their eyes turned sullen. They seemed bewildered by the events that their American counterparts were involved in.

For days, Wahid and I listened to the events that befell the young taxi driver and heard other former detainees catalog their own experiences in US custody.

During the evenings we sat underneath a sheltered veranda at the Governor's Guesthouse, lounging on long burgundy velvet cushions and sipping tea as the sun set. Wahid worked for hours, translating the events from Bagram and Guantanamo. He was groggy from sleeplessness; his nights were filled with vivid nightmares of lunging dogs and menacing figures.

"I just keep thinking ..." he mused. "If they can do this to a taxi driver—a nobody just carrying an electrical stabilizer—and they can capture, and then kill him ... then they can do this to anyone."

Dilawar's story, like others I encountered in Afghanistan and the Middle East, was an exception, I explained to Wahid. True, there were several documented cases of US torture in recent years, but that didn't represent how most US forces behaved. I couldn't gauge whether Wahid genuinely accepted this. And it was hard to explain why US forces turned to abuse, and how it became so aggressive that they would take the lives of Dilawar and Habibullah.

I told Wahid about one common explanation: Bush officials drafted memos that sanctioned coercive interrogation techniques for the military, and those practices spread first to Guantanamo, then to Abu Ghraib, and from there leached into other parts of Iraq. But this account could not be used to explain the torture of Dilawar and Habibullah. Like other prisoners who had been abused by the US military in 2002, their experience preceded the memos.

Due to legal decisions drafted by the Bush administration during early 2002 prisoners were regarded as "enemy combatants," and many US troops understood that al Qaeda and Taliban detainees weren't entitled to the minimum standard for humane treatment afforded in the Geneva Conventions' Common Article Three.[14] But the other memos pertaining to coercive interrogation probably had far less influence on troops—especially early on.

In August 2002, Jay Bybee, then head of the Office of Legal Counsel, signed off on a memo to provide the CIA with the legal framework for harsh interrogation. That memo, often called "the Bybee memo" (or the "torture memo"), defined physical torture as "equivalent in intensity to the pain accompanying serious physical injury, such as organ failure, impairment of bodily function, or even death." Later that year, in

December, the Department of Defense's general counsel, William J. Haynes II, sanctioned coercive interrogation, known as Counter-Resistance Techniques, exclusively for Guantanamo's interrogators. Secretary of Defense Donald Rumsfeld later approved the techniques contained in the Haynes memo. Additional memos and directives authorizing US forces to use coercive interrogation emerged after 2002.[15]

It is possible that there were other memos that haven't been made public, authorizing troops in Afghanistan to apply torture or abuse during 2002. Perhaps there is proof—through memos, verbal orders, or military directives—that senior officers directed soldiers to rough up detainees and even outlined the techniques that troops could employ. That such evidence exists has been a common belief among those who have researched and read about US torture.

"There seemed to be a regimen or a system in place where prisoners were routinely roughed up as a matter of policy," observed a human rights researcher I knew who had interviewed dozens of former detainees from Bagram and Kandahar. "Someone had to issue an order or directive. American soldiers just don't do that sort of thing on their own."

To date, no evidence has been found that senior military commanders issued explicit directives to soldiers in Afghanistan to abuse and torture detainees during the time Habibullah and Dilawar were in US custody. According to Reed College professor and noted torture expert Darius Rejali, high-ranking officers and government officials typically have not ordered torture policies in most documented cases of torture. Instead, in most historical cases, "torture began with the lower downs, and was simply ignored by the higher ups."[16]

If the cases of Habibullah and Dilawar mirror the same pattern of guidance and leadership (or lack thereof), they force us to ask: How do we account for cases in which troops lacked directives and still committed abuse? It is too easy, and sometimes inaccurate, to claim that heated combat operations lead to torture. So what happened?

It's hard to pinpoint exactly when US torture and abuse first emerged during the war on terror or to determine who first planted the seed—either with respect to the conditions in Afghanistan or the origins of the techniques themselves.

Chris Mackey, an Army interrogator who served in Afghanistan during the early years of the war and chronicled his experiences in his book *The Interrogators*, offers one of the few glimpses into this period.[17] Mackey and his interrogation unit started out in Kandahar during early 2002. It was the first time most of them had actually performed real-world interrogation work. Like other forces, they had to hastily learn about their adversary in order to conduct intelligence operations. It demanded hard work and long hours of study. Understanding the war and their enemies was confusing, and they grew even more frustrated through repeatedly questioning detainees who misled them.

"The interrogators were swimming in deceit, all day every day," wrote Mackey.[18] But once his unit transferred to Bagram in the spring of 2002, it encountered a far more hostile prison population. "And the interrogators' hostility toward them increased in turn."

Mackey wondered how this hostility would affect his work as an interrogator, and how the antagonistic environment would generally alter his troops' outlook and behavior toward their detainees. "It made me wonder sometimes whether we were becoming like the troops in Vietnam who had become so prejudiced against the 'gooks' and 'slopes' and 'Charlie,' " he mused.[19]

Mackey said that he and his fellow interrogators didn't apply any kind of coercive techniques for most of his tour in Afghanistan. "But during the coming months in Bagram, a combination of forces would lead us— lead me—to make allowances that I wouldn't have even considered in the early days at Kandahar," he admitted.[20]

They tinkered with their methods, making "tiny encroachments on the rules." The first technique they used was sleep deprivation, though Mackey referred to it as the "adjusted sleep routine." While in Bagram, Mackey worked with a seasoned military intelligence officer and interrogator named Steve (a pseudonym, as is Mackey's name), who seemed to have special insight into how sleep deprivation affected human behavior.

"[Steve] talked in almost academic terms about patterns of prisoner behavior," wrote Mackey. "He told us at one point that hard-core prisoners were unlikely to start cracking until about fourteen hours into an interrogation, and it was clear that he wasn't just pulling this number out of his head."[21]

Mackey further reasoned that Steve's informed understanding about the successes of this technique gave it further legitimacy. But the interrogators also wanted to impress the special operations forces they worked with and sought to match their toughness to prove to them that they were equally capable of producing successful interrogations.[22]

Steve didn't order harsh interrogation techniques, but implied that they should be used. "He made it clear to me," wrote Mackey, "that we would be letting him down, letting down [the task force], if we were to take our foot off the gas pedal. There was clearly more pressure."[23]

According to Mackey, in the summer of 2002, he and his unit met another intelligence officer at Bagram, a sergeant, who encouraged them to use the "adjusted sleep routine" more often.

"He was a very enthusiastic guy, always pushing us to be more aggressive in the booth," remembered Mackey, referring to the interrogation booth. Once, while he was giving interrogators pointers in the ICE (Interrogation Control Element) the sergeant suggested they combine their regimen with other techniques—and try to frighten detainees in the process.

" 'You've got to scare them,' he said, 'get right up in their faces and *monster* them.' From then on there was only one word that we used for keeping prisoners in the booth until they or their interrogator broke: monstering."

The name stuck. And so did the continued use of monstering and other coercive techniques even after Mackey's unit had left Bagram.

"By the time we left Afghanistan, we had come to embrace methods we would not have countenanced at the beginning of the war," wrote Mackey. "Indeed, as we left, it was clear they did not regard this as a method of last resort but as a primary option in the interrogation playbook."

Members of the Army's 519th Military Intelligence Battalion succeeded Mackey's unit in August 2002 and embraced the techniques that his unit left behind. What started out as "tiny encroachments on the rules" led to monstering. As Mackey further explained, his successors "took to monstering with alacrity ... What was an ending point for us was a starting point for them." He went on to say, "And during their stint in Afghanistan, they undoubtedly added their own plays, many of which were probably exported to Iraq."

Mackey has tried to distance himself from a system of abuse that he and his interrogators put in motion, explaining that the rise in violence compelled other units to turn to these harsh interrogation techniques. After Mackey's unit had left and was replaced by a new company, "the stakes got very high," he said.[24] "We went from losing three or four soldiers a month to scores of them. [The interrogators' command] must have been under a tremendous amount of pressure."[25]

Other soldiers have also maintained that the US and its allies sustained heavy attacks during this period in Afghanistan, and that this partly explains what drove troops to use torture during interrogation. But this justification doesn't square with the facts.

The rate of attacks on US forces in Afghanistan during 2002 in general—and especially during the latter part of that year—remains uncertain. But the military has provided information about the number of combat deaths and casualties for each month of 2002.

Mackey's unit, the 202nd Military Intelligence Battalion, left Bagram in August 2002. In 2002, there were 123 casualties among US soldiers in Afghanistan, including forty-nine deaths.[26] Forty of those deaths occurred during the first six months of the year, and the remaining nine died during the latter six months. Just fourteen of those earlier deaths were soldiers killed in action or who died as a result of combat wounds, and only four soldiers were killed in action during the latter six months.[27] As for casualties, seventy-four US soldiers were wounded in action during 2002. Fifty-one injuries occurred during the first six months, and twenty-three during the latter six months.[28]

If there were increased attacks on US forces during the latter part of 2002, they didn't translate into a spike in casualties and deaths in combat. In fact, the military's own figures show a drop in casualties during that period. There is no indication that "scores" of soldiers were killed during the time frame that Mackey referenced.[29]

Dilawar and Habibullah were detained in Bagram during November and December, when eight soldiers were wounded in action and one soldier was killed in action. The "high stakes" argument was at best inaccurate and at worst misleading.

American troops described how they abused detainees as they filtered into Bagram.

"Whether they got in trouble or not, everybody struck a detainee at some point," said Brian Cammack, a former specialist with the 377th.[30]

Jeremy Callaway, another Army specialist who served in the 377th from August 2002 to January 2003, told military investigators in sworn testimony that he, too, struck about twelve detainees at Bagram.[31] When military investigators asked why, Callaway answered: "Retribution for September 11, 2001."[32]

Sometimes MPs greeted detainees with dogs that had been provoked into frenzied barking.

"The K-9 unit from the Military Police would be called to the facility and normally he was there before the detainees arrived," remembered Sergeant Jennifer N. Higginbotham. "The detainees would be brought into the room and the dog would be barking. The MP K-9 handler would bring the dog into the facility on a leash and the dog was normally muzzled. Once inside the building, the muzzle would be removed to allow the dog to bark. The MP K-9 handler always kept the dog on a leash. If there were only a few detainees brought into the facility, he would stay for about fifteen minutes. If more detainees were present, he may stay longer."[33]

Detainees were also abused during interrogations. Interrogators from the 519th continued to use the same regimen of abuse handed down by their predecessors, and secured additional manpower to buttress their work. The interrogators asked members of the 377th Military Police Company to help them with monstering, and the MPs complied.[34]

Sometimes they improvised. Soldiers from the 377th admitted they slammed prisoners into walls, ordered them to hold straining positions for hours, twisted their flex-cuffs around their wrists to cause pain, and forced a detainee to consume water "until he could not breathe."[35]

Troops also used techniques from their training drills.

"We used to have the detainees do physical training," said Higginbotham. "Sometimes we would do the training with them—as in jumping jacks, push-ups, sit-ups, 'Iron Mikes' (lunges with your hands on your hips), wall sits where the detainee assumed a seated position along a wall without a chair and holding their hands out to their front … We would sometimes use stress positions as an interrogation technique. That would be anything from sitting on the floor with no chair, standing with a chair next to you, but not being able to sit down in it, kneeling on the floor with your hands interlocked behind your head, lying on your back with your hands and feet in the air. Some of us tried these stress positions to see how long you could stand to be in those positions. Once you knew how long you could stay in one of the positions, you never told the detainee to stay in the stress position for a period of time longer than you could stay in it."[36]

The MPs also added different methods of monstering to punish detainees and keep them from sleeping.

"If they would not stand up when they were told to, then we would cuff them to the ceiling to keep them standing," explained an MP from the 377th in a sworn statement. "We would use a leg chain, fixed to the ceiling and then affixed to the short handcuffs."[37]

But why force detainees to stand?

It was, as the MP explained, "so they wouldn't sleep, so they would be willing to talk to MI [Military Intelligence]. MI directed us to keep them from sleeping for specified periods of time. They would write it on the status board, for example, 'one hour up, two hours down.' "[38]

The MPs also turned to other techniques to discipline and monster their prisoners. These techniques didn't come from official Washington guidelines. Instead, MPs simply turned to their training. Soldiers from the 377th learned how to subdue and restrain detainees during their MP training at Fort Dix in New Jersey. Some of their instructors were police and corrections officers who had used these techniques in their work. Many of these techniques, such as "pressure-point control tactics" and "compliance blows," were designed to disable prisoners without causing lasting damage. Some troops became proficient with these techniques and earned nicknames because of these associations. One soldier was dubbed "the Knee of Death." Damien M. Corsetti, a specialist in the 519th Military Intelligence Battalion, was actually nicknamed "The King of Torture" or "Monster" and had the Italian word for monster (*mostro*) tattooed on his stomach.

One of the 377th MPs, Specialist Willie V. Brand, said that he was instructed how to use many of these techniques when he first arrived at Bagram. One of the most frequently used compliance blows that Brand and his peers used was the "common peroneal strike"—hitting a prisoner on the lateral side of the thigh. Striking detainees became "a matter of common practice," said Brand, and compliance blows were adopted as "standard operating procedure" (SOP) at the base since they were so effective at disabling unruly prisoners.

Brand used the strikes four times against one such defiant prisoner, who was hung by his wrists with chains: Habibullah. "It was morally wrong," Brand said in an affidavit. "But it was an SOP."

Even after Habibullah's death, soldiers weren't discouraged from using peroneal strikes—they were only instructed to record when they used them.[39] The day after Habibullah died, Brand had to contend with another detainee who, according to depositions, was "resistant to interrogation" and "eventually became combative."

That detainee was Dilawar.

Dilawar was suspended by chains from the ceiling at Bagram, and his handlers couldn't understand what he was pleading for. Fellow detainees heard him beg for help. Guards remembered Dilawar trying to shake the hood off his head and repeatedly kick one of the prison doors to gain the guards' attention.[40] The guards tried to ignore him, but grew annoyed by his conduct. Some of them were irritated with Dilawar after he spit up water when an MP took "a small [1/2 liter] bottle of water and shoved it in [his] mouth and squeezed water into his mouth."[41] One even remarked that Dilawar was "being an ass."[42] Brand had had it.[43] He struck Dilawar in the thigh several times to subdue him.[44]

"I told people I had to switch knees because my leg got tired," said Brand, who admitted he hit Dilawar about thirty-seven times.[45]

Brand may have delivered the final blow, but others contributed to Dilawar's abuse. Another MP pummeled him six times on both legs with peroneal strikes. A soldier who witnessed Dilawar's treatment remembered "the look [the MP] gave me when he came out, which seemed ... to me as if to mean, 'This is how you take care of business.'"[46]

Troops passed by Dilawar as they went on to deal with other prisoners.

"Dilawar was hanging limp in the chains," remembered Sergeant Thomas V. Curtis. "I thought he was sleeping. So I kicked the door and I could have sworn I got a response, a slight move of the head." Then, he said, "we took the hood off and uncuffed him and he was dead weight. He just dropped."[47]

The MPs tried to resuscitate Dilawar but failed.

His legs were "pulpified," according to the forensic report.[48]

Curtis summed up the way he felt about Dilawar's death: "It was more or less that he was the second one to die in our shift," he said. "I had no personal connection to him, I didn't [know] him, but it was unfortunate ... You can sit back now and see that we should have done things differently. It was like a war thing, us against them. We just did what we were trained to do."[49]

Even if high-ranking officers did not have a direct role in ordering the abuse at Bagram, they could still have contributed to it in other ways. According to a classified report given to the *Washington Post*, the 377th's command oversaw the abuse, knew soldiers "were striking detainees in Afghanistan," and that a "dereliction of duty contributed to routine prisoner mistreatment."[50] Perhaps more than issuing orders, officers simply chose to ignore maltreatment, and that inaction, in turn, helped allow abuse to continue, and to worsen, unabated.

After Wahid and I wrapped up our reporting in Khost, we set out to Forward Operating Base Salerno to catch our flight to Kabul. But we decided to visit one more place before we left. Sadat sped by the verdant fields that edged Khost's main road, drove past Salerno's gate, and climbed the same mountain road where Dilawar and his passengers traveled on their way to Yakubi.

There, just beyond a coarse, gravelly cemetery, lay an exposed saddle where the four travelers had been abducted five years earlier, explained Sadat. Wahid, conscious of our surroundings and our proximity to the Pakistan border, felt that we were now exposed. He grew edgy and suggested we move on quickly. We had only a few minutes to take in the surroundings and reflect on the journey that began there nearly a year after the war on terror was declared. Sadat drove us back to Salerno and deposited us at the gate.

"Thank you, brother," he said. We embraced, then Sadat waved and finally departed.

At Salerno, visitors had to pass three main checkpoints: Afghan forces manned the first two; US troops guarded the third. When we arrived at the first checkpoint, Afghan guards exchanged puzzled questions through rackety walkie-talkies about how best to announce our presence and who would give us clearance. Thirty minutes passed before we were granted permission. We passed the first two checkpoints and hiked several kilometers with heavy luggage along the hot, dusty road to the US checkpoint. I approached the gate first and walked towards a Pashto translator who shouted out to us as we advanced. His cries continued as we neared, and the American soldiers beside him raised their rifles. I suddenly remembered the way Tank, the Governor's security attaché, described how he identified suspected suicide bombers: they were often dressed in baggy clothes, carried some kind of gear (often strapped to their chest), and were almost always heavily sweating. I fit the profile.

"I'm American—I don't speak Pashto!" I declared.

The US soldiers were taken aback, then relaxed and lowered their weapons. They asked to see my passport and inquired about our business. The Afghan guards at the first gate had relayed confusing messages to the translator at the US checkpoint, which only heightened their trepidation. Wahid eventually caught up to the checkpoint and doubled over with laughter when he learned that I had been confused for an Afghan—and by my own countrymen. The soldiers were stunned that anyone other than an Afghan would travel "outside the wire" (outside the base, without a military convoy) in local garb.

"Takes a lot of balls," said one soldier, shaking his head in disbelief.

After clearing this last checkpoint, we went out to the airfield to catch our flight. Just as we were rushing down the base road, a call came from Kabul: our flight was cancelled due to technical problems. The travel company promised to try again the next day, but added there could be a two-day delay, given the foul weather that had formed around Kabul's mountains. Travel in Afghanistan comes with many hurdles and regularly includes these types of delays and cancellations. Our journey from Khost to Kabul was no different, and Salerno became our home for a spell.

Wahid and I sat beneath locust and poplar trees that hugged the roads, and paused to appraise our situation. Beige office buildings and long olive-green tents were wedged between the alleyways that divided the base. A small stream of Afghans ambled through Salerno, mostly filling their hours with construction work. American soldiers strolled by, often dressed in Army T-shirts and shorts, with M16s casually slung over their shoulders or pistols fastened to their sides. Movement around the base seemed unhurried, even calm.

I tried to convince Wahid that our time on the Salerno base would be tranquil, maybe even enjoyable. It would be safer at Salerno than in Khost, where suicide bombs seemed to strike regularly, I argued. True, we wouldn't have a jasmine-perfumed veranda, but there was a recreation hall—the Hard Rock—with ping-pong, pool tables, and a small movie theater with many DVDs. We would have access to the KBR mess hall that served a wide array of bland meals and junk food, which would likely ensure one less night of food poisoning back in the Governor's Guesthouse (I had already had many bouts of sickness there). We could enjoy a night of air-conditioning and avoid more malaria-bearing mosquitoes. And at last, we had access to bathrooms with fully functional plumbing.

Eventually, Wahid agreed to stay—albeit with some reluctance. A contract worker on the base overheard our discussion and offered to help us properly check in so that we could secure accommodation. We agreed, and minutes later she located a military escort who met us at Salerno's multi-denominational chapel (just across from a mobile Subway kiosk).

A young Army captain and mother of two walked us around the base facilities, first showing us our lodgings: a tent filled with twenty stiff cots that sheltered a handful of Navy reserves from Florida. Then the facilities: restrooms along the roads and the mess hall on the opposite end of the base. Finally, the bomb shelter. She reminded us about Salerno's pseudonym, "Rocket City," and instructed us to file into fortified bunkers if the sirens sounded off.

"Just wait for them to announce the all-clear. Then you'll be fine and can return to your tent," our escort explained. "There's usually not a lot of action with so much 'luminous,' and we nearly have a full moon now."

Wahid's face dropped; her words offered little consolation. It wasn't just the prospect of occasional incoming fire that was disconcerting. Together, dressed in local attire, we stood out among the throngs of American soldiers, and often caught suspicious stares. Tired, lost in thought, we sat by the road under the shade of the trees, calculating the time we'd have to stay on the base, when a patrol of GIs pulled up in front of us. The soldiers spilled onto the road and questioned us about our presence on the base. Our luggage, which we had just dropped off at the tent, was visible in the back of their SUV.

"You didn't properly check in, and you guys need to speak with the commander," said the sergeant.

The soldiers encircled us as we took our seats in the vehicle. Wahid's face looked strained with worry.

"Nothing will happen to us," I promised. "We haven't done anything wrong."

He nodded and turned away.

The SUV pulled up at the American checkpoint, and the soldiers brought us to one of the base officers who managed non-military visitors. I explained our situation, including our military escort's invitation to sleep over. Wahid offered to leave, insisting we really didn't want to cause any trouble.

"That's not necessary," countered the commander. They returned our luggage, but we temporarily had to surrender all electrical devices —computers, recorders, cameras, and a satellite phone—to prevent transmitting signals. Wahid carefully retained all of our notes about the detainee abuse we had just researched, and then together we checked in our personal effects. The soldiers at the office were helpful and courteous, and handed me a receipt for our equipment after they filed it away.

"See? No problem," I said to Wahid, patting his back as we exited the office.

He lit a cigarette, and quietly sighed.

"We were kidnapped," he said, half-joking. And then he repeatedly offered to return to Kabul by road, even though it was a dangerous journey.

My countrymen shuffled through the base. They spoke a language I could understand, ate familiar food at shared meals. Troops played basketball on paved courts, and raucously cheered during evening volleyball matches. But Wahid felt no such familiarity and comfort. He might even have felt less comfortable there—at the very base where Dilawar was first captured—after having spent several days translating accounts of how US forces treated his fellow countrymen.

There was a war on, and we were in a violent Taliban region. Soldiers had to prepare themselves for regular attacks. And yet the barricades and distant checkpoints, along with the availability of familiar American comforts peppering the base, seemed to insulate Salerno, to disconnect it from its locality.

Apart from brushing up against Afghan laborers and their military counterparts who worked at the base, I wondered how much contact American troops had with the local population, and whether this shaped their perception of local Afghans. How many Americans at Salerno had even heard about Dilawar?

Two days after our original departure date, a turbo-prop plane finally picked us up and returned us to Kabul. Days later I met with Nader Nadery, deputy director of the Afghanistan Independent Human Rights Commission. I asked Nadery about the extent to which American troops were still involved in detainee abuse.

"Since last April, complaints have been decreasing," he said. It was heartening to hear that there were fewer incidents. But, Nadery added, since 2006, "Americans were forcing Afghans to sign documents saying they should not describe what happened to them."

I had heard that US forces compelled detainees to sign papers before their release—especially if they had been held in Guantanamo. Nadery feared that released detainees were unsure of exactly what the documents contained, but felt intimidated by having to sign them, which may have kept them from reporting abuse. He and other human rights workers also felt that the limited redress offered in cases of US torture and abuse discouraged detainees from reporting their experiences. It reminded me of a discussion I had about the Dilawar case with a staffer of the Senate Armed Services Committee before my trip to Afghanistan.

"When we were briefed on the Bagram cases we were told 'this is a success story,' " he had said. "Of course we were briefed sometime in 2004, nearly two years after the incident occurred. But CID [the Army's Criminal Investigative Command, commonly referred to as the CID] said, 'We got this initial report in and we were told nothing really happened. But we didn't believe that and went back and looked into it some more until finally we realized they were serious homicides, and we needed to make recommendations.'

"They were touting that as a success story over at CID, really. But you wondered why it took so long in the first place. I mean these guys were beaten to a pulp. Literally." Even some CID officers were distressed by the outcome of the Bagram case.

Dilawar and Habibullah weren't the only detainees to suffer such a fate. To date, Human Rights First found more than 200 detainees have died while in custody of US forces since the launch of the "war on terror"; some were obviously tortured to death.[51] For former detainees, the sluggish pace of the investigation into the Dilawar case (and other similar cases) seemed to signal more than a slow bureaucratic response. For these torture victims, it indicated that the US wasn't genuinely trying to stamp out torture; to some, it even seemed to suggest a kind of sanction.

When Wahid and I interviewed former Bagram detainee Qader Khandan in Khost, he told us that military investigators visited him while he was incarcerated in Guantanamo from 2003 to 2006 and asked him about what happened to Dilawar at Bagram. He sketched out pictures of the holding cells, and the ways in which military personnel suspended prisoners with chains. His drawings looked strikingly similar to the ones that US troops submitted to investigators from the US Army's CID. Khandan was certain the investigation would help bring justice to those responsible for the torture and demise of Bagram's detainees. It didn't.

After we finished our interview with Khandan, we broke to eat lunch together and I told Wahid what ultimately transpired with the investigations and courts-martial. Few soldiers, and even fewer officers, involved in the deaths of Dilawar and Habibullah saw the inside of a courtroom. Military investigators recommended that twenty-seven Army personnel be criminally charged for the Afghans' deaths and related abuses that occurred in Bagram around the same time. In the end, only four troops were sentenced to jail time. None of the sentences exceeded five months.[52]

"I will not translate this to him," said Wahid, referring to Khandan.

I nodded in agreement. We both knew such news would only worsen his grief.

The stories of Dilawar and Habibullah represent only two examples of US detainee abuse in Afghanistan in 2002. Yet they were also two of about 128 cases that year in which Afghans were seriously abused in Bagram and at US bases in Afghanistan—often with the very same techniques that were applied to Dilawar and Habibullah.[53]

I later asked Wahid if I could quote him when writing about our experiences in Khost for Americans back home.

Yes, he said. "Tell them that after this I will not support them ... I will not trust them."

It was a halting remark. And it was then that I finally understood the enduring legacy of Dilawar's experience.

There has been plenty of torture in Afghanistan in modern memory—from the recent Soviet invasion and the civil wars that followed to this most recent conflict. Dilawar's experience is another tragic story in that continuum. It is also key to understanding early US detainee abuse.

The stories of Dilawar and Habibullah reveal that violent assaults and desperation cannot always explain why troops resort to torture. True, the American military was embroiled in a war with the Taliban. But US forces at Bagram can't explain away their acts of torture because they were under attack (as some soldiers have alleged).[54] Bagram didn't face an increase in combat deaths and casualties during the time that Dilawar and Habibullah were tortured. In fact, American casualties in Afghanistan during the winter of 2002 were comparatively quite low.

Dilawar and Habibullah's experience also showed that soldiers didn't need manuals or memos to lead them to torture. US troops in Bagram tortured their prisoners in banal and crude ways, informed by myths and memory. The sleep deprivation dreamed up by Mackey's military intelligence colleague, as well as his observation that "hard-core prisoners were unlikely to start cracking until about fourteen hours into an interrogation," were a product of folklore that spread through casual hearsay. The soldiers that enhanced sleep deprivation through "monstering" used techniques they remembered from their MP training (e.g., the "peroneal strikes"). Some learned compliance blows from three weeks of detainee training at Fort Dix, New Jersey, which, in some cases, were taught by police and corrections officers. Some said they learned peroneal strikes on the job at Bagram. One soldier referenced the techniques he learned while working in a juvenile detention center (though he didn't admit to applying those techniques on Afghan detainees).

The degree to which officers issued explicit orders remains uncertain. It's possible that mid-level officers ordered some of the abuse. However, at present, there isn't proof that high-ranking officers sanctioned abuse at Bagram. The soldiers' lawyers did not introduce such orders as exculpatory evidence during courts-martial. Dilawar's experience shows that directives, written or otherwise, weren't needed to enable abuse. Officers merely had to look the other way to facilitate the abuse—and they did, according to military reports.[55] In that regard, the stories of Dilawar and Habibullah reinforce the impression that overlooking abuse can (and did) help facilitate torture just as much as issuing orders.[56] Indeed, failing to stem abuse would contribute to more abuse elsewhere during the war on terror.[57]

In the end, some military personnel felt that the intelligence collected from Bagram's detainees during that period was dubious. According to a report on US detainee abuse in Afghanistan produced by the McClatchy Newspapers, Major Jeff Bovarnick, a legal adviser at Bagram from November 2002 to June 2003, "said in a sworn statement that of some 500 detainees he knew of who'd passed through Bagram, only about 10 were high-value targets, the military's term for senior terrorist operatives."[58]

There was another dimension to this story that I hadn't fully understood until my journey to Khost: the Afghan perspective.

I had a fleeting taste of what it was like to play "Afghan Like Me" because of my having dressed like a local in Afghanistan's provinces. That experience gave me a small sense of what it was like to live in fear, cautiously examining fellow countrymen and foreigners, and habitually trying to avoid attention. Associating with foreigners in public, even those who are friends and allies, attracts attention and, by extension, danger. Mixing with foreigners on their own turf, as at Salerno, also presents particular risks. Together, Wahid and I saw how soldiers were vigilantly skeptical of the unfamiliar, not out of malice but in the interests of self-preservation. I had a glimpse of this when I was almost targeted by young troops at Salerno's gate for being a suspected suicide bomber. It was a chilling encounter. A moment later, it was comical—at least for Wahid. Unlike others wearing Afghan garb, I could quickly dispel any distrust with an American passport and a casual conversation with US soldiers.

Seeing Salerno through Wahid's eyes during our brief tour there provided a starkly different perspective. He didn't have the American passport and couldn't disarmingly relate to the checkpoint guards. Salerno was an oasis of familiar culture and safe food for me, but it was a coarse, unwelcoming place for Wahid. He wasn't uncomfortable with the trappings of Western culture around the base (some of which he enjoyed), nor was he bothered by the American soldiers. Wahid was uneasy about something else. We had been engaged in extensive conversations with former detainees and their families for about a week. And the memory of Dilawar's sad fate lingered days later as we ambled through the very US base where his captors first sent him.

The US troops who stopped us at Salerno were respectful and appropriately vetted us. But it was impossible not to think of Dilawar at the moment of our brief capture. We were not detained, nor were we at all mistreated, but it gave us both a sense of what it was like to be distrusted and powerless in the hands of an awesome and imposing military.

I understood another dimension of Dilawar's legacy after Wahid and I visited Salerno. It was resentment. Dilawar's death wasn't just a tragic loss because of his innocence. It also exemplified the blithe disregard with which a poor Afghan kid was treated by a foreign army.

I'll always remember the time in the Khost prison when I interviewed Parkhudin, watching the guards' reaction when they heard how a young, fragile man perished under his captors' crushing blows. Wahid's arresting statement—"Tell them that after this I will not support them ... I will not trust them"—was also unforgettable. He wasn't in any way suggesting he had turned against the coalition forces. He was reacting to the way in which the US military had responded to Dilawar's torture, and the lack of accountability after his death. Dilawar's fellow detainees, like other victims of US abuse or torture, still have not enjoyed any redress or received any meaningful apology.

Wahid's response seemed to highlight that even though Americans, Afghans, and Iraqis had been engaged with each other for many years, they still remained far apart and disconnected in certain crucial ways—especially when it came to reckoning with torture.

Chapter 3:
"We weren't in the CIA—
we were soldiers"

TROOPS FROM BATTALION 1-68 were bracing for a fight. Like Adam Gray, there were many gung-ho soldiers who were members of the tank unit or working alongside it. Some became impassioned about fighting in the war on terror after the US was attacked. Jonathan Millantz fit into that category. September 11, 2001, filled him with renewed patriotic fervor and a hatred for terrorism. Six months later, he joined the Army. Millantz was assigned to the 4th Infantry Division, not as a tanker but as a combat medic for Battalion 1-68.

Adam Stevenson watched the World Trade Center crumble on television from his home in Danville, Illinois, and wondered how the attacks would affect his upcoming military service. He had enlisted several months before the terrorist strike and was slated to report to basic training on September 12, 2001. But it took two years for Stevenson to learn how the war on terror would influence his stretch in the Army.

A year and a half after US forces attacked Afghanistan, the war on terror dramatically extended its reach. The Bush administration claimed that Saddam Hussein's regime belonged to a pantheon of terrorist states and was a member, alongside Iran and North Korea, of an "Axis of Evil." Throughout 2002 and 2003, the US and its allies argued that the Iraqi regime posed an imminent threat.

On March 19, 2003, President Bush finally ordered US forces to attack Iraq, and Stevenson found himself serving alongside Adam Gray with Battalion 1-68, charging ahead in their Abrams tanks. "There was so much anticipation," Stevenson remembered. "It [was] like going from a crawl to a full-on dead sprint in two minutes."

In Iraq, Millantz met Daniel Keller, a slim, relaxed Southern Californian with short-cropped dark hair. Keller once described himself as a "a huge liberal" who "wasn't cool with war." But part of him also wanted to be a soldier from the time he was a young boy.

"I always thought being a soldier was this honorable and noble thing," said Keller. "You're doing a job that not many other people can do so that other people don't have to."

When he visited the Army recruiter's office, he explained that he wanted to find a job in the military that would enable him to "blow shit up." The recruiter suggested tanks.

Once Keller finally joined the Army he took pride in being a professional soldier. For Keller, Battalion 1-68, "was not a disappointment to me at all ... [it] was a cutting-edge unit, and the general soldiering skills were outstanding."

He and his fellow troops wanted to test their skills in combat and contribute to the war on terror. They finally got their chance when the Iraq war started. The US military gave it a code name: Operation Iraqi Freedom, and together with other coalition forces they swiftly tore through the country. The air attack—the "shock and awe" campaign—quickly decimated the Iraqi military.

By April 9, 2003, troops entered Baghdad and toppled Saddam Hussein's regime. "I arrived in Baghdad to a city blown apart, bodies lying everywhere, and ... just a total mess," remembered Millantz. The first wave of combat also left comparatively little fighting for other units. Conventional warfare, including tank warfare, was no longer in great demand. Many members of Battalion 1-68 recalled that during this period their enthusiasm quickly faded into dejection.

In Tehachapi, California, Cindy Chavez was glued to her television, eager for more news about the American military campaign in Iraq. She was able to exchange emails with her son, Adam Gray, and even an occasional phone call. Adam also sent her a microcassette audio diary from Iraq.

"Hey, mama, this is your baby boy ... just wanted to say hi," he said in the recording. "Maybe it could give you some release to make sure that I am doing all right so you don't have to worry ... The mail has been real slow here. We've been moving all around, so it's taken awhile for it to get in and out ..."

He casually talked into the tape recorder and rambled on about everyday life during his early tour in Iraq.

"It's hot as fuck during the day, usually 120–125 degrees during the day … We're just rolling around Iraq here, not doing much. Chain smoking like a nut, that's about it …"

Adam occasionally teased her, too.

"I was thinking about maybe coming over for supper tonight, what you making? Make some meatloaf and mashed potatoes. That'd be great."

He also told her about the scenery and his interactions with local Iraqis as his unit rolled through streets in their tanks.

"Mom, they have farms here. They have so many fruits and vegetables. The teachers bring the soft, sweet bread in the morning and … share it with all the soldiers."

Adam and his unit patrolled schools and took many pictures of smiling children playfully wrapping their limbs around him and his fellow soldiers. Handing out candy to local kids was a favorite diversion, and members of the unit would trade guard duty for the distribution runs.

Cindy assembled many care packages for him and figured one in ten of them would actually reach him. She sent pumpkin seeds, Kool Aid, candied necklaces, Copenhagen tobacco, and Pez candies—anything that wouldn't melt in the heat. She chuckled as she handed me a photo of Adam leaning against a tank in an olive-green jumpsuit with a Bart Simpson Pez container in his shoulder pocket. It was just the kind of levity and sweet distraction they needed. As the initial fighting wound down, the combat grew subdued. For a while, anyway.

"It seems like no one wants to mess with tanks anymore," said Adam. "Everyone sees us roll up and takes off hauling ass the other way. It seems like slim pickings for fights, so I might go 19 Delta [Calvary scout]. It just seems like I might see a little more action."

During that time, Adam's unit was settling into central Iraq, and he felt that their routine had become monotonous.

"I'm bored, I'm lonely," he admitted. "Got a shitload of ammunition and nothing to do with it. We got 10,000 rounds of machine gun ammunition and … not a lot of things to shoot. There's no killing left to do, mom. They didn't leave me any killing, those bastards."

Cindy said Adam was referencing a line in a military comedy, *Major Payne*—that's all. But even if he was joking, it still reflected how he and other unit members were frustrated by the lack of action they faced.

At one point on the microcassette tape he spoke in a low voice, cut away for a moment, and casually returned.

"All right I'm back," he said. "Somebody went over a landmine, and blew the shit out of their vehicle … supposedly there are 10,000 land-mines in Iraq. Too bad there's no action. Everyone pretty much turns ass and runs like a son of a bitch. I'm so freaking bored …"

Other soldiers in Battalion 1-68 admitted that they were equally disappointed by the lack of activity after their early incursion into Iraq.

"The excitement from the initial insertion into a foreign land wears off," said Keller. "You're just not excited by it anymore. The adrenaline rush of your life being under threat constantly is gone. You're contracted by the government to kill people—that is your job—and you're doing that under the threat of death."

Adam's good friend Tony Sandoval remembered how men in his unit wanted to destroy big targets with their tanks just to apply their training. But the Iraqi army quickly collapsed, and there were no tank battles, no heavy armor or targets to hit.

"We got there ready to flex our muscles and nothing happened," remembered Sandoval. "Everyone was getting really frustrated."

The lull in action seemed especially difficult for his friend Adam. "He was well trained and ready to go," said Sandoval. "He thought we were going to go over there and get to shoot some main gun rounds, fire down on people, and really beat up the bad guys. Instead it seemed like we were this big giant that kind of got slapped."

Some were also deflated by how their mission changed over time.

During the early part of their tour in Iraq in 2003, the 4th Infantry Division—the larger detachment that included Battalion 1-68—was tasked with searching for weapons of mass destruction (WMDs). Troops combed through the country to find the weapons, even scouring surfaces with metal detectors. In the end, the search for WMDs was a bust, and the war's links to Osama bin Laden and al Qaeda appeared to be ever more vague and questionable.

After Baghdad fell to US forces, Battalion 1-68 was stationed in the central Iraqi city of Tuz, a relatively quiet city at the time. Captain Sean Nowlan, the S2 or military intelligence officer for Battalion 1-68, remembered how calm and safe it was. "I would probably say the local populace was very welcoming and open and warm, and you could pretty much travel in the Tuz area with very little security," Nowlan remembered. But that changed in late June 2003, after the battalion pushed on to the city of Balad. "Once we moved from Tuz to the Balad area, that's when it started escalating," said Nowlan.

Balad is located in the heart of the Sunni Triangle, an area northwest of Baghdad that was regularly engulfed in violent clashes against coalition forces. By the autumn of 2003 the complexion of the Iraq war had markedly changed, and US soldiers faced new challenges. Pockets of resistance soon formed, and their attacks focused on the coalition forces and the nascent Iraqi police and military. US commanders called them insurgents, and their attacks became more frequent and lethal.

"After Saddam Hussein was captured, there was a brief lull [in violence] of a few weeks," said Major Bill Benson, the operations officer, known as the S3. "There were other times where we would have three or four attacks a day. I think the highest was probably five in any given day."

The US mission, once deemed "accomplished," suddenly seemed unresolved. It had also taken a new shape.

Troops remembered that the unit's approach to the insurgents, and the Iraq war in general, changed after the battalion's leadership rotation in Tuz. They were being confronted with new enemies, but they weren't yet entirely clear about who their new targets were and how best to root them out. Battalion 1-68 accepted its missions, and Adam Gray and his fellow troops were no longer bored.

Adam dutifully fulfilled his orders, but part of him still sympathized with the Iraqis and what they were going through. He told his mother, "There's a war going on and these guys are just trying to protect their family. But you never want to turn your back on them because they will kill you. They'll smile at you and blow your head off, so you can never calm down."

That kind of fear affected the troops' reactions to perceived threats.

Jonathan Millantz traveled seventy miles north of Baghdad to join his new unit, Battalion 1-68, in Balad at Forward Operating Base Lion (FOB Lion, later known as FOB O'Ryan). During his journey he saw parts of the country that had been razed by battle and bombs, and areas where Iraqis happily greeted him and his fellow troops.

"When we first arrived we were handing out water, candy to kids … and it was all right for the first few days," he said, mirroring Adam's early memories of Iraq. "Getting to our operating base wasn't too bad—until we started going on patrols."

Sergeant Oral Lindsey, Adam's tank commander, remembered how he and his crew had to adjust to the patrols and the ever-changing operations.

"The patrols, the raids, and the traffic control checkpoints ... [It] wasn't really our kind of job," said Lindsey. "We were tankers, come on, man. We were supposed to be out there blowing stuff up, not stopping traffic, trying to interpret the Iraqi language—that wasn't our responsibility. Well, it was everybody's responsibility to do it, but it just wasn't what we were trained to do."

I met Lindsey shortly after I visited Adam Gray's mother in Tehachapi, California. He worked for a fuel company roughly seventy-five miles west of Tehachapi and lived in the desert amidst oil drills, pump jacks known as "nodding donkeys," and bulging, bent gas lines. It was a landscape that seemed similar to Iraq and reminded me of the images that Adam referred to as he drove back to Tehachapi after his tour. Cindy believed Lindsey might have some answers about what happened to her son and urged me to meet him.

Lindsey recalled one incident in particular. It happened on a night when they were on patrol.

Adam and his crew did routine counter-IED rounds with their tanks just outside of Balad to locate makeshift bombs hidden along the road as well as the insurgents who planted them. They routinely took machine gun fire from a small village on the side of the road as they went on patrol. Troops looked through their night scopes—a thermal imaging system—to identify targets. One night, they spotted a silhouette and quickly read its heat signature: it appeared to be a cluster of insurgents and a weapon.

Lindsey was manning the tank's gun, and he engaged the target and opened fire. The gun discharged tracers into the night and sliced through a pile of hay that burst into orange flames. He ceased firing as smoke wafted off the gun. A pair of soldiers left the tank and trekked into the darkness to assess their target. But they hadn't hit a cluster of insurgents. Instead, they'd fired upon a small family—a man in his mid-forties, a young man in his twenties, and a little girl. One of the men was carrying an AK-47—many Iraqis were allowed to carry one for personal protection.

The crew radioed for help. A Blackhawk helicopter arrived and swiftly flew the three injured Iraqis to the Balad Air Field. Only the young man survived; the older man and the young girl were soon pronounced dead.

"Not a day goes by that I don't see a little girl's face, and it's hard," Lindsey told me, his throat tightening as he reflected on the incident nearly three years later. "Especially [since] that little girl was the same age of my daughter, my oldest daughter. I tell you what … it's hard to deal with."

I later relayed his account to Cindy, who didn't know that Lindsey had been so affected by the experience. Adam had already told her about the shooting incident during a night of heavy drinking, and Cindy knew that it deeply upset her son. During that same night of boozy confessions, Adam told his mother about more events that occurred in Balad that also troubled him, and had traumatized others in his battalion as well.

In mid-2003, violence increasingly engulfed the Sunni Triangle as militant groups gathered throughout Iraq. The insurgency was becoming more organized and began launching regular strikes on Americans and their allies. Battalion 1-68 could count on a rocket or mortar attack just about every night and struggled with how to respond.

Major General Raymond T. Odierno, who commanded the 4th Infantry Division, ordered his units to aggressively round up Iraqis involved in the insurgency. Part of Battalion 1-68, like some of the units from the 4th ID, were assembled as a Quick Reaction Force (QRF), tasked with locating and capturing insurgent suspects. They conducted house raids, made arrests, and carted away detainees. Later, an investigation by the Army's inspector general's office found that units of the 4th infantry division (to which Battalion 1-68 belonged) were "grabbing whole villages because combat soldiers [were] unable to figure out who was of value." The mass detentions swamped the US interrogation system and alienated local Iraqis.

"There was a tendency early on to do larger, battalion-type … operations—they were cordon-and-search operations," said Benson. "That's what folks are comfortable with … those are the typical types of military operations that we were all trained to do. But the second part of all that is, we just didn't have the detailed intelligence needed to conduct this specific targeted missions that we really wanted to do. And we got much better at that over time … There was no Iraqi government official, Iraqi police official, Iraqi leader, that gave us any help and any information at all with regards to the enemy situation there. I mean none."

Soldiers from Battalion 1-68 knew tank warfare, yet they were suddenly embroiled in a different type of combat that made conventional arms and combat impractical. The Abrams tanks they drove were faster than their predecessors, but the treads wore out quickly and the tanks needed constant maintenance as they drove over Iraq's hot roads. Crews baked in the tanks' steel bellies, which lacked air-conditioning at the time. The battalion needed to be lighter and more nimble, so they operated Bradley Fighting Vehicles in place of most of their tanks.

It was a blow to many tank operators, who prided themselves on their menacing armored cavalry. The same crews that were once assigned to Abrams tanks were transplanted to the Bradleys, with gunners and loaders often sitting in the back, poised to jump out when needed. Even though they went through aggressive military training, some soldiers from Battalion 1-68 told me they were unprepared for house raids and detainee operations, and hadn't been briefed on some of the most elementary procedures for handling prisoners.

"We never dealt with zip ties," said Sandoval, referring to the plastic cuffs that soldiers used. "We just made it up as we went."

Before they started going out on raids, they first needed to assemble an area to contain suspects they captured. Part of Battalion 1-68 was assigned to FOB Lion, just outside of Balad and about five miles from Camp Anaconda (also known as Logistics Support Area, or LSA, Anaconda), a much larger American military base.[1] Soldiers there didn't have as much oversight as at a larger base, and with fewer resources they needed to work with the existing structures to set up a jail. The troops found a guard shack alongside a bombed-out ammunition depot with missing doors and bathrooms that didn't work. They strung up lights inside it, filled the windows with concertina wire, and draped coils of it from the ceilings to the floors where doors once hung. Soldiers described the jail they built as a slapdash, makeshift operation.

"It was very *Sanford and Son* around there," said Adam Stevenson, invoking a 1970s television show about a California junk dealer. "There was a lot of stuff that was duct-taped together, so to speak."

"We were very isolated," recalled Nowlan. "I mean, at [that] time, I literally had one computer with no connectivity. It was very World War II-ish, where we were just out there on our own."

With a holding pen ready, soldiers from Battalion 1-68 were better able to manage the Iraqis they captured. They hauled away fighters overtaken in ambushes, as well as prisoners from house raids. During those raids they relied on haphazard methods to identify and seize suspects. Some of their targets were identified through wanted posters that the battalion put together to identify insurgent suspects.

Troops also carried blurry photographs of suspects and picked up anyone who resembled them.

Benson said some Iraqis approached his unit, wanting to volunteer information. But, he said, the Iraqis told him they could talk to him only if their neighbors could see them being arrested in their homes.

"It was not unusual for an Iraqi who wanted to help the Americans or wanted to pass information to say, 'Hey, come to my house, do a raid and arrest me, and that way I won't be seen by my neighbors to be helping the Americans. It will give me credibility in the community but I'll still be able to pass you information,' " recalled Benson. "I mean that kind of thing happened countless times."

Sometimes the unit hauled in twenty or thirty prisoners a night. They cinched plastic zip ties around their wrists, slipped an empty sandbag over their heads to blind them, then carted them to the jail on a flatbed truck. To some soldiers it seemed like a scattershot approach, aimed at seizing and sorting through suspects. But the troops were doing the best they could for a mission that demanded improvisation.[2]

"The lines were certainly blurred at the beginning of the war, as people were put in situations that they were not necessarily used to operating in," said Benson. Soldiers, he said, were operating "out of a desire to do [their] job, and to save people's lives … you had people who were trying to do their job the best way they could."

Those who weren't tasked to do patrols or QRFs had to watch over prisoners at the jail. FOB Lion didn't hold as many prisoners as the larger bases or detention facilities in Iraq, but the tankers still needed to guard and tend to them. In some cases, they had to keep order among their prisoners, and there, too, they improvised.

Members of Battalion 1-68 went through tanker training and also, like all US soldiers, basic training. Drill sergeants put their new enlistees through strenuous exercises to improve their fitness and toughen them up, but also to discipline recruits.

"In basic training when we screwed up as a whole they'd 'smoke us'— that's what they called it," Sandoval said. "They found ways to make you sweat if you screwed up." He recalled the various punishing exercises recruits were ordered to do when that happened: holding heavy duffle bags upright with their arms wide apart while standing in formation for a half hour; crawling on their bellies on the rough forest floor; and doing endless series of push-ups in various positions in the sweltering heat.

In the jail at FOB Lion, troops borrowed some of these disciplinary tools to punish their prisoners.

"Sometimes if they wouldn't shut up you'd say, 'Okay, start doing push-ups or get in some physical position,' " Sandoval remembered. Soldiers from Battalion 1-68 recalled how the techniques used to discipline detainees bled into the regimen applied to soften up detainees before or during interrogations.

Many soldiers from Battalion 1-68 reasoned that since the military forced them to do such grueling exercises during their training, it wasn't unreasonable to make accused terrorists do them too.[3]

"Basically the same things we did to those people in Iraq were the same things that were done to us and taught to us," said Millantz. Sometimes they forced detainees to march, maintain forced positions, and hold heavy wooden boards until their limbs strained.

"To our eyes this stuff wasn't that bad [since] some of it was done in basic training," said Millantz. But deep down inside, he knew it really was "that bad."

"It's painful," he conceded. "Especially if you have twelve soldiers from a different country yelling at you, screaming at you, pointing guns at you and having stuff done [to you]. I can only imagine how traumatizing that would be to someone."

Once, Millantz even saw a detainee's wrist break from one of the forced exercises. Yet that didn't deter everyone from experimenting with other techniques and using them for various purposes.[4]

Just beside the jail sat interrogation booths where military intelligence officers questioned detainees. Daniel Keller was underwhelmed by the early interrogations that he witnessed and was struck by the ways in which Army personnel tried to arouse fear in their detainees.

"One of the first times I saw someone interrogated I was really disappointed," said Keller. "It was uneventful; it wasn't frightening, it wasn't scary. It was nothing. It was a bunch of really loud music being played in a dark room with a guy yelling … in an Arabic dialect and some guy … yelling at [detainees] in English."

Interrogations changed over time, and some troops said they helped provide ancillary assistance. Troops from Battalion 1-68 had varying accounts about where particular techniques originated and what compelled them to rough up prisoners for interrogations. None of the soldiers with Battalion 1-68 whom I interviewed admitted they had any knowledge of memos, directives or orders handed down by high-level officers or officials. Several alleged that officers looked the other way while prisoners were being abused.

"Interrogations happened at night, around two in the morning, while no one else was awake on the base except us and the guys right outside on the firing line," remembered Millantz. He and other soldiers recalled, however, that "colonels and generals were walking around—they knew damned well what was going on. It was a dog and pony show."

Benson and Nowlan had a different perspective on the intelligence operations. Nowlan denied any knowledge of detainee abuse. "No, I don't remember that—no, absolutely not," he said. "I don't remember, I don't recall any of that." And Benson said he was "very surprised to hear" about allegations of abuse. "I had a pretty good handle on the things that were going on, particularly in our holding area, which was literally 200 meters from where I slept, and it was at our front gate," he said. "If I went more than a day without checking on our holding cell, that was a rare occasion. I mean, it was that important ... Things might have happened, but it would not have been because it was a policy. And certainly if I knew what was going on, it would have been stopped and these guys would have been called to task for it."

But Nowlan and Benson also objected to the characterization that they were conducting interrogations.

"By regulations we're not allowed to [interrogate]—you have to be a trained interrogator in order to do that. We ... conduct[ed] tactical questioning," said Benson. "The difference is that we [were] authorized to ask direct questions. In other words: What is your name? Where were you last night? Do you know Mohamed Mohamed? Those are direct questions."

Even Nowlan, the battalion's military intelligence officer, hadn't been trained in interrogation. He explained that Tactical Human Intelligence Teams (or THTs) would come from Camp Anaconda to Balad to assist with interrogation operations when FOB Lion's jail contained prisoners.

"They were trained, they were just not very good," said Nowlan, referring to the interrogators on the THTs. "They didn't have any situational awareness. They lived on Anaconda, you know? They went to a dining facility and they had all the luxuries of good living. We lived not amongst the populace, but very close to the fight."

"I would just say that our interrogation and our questioning techniques were very immature at the time. And rightly so. The Army hadn't had a lot of experience doing that in a large, real-time way," said

Benson. "We were doing the best we could with what we had … the Army didn't have a lot of trained, seasoned interrogators who understood the culture, and so forth. Certainly I had never read the Army manual on interrogations and tactical questioning … That had never been anything that I had come in contact with in my military career—at that point, you know, fifteen, sixteen years."

I asked Benson if he or his unit received specific directives on interrogation techniques during Battalion 1-68's first tour in Iraq during April 2003–March 2004.

"You mean to use certain kinds of techniques? No. Absolutely not," he replied. "There was never anything as far as I know [that said] 'Hey, use these types of techniques—this will help you in your mission.' … I can remember talking about techniques, and what was appropriate, and what was not, and we did start having those conversations. But again we were kind of learning and we were trying to figure that stuff out as we went along, and what we were allowed to do and not allowed to do."

Benson added, "In the absence of direct orders or guidance, guys are going to do what they think is the best thing to do, and everybody has a little bit of a different take on that."

Several soldiers from Battalion 1-68 indeed had "a different take." Some felt that there were tacit suggestions from higher up that the abuse of prisoners was necessary.

"It's a tricky subject," said Keller. According to him, some of the officers on the base "kind of implied that you should soften [them] up, but not necessarily for interrogation purposes. And it doesn't necessarily come from anyone higher than your own [commander]. While it's not a direct order, a lot of people kind of make it sound like you should be hurting him a little bit. And of course, the higher-up NCOs [non-commissioned officers], platoon sergeants, and stuff like that will always tell you, 'Don't actually do it.' But then there's always also that sideways glance, or you hear about the situation where they might have done the exact same thing."

"It wasn't like they'd say, 'Go in there and clock this guy,'" said Adam Stevenson. "But they'd say, 'Make it uncomfortable … don't let him sit down for a while.' Stuff was changing all the time. It was trial and error. After a while, if stuff didn't work—if we weren't getting good intel [military intelligence]—we'd leave them alone. We were always changing our method. Sometimes with certain people, stress would work. For certain people, it would have an adverse affect."

Oral Lindsey, Adam's tank commander, said someone within the battalion's military intelligence section, known as "S2," specifically ordered sleep deprivation.

"S2 may have come out, or one of their NCOs may have come out, and said, 'Hey guys, we can't let these guys sleep,' " said Lindsey. "Somebody from S2 had to do that. I couldn't just go out and say, 'Hey man, I'm not gonna let these assholes sleep.' "

Lindsey had a Sony boombox that his mother sent him, and he often played a Kid Rock CD, *American Bad Ass*, to keep detainees awake. "I'd put that thing in and crank it up as loud as it goes," said Lindsey. He would start blasting the music at one or two in the morning, wander off for a while, and return much later to ensure no one was napping.

"Apparently it works," he said. "When I was in basic training, sleep deprivation is a very, very useful tool. And it still is with the Navy Seal training and Army Ranger training. Sleep deprivation ... breaks you down, you know? You'll do anything for sleep, man."

Lindsey said the ordeal of sleep deprivation built "unit cohesiveness" among members of his platoon and other troops who had undergone the same experience during their training. But he also conceded he didn't know how or why it was successful in eliciting meaningful intelligence from detainees.

"I don't know how it's going to work in interrogation and stuff," he said. "I mean, I have no idea."

Yet some in Battalion 1-68 reasoned such measures were necessary under the circumstances.

"If you've never seen that stuff, it sounds cruel and inhumane but till you've been there and done that, shit, you lose your morals," explained Lindsey. Insurgents were "out there making bombs ... trying to kill you. And all you want to do is go home to your family. You do what you gotta do."

"We were stressed out and we needed to know what was going on," said Stevenson. "We were getting shot at all the time so we needed to know what they knew."

But some soldiers turned on their detainees for reasons other than the need to gather intelligence.

Many in Battalion 1-68 were frustrated that they weren't making tangible strides with tamping down on the insurgents who were attacking them. At times, that frustration boiled over.

"I threw another human," remembered Sandoval. He was "tied up and I picked [him] up and threw him. At that point [I] wasn't thinking about another human being—wasn't worried about how he thought, if he was embarrassed. I just picked him up and threw him in the back of the Humvee. At that point, I was thinking, 'That was fun—that was funny. We're getting bad guys. Something accomplished.' When the tangible was happening it felt good."

Some soldiers felt sorry for their detainees. Stevenson said he found himself sympathizing with many of his prisoners and understood the source of their anger.

"I can totally understand why a lot of them do what they do," he said. "If somebody kicked my door in at two a.m. and took my dad and put a bag over his head and zip-stripped him, I'd be out there the next night with a rocket too. And if you say you wouldn't, you're a liar. Or a wuss."

That resentment cut both ways. Sandoval felt that watching over the detainees in the jail was grating for many soldiers, and he and others increasingly resented them.

"You have to watch these prisoners—they're the reason why you're in the damned country," he said. "They screwed up or whatever. They're the reason you're tired. They're the reason you're hungry. They're the reason you're thirsty. They're the reason you're miserable. And here you have to babysit them."

Nowlan remembered how detainees were either released or referred to other bases for follow-up questioning. He estimated that during "the first three or four months" of their stay in Balad, "50 percent" were first referred to "a brigade level, which was Anaconda … then they would say 'Okay, we're going to send them forward to division, and eventually division … extended into Abu Ghraib or other prisons in the area."

Over time, Nowlan saw the number of detainee referrals begin to level off. "As we went along, and our experience increased, [in] the end it would be less than 10 percent of the people that we would take in."

Some troops grew aggravated by the way in which prisoners had been discharged after their detention. "At first, a lot of them were suspected of attacks," said Keller. "But later, a lot of the guys we ended up releasing on the same day."

For some, the detainee turnover seemed to show that the battalion's operations hadn't deterred the attacks against them. As a result, "we just got mad at people," said Keller.

"You [would] see people ... get frustrated," said Nowlan. He remembered troops bringing in people they thought were guilty, "And I was the guy who said, 'I don't know anything about this guy. I don't think he's done anything—there's no evidence. We need to let him go.' And the younger soldiers were very frustrated with that."

Soldiers sometimes took their frustrations out on their prisoners.[5]

"It's not like I'd ever seen some guys go in and tell them to get naked and stack up on each other—I think that's gross," said Sandoval. "None of us were that stupid. But there were other times when you wanted to pull out a pistol and put it to the back of their head. Everyone had that sort of tension. It was very uncomfortable, it was miserable."

Several soldiers from Battalion 1-68 said they were numbed, almost dulled by their monotonous wartime routines. Shifting to more mundane work, such as patrolling and detaining prisoners, could make a soldier "bored ... so eventually you start to lose those feelings," said Keller. "And the only thing that really does excite you is when you get to ... torture somebody."

Then Keller added, "Honestly, a lot of the things that were done to the detainees were ... just someone's idea of a good time."

Some troops said they beat their prisoners. Daniel Keller described how he dragged detainees through concertina wire that was lying on the floor. At times he just used zip ties to force detainees into painful positions for hours—sometimes days. "I once left a person zip-tied to a cell door for two and a half days, suspended on his own weight," Keller remembered.

During one unit meeting, mid-level officers discussed detainee operations. They weren't intelligence officers, but they still traded war stories about detainee treatment during previous wars.

"One of the NCOs described ... what they did to get information out of detainees in Vietnam," recalled Keller. "And then they'll give you a detailed description of torture techniques, and then you go and perform torture."

According to Keller, one of the NCOs described a technique that involved the use of water to extract information from prisoners in Vietnam. "Then I went ahead and tried it," he said. "The difference was that I didn't want information, I just wanted to hurt [a prisoner]."

In this technique, soldiers would pin a detainee down on his back and brace his torso so that he couldn't wriggle free. "They will now feel like their life is in danger," said Keller, who methodically described how it worked. "Then you take a five-gallon jug of water, and you slowly start pouring it over their face in the mouth and nose area so that it's not enough for them to really suck in and die, and they can still move their head to the side and catch a breath ... It simulates drowning without permanently injuring [detainees]."

The water torture wasn't combined with questioning.

"We were doing things because we could. That's it," said Keller. "And the objective just got less and less important."

Troops didn't have to rely on brute force to wear down detainees. Prisoners asked Keller if they could urinate. He would oblige, but first hooded them, cinched zip ties around their wrists, and took them out back. A gunner manned the front gate of the jail in a machine-gun nest, and had to test-fire his weapon periodically to ensure it worked properly. Keller would deposit the detainee just outside the jail after they had relieved themselves and signal to the machine gunner to fire a round each time he marched another detainee outside. He would leave the first detainee outside and return to the jail to see who else sought relief. Detainees heard their friends requesting the bathroom, saw them cuffed, blindfolded, and escorted out of the cell, then they would hear a shot, and their friends didn't return. Keller repeated the same routine and slowly emptied the jail. And it consumed detainees with fear.

Eventually, Keller would force detainees outside and tell them, "You've got to go to the bathroom"—even if they didn't have to.

"They would be crying whenever we came in to take someone to go to the bathroom because they thought they were about to be executed," said Keller. "And we thought it was fun as hell."

The soldiers involved in detainee abuse at FOB Lion denied that everyone in Battalion 1-68 had been equally involved. It remained unclear how many troops actually participated, as was the extent to which abuse was ordered or overlooked. Some soldiers denied that abuse had been widespread. Most troops and officers I spoke to insisted they performed with honor and distinction as they carried out their service in the face of lethal dangers.

"The guys that I dealt with were professionals, and good soldiers and good officers," asserted Benson, who said that detainee abuse and torture "were not things that were indicative of that unit or any of those people that I'm associated with ... I'm not going to indict any soldier because somebody was put in a stress position." He said that "people were getting killed and maimed over there all the time," and added, "Sure, [detainee abuse] could have happened. But I have never been told about it and I never found that kind of thing happening … If one of our subordinates had found it happening, they would have stopped it."

Those in Battalion 1-68 who admitted they abused detainees did so for many different reasons. When they returned home from Iraq, they began to reconsider what had compelled them to torture and abuse detainees.

"It makes you wonder," mused Keller. "Did I do this because of the stress? Did I do this because of the situation? Should I have known not to do this anyway? Am I at fault here? Does that make me a bad person?"

"I was consumed by hate, and that's the best way I can describe it," said Millantz. "I was pissed off, and [wondered], 'What the hell are we doing here? What's our purpose?' Innocent people were getting killed— poor soldiers, poor mothers have to … see their kid in a body bag."

Sandoval maintained he only forced detainees to perform strenuous exercises in order to discipline them, and denied seeing much detainee abuse in his unit. Sergeant Oral Lindsey claimed that the officers connected to the battalion's military intelligence attachment ordered him to blast music next to detainees' ears to keep them up all night. Lindsey insisted that he couldn't have done so without their consent. Others in the unit said they were simply encouraged and given tacit approval or oblique instructions. Some insisted that their officers just looked the other way as they experimented with a range of techniques. They didn't rely on directives. Instead, they often turned to anecdotes—"what they used to do in 'Nam," as Keller recalled—or used what was familiar to them from their training.

"We weren't in the CIA—we were soldiers," said Millantz. He added that it was reckless "to give that much power and responsibility to a bunch of guys who were full of hate and resentment—getting shot at and watching their friends get killed … seeing people decapitated [in videos]—and then putting those guys in direct control of the people who did these things. [That] was very ironic to me. And I think any human being in that situation would have done similar things."

The reasons for roughing up prisoners shifted and blurred. Some soldiers said they felt growing resentment toward their prisoners, and abuse became an outlet. Some troops regarded the abuse as a way of breaking up the tedium; others got into it and felt that the abuse and torture were "fun as hell."[6]

I asked soldiers from Battalion 1-68 about Adam Gray's involvement. He had already told his mother about how he mistreated detainees, and fellow unit members confirmed that he was involved in detainee abuse, though I wasn't able to get a consensus on how much he contributed and what exactly he did.

"Gray was no less than the rest of us," said Keller. "I'm sure Gray wasn't always that bad … I'm not going to say he was like the worst or anything like that, by any means. I'm not trying to put that across."

Neither the individuals in Battalion 1-68 nor the battalion itself were unique in their involvement in detainee abuse.

"One perception was that what happened in Abu Ghraib was terrible and reprehensible, but it was really a few kind of rogue people," said Keller. "The thing is, it's not a few rogue people … there were a lot of us doing it."

Abusive detentions and interrogations extended well beyond the reach of the units of the 4th Infantry Division. Other units followed the same basic course taken by troops from Battalion 1-68—a trajectory of common experiences, behavior, and beliefs that led them to engage in torture. Such was the case even for trained military intelligence officers and the officials who approved harsh interrogation.

Chapter 4:
Shock the Conscience

TIM JAMES WAS one of the Special Agents in Charge for the Criminal Investigation Task Force Guantanamo Bay during 2002. On December 4, 2002, while poring over a new batch of memos from the Department of Defense, he came across one dated two days earlier. He had heard about a memo that Secretary of Defense Donald Rumsfeld had signed that approved coercive interrogation techniques. But it was hard for James's staff to secure a copy for him; the memo had only been distributed to select personnel involved in a highly sensitive interrogation. When James read through the memo, he spotted a handwritten statement on the bottom of the page that read, "I stand for 8–10 hours a day. Why is standing limited to four hours? D.R."

James reread it several times, until he finally understood that the remark referred to a section of the memo that spelled out the amount of time that interrogators were permitted to engage detainees in forced standing. But he wondered what the initials "D.R." signified.

Is this Rumsfeld's note on this thing? he wondered.

It was. James turned to a colleague in his office and pointed to the memo.

"This is the dumbest thing I've ever seen," he said. "Because this thing is going to get out."

Yet some of his counterparts in Joint Task Force 170 (JTF-170), the intelligence task force charged with obtaining "actionable intelligence," saw it as a validation of their commanders' agreement that coercive interrogation was justified and permissible.

James worked on the Criminal Investigative Task Force (CITF), which was designed to put together prosecutable cases against all imprisoned terrorist suspects—in Guantanamo and elsewhere in the war theater. At times he openly disagreed with his colleagues. He often argued with a colonel on JTF-170. The colonel condoned harsh interrogation, and he now pointed to Rumsfeld's memo as proof that his position was right all along. "Tim, tell me, why are you guys refusing to accept this?" asked the colonel. "My God, Sec Def [the Secretary of Defense] has said this is okay. What's the problem?"

James shook his head.

"Look, it's wrong—it's just wrong thinking," he said. "Quite frankly, this is a felony."

Fourteen days after James first spotted that memo, Alberto Mora read the same document from within the Pentagon, and he was equally shocked.

When Mora, the Navy's top lawyer, first learned about harsh interrogations at Guantanamo, he didn't believe a higher authority outside the base had approved them. Instead, he felt such behavior had all the marks of rogue interrogators who were inexperienced, undisciplined, and poorly supervised.

Before the September 11 attacks, Mora, the Navy's General Counsel, chiefly managed military legal issues and other departmental responsibilities. "After 9/11, all of that changed fairly dramatically, and we all became more engaged in the problems of finding terrorists and in war fighting," he told me.

On December 18, 2002, Mora met with David Brant, head of the Naval Criminal Investigative Service (NCIS), and other colleagues, including Dr. Mike Gelles, a respected Navy psychologist.

"Mike was regarded as not only a treasure within NCIS but also as a national asset," said Mora. "He was consulted by CIA, the FBI, and other law enforcement services. He was seen as a leader within government, not only within the Navy, but in the application of psychological techniques and tools to solve problems of law enforcement and national security."

Brant set the tone of the meeting. He introduced the matter of detainee abuse at Guantanamo, then asked Gelles to brief them on what had happened there. Gelles had come armed with several reports collected from interrogation logs saved on Guantanamo's computers. Gelles introduced one transcript in particular that detailed a troubling interrogation that had occurred at Guantanamo. It showed abuses that JTF-170 personnel had allegedly committed.

"It didn't mention any names," remembered Mora. "It was one unidentified detainee."

But it appeared to be a detainee of some significance. Guantanamo interrogators abused him over the course of several weeks. In one instance, he was tortured so badly that his heart rate dropped to thirty-five beats per minute—about half the average heart rate of a healthy adult (sixty to eighty beats per minute).[1]

"It was just … it was absolutely shocking," said Mora.

He and his colleagues lingered around the conference table after Gelles's presentation and absorbed all that they had just heard. That meeting became one of Mora's most disheartening experiences at the Pentagon. But he pressed on to discover what had happened.

The following day, December 19, Mora called his counterpart, Steven Morello, the general counsel of the Army.

Had he heard about the abuses in Guantanamo?

Yes.

Morello invited Mora to his office and presented him with "the package"—a set of documents that detailed the dispatches between Guantanamo's officers, the Southern Command (which oversees US military operations in Latin America and the Caribbean), and Washington, DC. Reading through this chain of cables and memos, Mora began to grasp how and why torture emerged in Guantanamo.

At first, said Mora, "I thought it was all a mistake. Never did I think this was anything other than just failure to read carefully and to think through carefully and to imagine what the consequences of this were."

To his dismay, this case didn't represent a rogue group. Mora was distressed that the abuses had taken place. But worse, he was even more troubled that some of these practices appeared to be sanctioned by Bush administration officials—from an administration that Mora supported politically and protected legally.

Mora did not normally receive reports about events in Guantanamo, which fell outside the typical matters that he and his office worked on. Even Gelles, who supported the CITF in Guantanamo, wasn't privy to what his counterparts in JTF-170 had been doing or the information they collected from interrogations. He and other CITF members had heard rumors about abuse, but had access to only fragmentary interrogation transcripts that did not account for the full scope of what had taken place. The clues to understanding these developments stemmed from the interrogation log that Gelles provided to Mora about that one unidentified detainee.

★   ★   ★

Mohammed al Qahtani traveled to Florida on August 4, 2001, where he planned to meet a friend from Egypt. He carried a legitimate Saudi Arabian passport, had a valid visa, and spoke choppy English.[2] But Qahtani aroused suspicion when immigration authorities at Orlando International Airport discovered he had little money on hand, no hotel reservations, a one-way ticket, and could not give a coherent account of his plans for his stay in the US.

According to the immigration official who interviewed him, Qahtani said that "a friend of his was to arrive in the United States on a later date, and that his friend knew where he was going."[3]

His story seemed shifty to the immigration official. Qahtani's conflicting explanations about his travels didn't add up, so the officer didn't let him pass through the checkpoint. Qahtani grew angry, but the immigration authorities didn't budge. They denied him entry into the US and deported him to Dubai. His travels continued—from Dubai to Pakistan, and eventually to Afghanistan.

During the US invasion of Afghanistan, Qahtani was captured along with other foreigners who were fighting alongside the Taliban at Tora Bora. After passing through a chain of detention facilities, he successfully landed in a US area—an American military base.

Qahtani was one of many foreigners captured in Afghanistan and shipped to Guantanamo. Once there, that "one unidentified detainee" languished for roughly seven months before US authorities finally identified him as Mohammed al Qahtani and established who he was.

Qahtani wasn't a mistreated victim of American immigration screening. The Egyptian "friend" in the US whom he planned to meet turned out to be Mohamed Atta, the man who orchestrated the September 11 attacks from within the US.

Qahtani missed his chance to join Atta and the other eighteen hijackers as the twentieth man involved in those attacks. Once federal officials positively identified him through fingerprinting identification, the FBI was allowed to question him. Interrogators drank tea with Qahtani and prayed with him on occasion. Over time, he did provide the FBI agents with some useful information about terrorist plans and operators.

Yet military officials feared he still might be withholding information. If anyone at Guantanamo had actionable intelligence, it was Qahtani, they reasoned. His case, some argued, was exceptional, and so extraordinary measures were justified.

In November 2002, military interrogators took over where the FBI left off, and they ratcheted up the pressure on Qahtani. FBI officials at Guantanamo documented Qahtani's harsh interrogations and observed that he was "subjected to intense isolation for over three months" and "was evidencing behavior consistent with extreme psychological trauma (talking to non-existent people, reporting hearing voices, crouching in a cell covered with a sheet for hours on end)."[4]

Instead of considering whether hallucinations and "extreme psychological harm" would compromise the quality of the intelligence, military interrogators and their commanders pushed for more latitude when questioning prisoners. They received official permission to use coercive techniques on December 2, 2002, when Rumsfeld signed the memo titled "Counter-Resistance Techniques in the War on Terrorism." It was the very same memo that Mora, James and others found so distressing.

Mora was a longtime Republican who had supported the Bush administration. He feared that news about the abuses (along with the memo that sanctioned them) could damage the president politically, have adverse effects on foreign and defense policies related to the war on terror, and leave senior military and political leaders vulnerable to legal actions.

"I never would have imagined that Donald Rumsfeld of all people would approve these kinds of techniques," said Mora. "I thought that what we had there, both in terms of the actual treatment of the detainees and the fact that it had been authorized personally by the Secretary [of Defense] after going up the chain of command, was a series of disasters in the making that could profoundly harm their own interests."

In the autumn of 2002, officers at Guantanamo cabled the Pentagon with a wish list of coercive techniques for interrogation. In response, Rumsfeld spelled out in his December 2 memo which of those techniques he did or did not approve in the following categories:

Category I: Use of mild and fear-related techniques (e.g., shouting and deception).

Category II: Use of stress positions; use of falsified documents; isolation for up to 30 days; removal of clothing; preying on fears (e.g., dogs); interrogation outside standard interrogation rooms "so long as no severe physical pain inflicted and prolonged mental harm intended."

Deprivation of light and sound, use of hoods, and use of 20-hour interrogations.

Category III: Use of death threats or threats of imminent physical harm. Exposure to cold, water, or use of wet towel to suggest suffocation not approved.

The officers didn't get authorization for every technique they had requested, including "water, or use of wet towel to suggest suffocation," although most were approved. But their requests reflected the base commanders' frustrations with the pace and volume of information that interrogations were yielding. One officer, Lieutenant Colonel Jerald Phifer, sent a memo to his superiors on October 11, 2002, that reflected this sentiment: "PROBLEM: The current guidelines for interrogation procedures at GTMO limit the ability of interrogators to counter advanced resistance." Phifer's memo was based on the belief that Guantanamo mostly held valuable detainees and explained why interrogators supposedly weren't getting enough information. Some interrogators contended that they faced detainees schooled in "advanced resistance," and that their "guidelines" hampered their ability to successfully question prisoners. But what was this "advanced resistance" that Guantanamo's interrogators faced? Many pointed to the Manchester Manual—a document that quickly became well known among counter-terrorism experts.

British police discovered the Manchester Manual in 2000 when they searched an al Qaeda suspect's house in Manchester, England—hence the name.[5] It contains eighteen chapters that detail al Qaeda tactics in very straightforward and simple language. Military and intelligence officials have often invoked it as proof that terrorist suspects had trained to brace themselves against interrogation and torture.

Tim James confronted coworkers at Guantanamo who cited the Manchester Manual to explain their limited success and to justify the coercion.

"Have you read it?" he asked. Most of the time they answered no.

"If you had, you wouldn't be so worried about it," he said to them. "The material in it is nothing earth shattering, nothing that you wouldn't really expect—it's common sense."

The core components of the manual's counter-resistant techniques include the following:

- Patience, steadfastness, and silence about any information whatsoever. That is very difficult except for those who take refuge in Allah.
- If the brother is the first subject in the interrogation, he should adhere steadfastly to the security plan in order to avoid trouble for the brothers that will follow.
- The worse case—Allah forbid—is when the brother breaks down totally and tells all he knows, which is due to a poor choice in the brother. Thus, it is important to test individuals prior to such work in order to ensure their steadfastness and minimize the likelihood of their breaking down. Testing may be done by accusing him of being an enemy agent and lying about the reported information, in the event he is supplying detailed information.
- Important information should not be discussed with the brothers, as they might reveal it during the interrogation.

It turned out that the description of the manual's counter-resistance techniques were plainly exaggerated. Nevertheless, some interrogators blamed their failure to elicit information from detainees on how al Qaeda recruits had allegedly absorbed the manual's wisdom.

Alberto Mora was in Guantanamo when the second planeload of prisoners touched down in January 2002.

"It's kind of bizarre that it [was] a beautiful, balmy Caribbean day—the bright sun and the sparkling sea," Mora recalled. "Then to see these guys in the orange jumpsuits and understand that this was the focus of the American 'war against terror.' "

Guards were exceedingly careful about the way they transported detainees. They bound prisoners' hands and feet, and placed each prisoner on a stretcher fitted with two large wheels to cart them to and from the interrogation booths. Such measures were used to ensure that prisoners were totally immobilized during transfers.

These prisoners were regarded as dangerous and malign. They were described as cunning. And, as evidenced by the smoldering rubble in Lower Manhattan, they were considered capable of terrible destruction.

"All of us were laboring under the belief that these individuals would chew hydraulic lines with their bare teeth if they had had the chance, to do anything possible to immolate themselves so they could kill Americans," said Mora, recalling a description of the detainees made by General Richard Myers, then Chairman of the Joint Chiefs of Staff.[6] "Another anecdote that I recall hearing at the time was that these are the kind of guys that, if they were in a prison infirmary, they could take a syringe and drive it into the eye of a nurse or corpsman—just out of sheer hatred of Americans."

Military personnel took these threats seriously. Mora himself had been in the Pentagon on September 11 when one of the hijacked planes ploughed into the building, incinerating coworkers.

"There was a sense that other terrorist attacks could occur any moment against the United States—one or many more attacks," recalled Mora. "Nobody really knew. But there was the real possibility that many Americans would die unless we got intelligence that could help us thwart those attacks. That was very much the mood in the Pentagon at that time."

Defense Secretary Rumsfeld famously described Guantanamo as a repository for "among the most dangerous, best-trained, vicious killers on the face of the earth. This is very, very serious business."[7] Vice President Dick Cheney declared that "the people that are at Guantanamo are bad people ... these are terrorists for the most part. They are people that were captured in the battlefield of Afghanistan or rounded up as part of the al Qaeda network."

And yet, by many estimates, those impressions turned out to be inaccurate.

In February 2006, Seton Hall University School of Law and two lawyers who represented Guantanamo prisoners—law professor Mark Denbeaux and his son Joshua Denbeaux—produced a report that comprehensively broke down Guantanamo's detainee population, using unclassified government data. Their analysis found that

> 55 percent of the detainees are not determined to have committed any hostile acts against the United States or its coalition allies. Only 8 percent of the detainees were characterized as al Qaeda fighters. Of the remaining detainees, 40 percent have no definitive connection with al Qaeda at all and 18 percent have no definitive affiliation with either al Qaeda or the Taliban ... Only 5 percent of the detainees were captured by United States forces. Eighty-six percent of the detainees were arrested by either Pakistan or the Northern Alliance and turned over to United States custody. This 86 percent of the detainees captured by Pakistan or the Northern Alliance were handed over to the United States at a time in which the United States offered large bounties for capture of suspected enemies.[8]

Even Bush administration officials knew about similar reports that disputed the number of serious terrorist suspects imprisoned at

Guantanamo. According to journalist Seymour Hersh, CIA director George Tenet sent an analyst to the base to interview detainees, assess the intelligence value they possessed, and evaluate interrogators' work. He reported back to his superiors during the fall of 2002, telling them that more than half the detainees were neither jihadis nor possessed actionable intelligence, and clearly should not have been incarcerated there.[9]

Lawrence B. Wilkerson, a retired US Army colonel and former chief of staff to Secretary of State Colin Powell, agreed that "to have admitted this reality would have been a black mark on [the Bush administration] leadership from virtually day one of the so-called Global War on Terror."[10] Wilkerson explained myriad systemic problems that led to capturing the wrong suspects in the first place. He concluded, "It did not help that poor US policies, such as bounty-hunting, a weak understanding of cultural tendencies, and an utter disregard for the fundamentals of jurisprudence prevailed."[11]

Instead of reckoning with these operational problems, senior political and military officials focused on what to do with detainees who had allegedly been trained in "advanced resistance," reasoning that it was the source of interrogators' frustration with uncooperative detainees.

On September 4, 2002, a review by the Chairman of the Joint Chiefs of Staff had "concluded that the JTF-170 had limited success in extracting usable information from some of the detainees at Guantanamo because traditional interrogation techniques described in FM 34-52 [the standard Army Field Manual] had proven to be ineffective."[12]

To remedy these problems, military commanders and senior officials made a bold decision. They turned to a specialized military training program known as Survival, Evasion, Resistance and Escape, or SERE. On September 16, 2002, some of Guantanamo's interrogators reported to Fort Bragg, North Carolina, where, according to a DoD Inspector General report, "personnel briefed JTF-170 representatives on the exploitation techniques and methods used in resistance (to interrogation) training at SERE schools. The JTF-170 personnel understood that they were to become familiar with SERE training and be capable of determining which SERE information and techniques might be useful in interrogations at Guantanamo."[13]

The SERE course was created after the Korean War in order to furnish airmen and select military personnel (including special operations forces) with survival skills. Each branch of the military has its own SERE training, so there is some variation, but it generally involves first aid, outdoor survival (e.g., building tools and shelters, navigation), water survival, and camouflage.[14] SERE also includes a kind of torture-resistance training. According to former students and teachers, trainees undergo sleep deprivation, "mock rape" scenarios, sexual and religious degradation, "noise stress," deprivation of food, exposure to extreme temperatures, and simulated drowning.[15]

SERE's alumni describe the torture exercises as a physically taxing and emotionally draining experience, and the military is mindful of its effects.[16] Mental health specialists watch over the torture training portion, and clinicians check the trainees during and after the sessions, measuring cortisol levels, to ensure that the stress doesn't become too taxing.[17]

CITF members were stunned that SERE techniques were being used on detainees. "That's not what they were designed for," said Gelles, the Navy psychologist. "But because they were techniques used to train people to resist, they figured, 'We know that people from our experience get pretty stressed out doing this ... We know this works.'"

Eventually he saw fellow psychologists operating under that same conviction.

Tim James helped organize briefings at Guantanamo to better prepare CITF agents for questioning detainees in the interrogation booth, also known as "the box." As part of their briefings, CITF required its agents to take a "box etiquette" class, which addressed interrogation protocol and safety, as well as what was and was not legally permissible during interrogations. Agents also went through one or two days of classes on legal issues, Islam, al Qaeda, and interrogation approaches. (These classes were offered to JTF-170 and others.)

Mike Gelles helped inform CITF staff about some of those issues and sharpen interrogators' understanding of the detainees' backgrounds and culture.

During one afternoon at Guantanamo, Gelles was informally chatting with his friend Mark Fallon about the new team of behavioral specialists who had been assembled at the base. Fallon was CITF's chief investigator and had worked with Gelles for years on all kinds of criminal cases and counterterrorist operations, including the bombing of the USS *Cole* in 2000.

It wasn't the first time that Fallon worked with a group of psychologists on a mission. But the size and scope of the psychologists' operation at Guantanamo was different and required a new approach to organization and coordination.

"Hey, what do you want to call this thing?" Fallon asked, referring to Gelles's group.

"How about the 'behavioral science consultation team'?" Gelles replied.

BSCT. The name stuck. Gelles and the other BSCT members— a team of psychologists, psychiatrists, and behavioral specialists from various government agencies—were instructed to advise on, but not to be involved in, interrogations at Guantanamo. The BSCT team was responsible for helping build criminal cases against detainees, but it didn't help JTF-170 interrogators pursue actionable intelligence.

"We understood how to interrogate and interview these guys," said Gelles. "We understood appropriate approaches that were consistent with US and international law, but we also understood that the rapport-based approach was the best approach."

Building rapport with detainees wasn't anything new. Seasoned interrogators often consider it the best approach, and it involves developing a relationship with the subject over time.[18] But building rapport with Guantanamo's detainees demanded an informed understanding of the Middle Easterners and South Asians they were questioning.

In the course of their imprisonment, detainees repeatedly described their experiences to interrogators. It was a lengthy, exhausting process for both sides. Gelles reminded interrogators that their detainees would relate to things like maps and directions differently than Americans do. He explained that some prisoners relayed experiences circuitously, through personal stories and idiosyncratic memories, but it didn't mean detainees were necessarily misleading them.

Once a relationship was formed with a detainee, interrogators could use coercion more effectively—not by physical means, but through shame, said Gelles. Some officials sought to replicate BSCT's success and had other ideas about how psychologists could use coercion when questioning detainees—especially for collecting actionable intelligence.

Major General Michael Dunlavey, commander of JTF-170, assembled his own BSCT team. If BSCT successfully helped law enforcement officials build prosecutable cases, why not use a similar team to advise those who were gathering the intelligence on people who were, as he put it, "implacably committed to apocalyptic terrorism"?

The clinicians and psychologists who formed the team had varied military backgrounds, but not many had experience with interrogation.

"We were consulting for law enforcement … consulting on interrogations and [had an] understanding of these issues for many, many years," said Gelles. "Those folks were just straight clinicians who you went to see for anxiety, depression, in the hospital one day. Now [they're] in Guantanamo—in this detention facility—without any training, without any experience and just doing what they knew. The concern [was] the clinicians [would] then get caught up or swept up in the whole adrenalin of the operational environment."

Dunlavey's new BSCT team included psychologists who oversaw the training at SERE schools—the same ones who oversaw the stress and duress that US troops experienced during their training. Gelles didn't object to using psychologists to help supervise SERE trainings. They "provide a valuable service—they teach and they monitor [training] to make sure that things don't get out of hand," he said.

But once SERE psychologists arrived at Guantanamo, they were asked to apply skills that went beyond their areas of expertise, said Gelles. In the absence of interrogation experience, they drew on what they knew—the torture exercises used in SERE schools and their ability to gauge a subject's level of stress throughout the training.

Several former CITF personnel told me they were surprised that such methods were even considered. No one predicted just how strongly those ideas would take root or how far those beliefs would travel.

Coercive methods had already been used at Guantanamo even before Rumsfeld's "Counter-Resistance Techniques" memo of December 2, 2002, arrived at the base. There were, in fact, at least twenty-three documented cases of detainee abuse that occurred in Guantanamo during 2002 before Rumsfeld's memo was signed.[19] In November 2002, Guantanamo interrogators started to use coercive techniques on Qahtani; they threatened him with a dog, deprived him of sleep for hours, forced him into a cold, isolated room, and sexually humiliated him. But Guantanamo's interrogators were finally able to enjoy legal cover for using harsh techniques once Rumsfeld issued his memo.

Army Colonel Britt Mallow, a Middle East Foreign Area officer with twenty-nine years in the military police and the Criminal Investigation Command (known as CID), headed the CITF. Mallow had been to Afghanistan during the early part of the US military campaign there. He had been to Bagram Air Base and forward operating bases in Afghanistan that had just been formed as US forces dug into the country. In his travels through Afghanistan, he heard disquieting stories about the treatment of Afghan detainees. Some soldiers, he learned, were experimenting with different kinds of force and stress positions during prisoner interrogations and detentions.

In the summer of 2002, he was at Guantanamo when CITF operations started up. Mallow discovered that some interrogators there were using coercive tactics he had heard about in Afghanistan and elsewhere. Some of these techniques included blasting loud music next to detainees' ears to prevent them from sleeping, keeping them in hot or cold rooms to induce discomfort, yanking them out of their cells at odd hours of the night, and subjecting them to intense interrogations.

Mallow feared that a self-generating feedback loop was emerging as soldiers traded ideas about what they had heard about or done elsewhere and relied on hearsay about the supposed success of such tactics used in other places. But there were other sources of inspiration. Some of Mallow's colleagues learned that interrogators had bandaged a detainee's head with an entire roll of duct tape. The episode was upsetting both because it was abusive, and because to some it seemed to resemble hazing.[20]

On one occasion, Randy Carter, former chief of operations for CITF at the interrogation booths at Guantanamo, "actually saw two cowboys —chaps, cowboy hats, neckerchiefs on and what have you—and they were just coming out of the interrogation."

For Mallow, such kinds of role-playing and experimentation seemed to show how coercive interrogation techniques turned into "low-level people 'freelancing' with it, and high-level [officials] authorizing it." He said, "The island would have sunk if ego had been a weight factor. There were folks particularly from various communities that were involved down there—operational community, intelligence community, law enforcements community—and everyone thought that they knew about [interrogations]."

Since the summer of 2002, CITF members had heard about sporadic cases of abuse from their colleagues on the base. "Then we started to hear stories and rumors," said James. He recalled hearing about "felonies … being committed by people that should be on our team" and remembered that the frequency and severity of abuses seemed to increase during the autumn of 2002.

The more they heard about the abuses by JTF-170, the more fissures seemed to emerge between the two task forces; the intelligence interrogators increasingly worked on their cases independently, and CITF interrogators paired up with the FBI with greater regularity.

CITF personnel continued to report on the abuses they had heard about and urged their superiors to advance their concerns up the chain of command. As head of the task force, Mallow tried to get officials to take corrective action. But instead of hearing outrage over the abuse, he found that many commanders supported the harsh methods that Guantanamo's officers had requested. Mallow met with military and civilian leaders, both in Guantanamo and in the US, many of whom presented arguments such as, "These guys are used to living in damp caves. How difficult is it going to be for them to put up with a little bit of extra air-conditioning in the interrogation room?" The prisoners were, they insisted, battle-hardened terrorists with counter-resistance training. Interrogators weren't going to kill them through coercive techniques, the officials argued, and so they advocated pushing detainees even further.

Sometimes advocates of coercive interrogation told Mallow and his colleagues that they had first-hand information of success stories from senior Pentagon officials who supported using more aggressive forms of interrogation.[21] But, he said, they never offered concrete examples to back up these accounts.

"I never saw any hard proof of anything," said Mallow. "But there were references made to detainees from other places."

That argument seemed strikingly familiar. It was, in fact, exactly the way Mallow had heard soldiers in Afghanistan referencing the so-called success stories that they learned about from their peers to justify using coercive interrogation.

"It just absolutely galled me that people would make decisions based on this kind of stuff, and then ... face [down] logic and everything else," said Mallow. He said he asked advocates of torture, "How are you going to make operational decisions based on unreliable information?" And he told them, "You're staking lives on this."

During meetings about interrogation, senior officials considered whether approving harsh techniques passed the "shock the conscience" test. That legal phrase is defined as "a determination of whether a state's action falls outside the standards of civilized decency." This standard has been used to determine whether harsh techniques are considered cruel or inhuman. Some military personnel voiced concerns about such moral considerations.

"Once you've crossed that line, you've now gone into a whole different area—you've changed the dynamic," said Mallow. "Are you prepared to escalate it if it doesn't work? And if you're not, isn't it kind of useless? One of the basic problems with the whole coercive strategy is [that] unless you are prepared to go to the next level, don't threaten it."

Gelles and other CITF staff members feared what would happen if interrogators did, in fact, go to the next level. Gelles specifically warned about "force drift."[22] According to this theory, whenever interrogators become dependent upon physical force, they tend to escalate it; if they reason that some force is useful, then more force would seem to be even more productive. And if their harsh techniques don't achieve desired results, interrogators may intensify force until it develops into torture.

Mallow and his colleagues also said they worried about other ways in which the use of force could drift, escalate, and possibly be replicated elsewhere. Once sanctioned, harsh interrogation could presumably migrate from one theater of war to another. The effects of introducing physical coercion into interrogation would therefore seem to ultimately make it *harder* to question detainees.

Chris Mackey, the former Army interrogator in Afghanistan and author of *The Interrogators*, repeated a common question I had heard in the course of my reporting: "If coercion doesn't work, why would the agency [CIA] go to the trouble?"[23]

It's a loaded question, which suggests government agencies would not use such means unless they knew they were effective. Even some critics of US torture thought that the approved harsh interrogation techniques were indeed based on actual research or scientific application. Like Mackey, they asked, Why else would the government sanction harsh interrogation?

The approved exploitation of phobias and the sanctioned use of psychologists seemed to indicate that the government held scientifically informed ideas about torture.[24] Some human rights attorneys have a different read on SERE: they believe that since US forces had experienced harsh interrogation scenarios during their training, government officials would be more inclined to approve such techniques for actual interrogation.[25] Dave Becker, a former senior Guantanamo interrogator and employee of the Defense Intelligence Agency, referenced US military training and said, "If it was okay to subject our soldiers to twenty-hour days, then in our minds it was okay to subject the terrorists to twenty-hour days." During my research for this book, I found that many critics of torture claimed that the techniques of harsh interrogation demonstrated a scientific knowledge that could only come from above, proving that detainee abuse was principally engineered from the top down. Yet I found little proof that psychologists had actually exploited many detainees' phobias during military interrogations. (The CIA's interrogations, which appear to have been far fewer in number than the military's, allegedly used psychologists more often.) I repeatedly asked human rights groups to identify specific cases in which psychologists had exploited detainees' phobias during military interrogations.[26] In the course of my research, I learned about only one phobia that had been repeatedly exploited by military interrogators: barking, lunging dogs. There was one known example in which interrogators exploited a detainee's fear of the dark during interrogation. And the CIA threatened one prisoner with a poisonous insect, which turned out not to be poisonous at all.[27]

Perhaps the presence of psychologists, more than what they imparted, helped buttress beliefs about the efficacy of torture among US forces. Or, as one human rights researcher described it, the presence of medical personnel and psychologists created a "patina of pseudo-science that made the CIA and military officials think these guys were experts in unlocking the human mind. It's one thing to say, 'Take off the gloves.' It's another to say there was a science to it. SERE came in as the science."[28]

SERE also came in as an excuse. Like psychologists and policymakers, SERE personnel have been implicated in detainee abuse that extended beyond their sphere of influence. In many cases, interrogators and guards seriously abused and tortured detainees in Bagram and Guantanamo before officials drafted and disseminated memos that authorized harsh interrogation (except for loosening the Geneva Conventions protections for prisoners) or before SERE personnel exercised any significant influence.[29] Yet some troops ascribed the torture they used to their SERE training—even if they hadn't gone through the course.

The case of one tortured Iraqi general is especially instructive. In Iraq, during November 2003, US interrogators and soldiers tied up an Iraqi prisoner, Major General Abed Mowhoush, in a sleeping bag for several hours and asphyxiated him. The general died, and the soldiers were charged with murder. In their defense, they claimed that "the sleeping bag technique" was used in SERE training. This contradicted their earlier explanation; the soldier who suggested using "the sleeping bag technique" hadn't gone through SERE training at all, and according to his earlier deposition, he actually "remembered how his older brother used to force him into one and how scared and vulnerable it made him feel."[30]

In Afghanistan and Iraq, US dog handlers have forced barking, lunging dogs on detainees in order to frighten them. Some might have learned from articles (e.g, anthropological studies) or military folklore or even a psychologist that Arabs have a particular fear of dogs and forced nudity.[31] But troops certainly didn't need to rely on a psychologist to understand that they could instill fear in hapless detainees by turning dogs on them.

This raises another important point: no hard proof establishes that science has had any special insight into the effectiveness of torture. If anything, the opposite has been established.[32] Studies have consistently shown the variability of pain experienced in each individual, making it virtually impossible to calibrate how torture should be applied to elicit accurate information from prisoners while also ensuring that such pain doesn't cause mental damage, thereby corrupting the quality of the intelligence.[33]

Lawrence Hinkle, one of the neurologists who helped advise the CIA on brainwashing research, saw that torture also had a straightforward impact on memory. In a paper titled "The Physiological State of the Interrogation Subject as It Affects Brain Function," Hinkle wrote, "Any circumstance that impairs the function of the brain potentially affects the ability to give information, as well as the ability to withhold it."[34]

Even US government-sponsored studies on interrogation recognize that pain and duress during interrogations damage the quality of intelligence. The CIA's own KUBARK Counterintelligence Interrogation Manual and the Human Resources Exploitation Training Manual, or HRET—produced in 1963 and 1983, respectively—researched, but did not endorse, torture techniques. The HRET manual found that the problem with torture, regardless of the technique (e.g., drugs, noise, sensory deprivation), was that "intense pain is quite likely to produce false confessions, fabricated to avoid additional punishment."[35] For most researchers on interrogation, the "science of torture" remains a pseudo-science.

It became increasingly clear to me that this was a circular argument based on erroneous information. That "patina of pseudo-science …

unlocking the human mind" has been, and remains, a seductive myth for torture advocates and critics alike.

It turned out that senior government officials and low-ranking troops at Guantanamo had much in common. Everyone feared terrorist threats—the interrogators and their officers, the psychologists and clinicians, SERE trainers, and Ivy League–educated government lawyers. They were desperately trying to collect intelligence from Guantanamo detainees and grew frustrated by how little information they actually extracted. Some feared that al Qaeda detainees had steeled themselves against tough questioning through counter-resistance training. Troops and officials turned to torture because they believed it was necessary. Washington officials, along with personnel from SERE and elsewhere, brainstormed about which techniques could be used to effectively question prisoners.[36] Eventually, these techniques were approved by the Pentagon and used at Guantanamo.

But the basis for engaging in torture in the first place was predicated on false information and misguided beliefs. Descriptions of Guantanamo's population ("the worst of the worst") were often based on poor intelligence, sometimes gathered in Afghanistan, frequently by inexperienced interrogators with no reliable means of identifying terrorist suspects. And claims about detainees' counter-resistance training turned out to be overstated.

Leaving aside the political, legal, and military wrangling that led to the approved use of harsh interrogation, one question remained unanswered: At root, where did ideas about the effectiveness of torture come from? I put the question to those who were present at Guantanamo when people were tortured there.

Mora speculated that "there must have been enormous communication between CIA and the Justice [Department] and the White House. The CIA probably had a greater body of knowledge, at the time 9/11 occurred, than the military concerning interrogation techniques [and was] certainly more in contact with the Israelis, the Syrians, the Egyptians, and others."

Indeed, some CIA personnel have claimed they effectively employed torture during the war on terror. As evidence, former agents have pointed to the way in which they compelled al Qaeda principals like Abu Zubaida and Khalid Sheikh Mohammed (also known as KSM) to confess to planning myriad terrorist plots.[37] Like many such accounts that have professed to show how torture works, these cases remain uncorroborated and offer unconvincing evidence.[38] Nevertheless, these stories, like other anecdotal evidence, fueled beliefs about the utility of torture.

But many military officials and seasoned intelligence professionals told me they believed something else beyond anecdotal success stories informed ideas about the efficacy of torture—something even more rudimentary.

"By and large, there's just this implicit assumption that torture and cruel interrogation techniques are effective," said Mora. "Individuals who did not have necessarily any background or experience or training in these kinds of matters [made] ... decisions based upon an implicit assumption that they would be effective."

Mora further contemplated the question and went to say, "I think part of it was popular culture."

Mallow agreed.

"I hate to say this, but I do think there's kind of an urban legend," he said. "I think some of the experimentation came from folks who thought it worked in other places. Others [reasoned], 'I've seen this stuff portrayed in other places. I've read about it. I've heard about it. I've seen it in movies ... Why shouldn't we give this a try?' "

The origins of harsh interrogation in Guantanamo and Washington and the pattern of behavior that led to abuse and torture provoked dismay. But it was especially alarming to hear that ideas about the effectiveness of torture may have been rooted in anecdotal accounts and pop-culture folklore. It seemed too far-fetched. Yet I kept hearing the very same explanation echoed in cases beyond Guantanamo and Washington, especially as the war on terror expanded elsewhere.

Chapter 5:
Rumors, Myths, and
Ticking Bomb Stories

ADAM GRAY'S FELLOW unit members in Battalion 1-68 were tankers, not interrogators. They were excited about battling Saddam Hussein's forces as they proudly charged into Iraq in their M1 Abrams tanks. As one of Adam's battle buddies, Daniel Keller, put it, "We were outstanding when we first got there."

For some in Battalion 1-68, their mission soured when they became involved in Forward Operating Base Lion's jail. The troops who admitted their involvement with torture and abuse had various explanations. Some said they were untrained and ill-equipped to do detainee operations. Others said they were encouraged to "rough up" prisoners, and some admitted they were bored and venting their anger and frustration.

Captain Sean Nowlan, the S2, or military intelligence officer, for Battalion 1-68, said he didn't know that any abuse occurred or was ordered. "I certainly wouldn't have," he said. "I don't recall ever ordering anything like that." Nowlan also differentiated the "interrogation" from the "tactical questioning" that they did.

"It wouldn't be interrogation, it would be screening," said Nowlan. "Interrogation is a whole other, different level that you have to have—there's a whole lot of rules and regulations and laws that you have to abide by when you do interrogations, so we rarely would do interrogations. It would be screening and tactical questioning just to determine if these individuals were to be interrogated at a higher level."

So why did trained interrogators engage in abuse? For answers, I turned to Tony Lagouranis, a former Army specialist who served in Iraq during 2004 and wrote about his experiences in his book *Fear Up Harsh*.

Lagouranis, a graduate of St. John's University in Sante Fe, decided to enlist in the Army because he wanted to study Arabic. He attended the

Army's Defense Language Institute in Monterey, California, and later trained to be an interrogator at Fort Huachuca in Arizona.

In 2004 Lagouranis was assigned to a four-person Mobile Interrogation Team that traveled throughout Iraq under the leadership of Staff Sergeant Shawn Campbell. When Lagouranis arrived at Abu Ghraib in January, he heard almost immediately that "something bad" had happened, although the photographs hadn't surfaced yet.

In March 2004, Lagouranis, Campbell, and their team took a C-130 plane to a base at the Mosul airport, sometimes referred to as Camp Diamondback and Camp Glory. That same month, Battalion 1-68's deployment was drawing to a close about two hundred miles north of Balad.

The team had already worked in two other facilities in Iraq and could sense that the interrogation operations in Mosul were haphazard. The physical infrastructure of the base was in poor shape; some of the housing lacked adequate shielding. Their interrogation office was in a bunker that had been hit with a missile during the 1991 Gulf War, but they managed to salvage it as a workplace.

A warrant officer oversaw the base's interrogation team. Those who worked with him described him as a driven officer in his late thirties, balding, with a mustache. "A normal Army guy ... A truly nice guy who had a sense of humor," recalled Lagouranis. Even though Lagouranis had studied Arabic, he wasn't fluent enough to do full interrogations without assistance. In Mosul and elsewhere in Iraq, translators from the Titan Corporation helped them during interrogation sessions.

After his first interrogation at his new posting, Lagouranis's interpreter complained about the amount he was being asked to translate.

"I hope you're not expecting us to do that every day," he said.

"Of course," answered Lagouranis.

The interpreter explained that they had been conducting interrogations in Mosul for a maximum of twenty minutes. That stunned the new interrogation team. In Abu Ghraib, they had been doing forty-five-minute interrogations, and even that rarely provided enough time for gathering useful intelligence. The new interrogation team would soon confront other startling protocols at Mosul.

Tall, sloping hills overlooked the American complex at Mosul. Although troops could scarcely make out the city beyond their fortification, they could see a darkened factory building near the base's perimeter

—what troops referred to as "the wire"—that faced their detention facility and could provide cover for sniper fire. Insurgents occasionally hit the base with waves of mortars, and patrolling soldiers regularly sustained casualties. It was even risky to grab a meal.

"We were getting mortared—smashed," said Lagouranis. "We wouldn't even go to the chow hall anymore because it was such a target."

Campbell recalled the same dangers. "I remember we were standing outside, and some soldiers were coming in and talking about how they got grazed by a bullet or some other unit got hit," he said.

Lagouranis's team believed that these dangers proved the need for serious, thoughtful intelligence work. Patrols varied the times they crossed the wire by day or night. Some had a specific mission; others went out to do rounds in the area and picked up suspected insurgents along the way. Campbell said soldiers who went on these missions usually brought back five to seven suspects a day, and sometimes more. Suspects arrived at the base with sandbags over their heads and handcuffed with plastic flex-cuffs. Soldiers left prisoners in a holding pen, a small area surrounded by concertina wire. Troops processed paperwork on detainees from the guard shack while each prisoner underwent a medical checkup. Finally, interrogation teams did an initial screening on the detainees.

New prisoners were asked a uniform set of questions: What's your name? Where do you live? Who do you live with? Have you ever been in the military? Were you ever a member of the Ba'ath Party? Do you know anybody who has been in a terrorist organization?

When interrogators finished their screenings, they handed the prisoners over to guards. Each was assigned a uniform, given a blanket and water, then ushered into a jail designed to house about 150 detainees, said Campbell.

Sifting through and triaging incoming detainees could be a catch-22 situation. Interrogators were supposed to make prudent referrals based on the information gleaned from initial interviews and arrest sheets, no matter how flimsy or incomplete. Some felt that if they downplayed anything suspicious in a detainee's background, their superiors regarded them as too lenient and questioned their judgment. If they erred in the opposite direction, detainees could be sent to a larger, more permanent facility such as Abu Ghraib, even if it wasn't warranted.

"We played detective and lawyer and interrogator and intelligence

guy all in one piece," said Campbell. "[The] guys that got released were
way low. If you got caught, you were probably going to Abu Ghraib.
There was no doubt about it in my mind—95 to 98 percent of those
guys went to AG [Abu Ghraib]. I can say that pretty comfortably."

Over time, Mosul's detention facility became increasingly overcrowded.
But the violence didn't abate.

"[Troops] would bring us people every day and say, 'These are the
guys who are mortaring us,' " Lagouranis recalled. "Every day. And the
guards would start to ask me, 'How is it they keep getting the guys that
are mortaring us, and we keep getting mortared?' The answer was
obvious: They weren't getting the right people."

Soldiers often picked up suspects who fit an age profile or had vague
connections to the Ba'ath Party, said Lagouranis. But the evidence—
such as a photo of Saddam Hussein, or something that struck troops as
anti-American propaganda—lacked any coherent pattern.

"A guy brought a detainee in because he looked suspicious," said
Campbell. "A lot of [Iraqis] would … get caught up in a system that
would basically keep them in jail anywhere from three weeks to probably six months—for absolutely nothing."

Campbell grew frustrated by the kinds of suspects his fellow soldiers
hauled in. "Nothing against those guys on patrol … they were laying
their lives closer to the wire than I was," he said. But he was annoyed by
some of the military's tools for identifying suspects.

"[The] number one thing that I used to hate was the GSR [gunshot
residue] test," Campbell said. The test involved swabbing suspects' hands
with a chemical agent that changed color if they had handled explosive
residue or munitions. But, he pointed out, cigarette lighter fluid and fer-
tilizer were easily mistaken for gunpowder and other explosive chemicals.[1]

"I think a lot of people watch the [TV] show *CSI*, and everybody sees
how they used the test to [determine] if you have gunshot residue on
your hands," said Campbell. "So if you pick up an … Iraqi [farmer], and
you test him and he comes out positive, it's like 'No shit. Really? And
this is all you got?' "

Whenever Lagouranis prepared for a round of interrogations, he
looked over the paperwork that troops filled out to describe why their
captives came under suspicion. "It was supposed to be information that
would help you try and figure out what this guy was guilty of and what
he might know," said Lagouranis. But he found that forms typically

contained little more than a description of the arrest. "It basically was a blank page with one statement—just completely useless information."

In some cases, detainees had come under suspicion because they were driving in an area where improvised explosive devices (IEDs) had detonated. There was talk that insurgents drove black Opels (which was true in some cases). But this resulted in many seemingly arbitrary arrests of drivers of black Opels.[2] In one case, a teenager who was carrying benzine, a cleaning solvent, was arrested because benzine could have been used for a bomb, recalled Lagouranis. Iraqis were arrested for carrying cell phones, which could be used for triggering IEDs—despite the fact that cell phones were a common possession.[3] Interrogators found reports on detainees who had been picked up near mosques for "suspicious activity." Sometimes troops included photographs showing piles of rocket-propelled grenades and AK-47 rifles in their reports. "So anybody who looks at that is going to say, 'This guy is fucking guilty,' right?" said Lagouranis.[4] But often those photos had missing or incomplete information—nothing that provided a context about the pictures or gave the interrogators a sense of how the weapons were related to the arrests. "Like a guy standing in a store buying a Pepsi," said Lagouranis. "He'd get arrested and all of a sudden he's charged with having these weapons. It happened all the time. All the time …"

Both he and Campbell thought that soldiers were picking up local Iraqis for trivial reasons, based on flimsy evidence and questionable clues.[5] It felt as if success was being measured by the volume of arrests instead of the quality of the intelligence being gathered. Lagouranis estimated that 90 percent of the detainees he interrogated were not involved in opposition to the Americans in any way.

Campbell tried to guess how many detainees he interviewed were legitimately suspicious. "Maybe 5 percent," he said, after a long pause. "Maybe."

Their assessment of US detentions of Iraqis during 2004 was widely shared. A confidential International Red Cross study found that 70 to 90 percent of US prisoners in Iraq "had been arrested by mistake" in 2004.[6] A sergeant who was part of the Detainee Assessment Board that contributed to screening prisoners at Abu Ghraib maintained that "85 percent to 90 percent of detainees were of either no intelligence value or were of value but innocent and therefore should … not have remained in captivity."[7]

*   *   *

In Mosul, Lagouranis said, his superior officers seemed to believe that interrogators could quickly obtain information to determine who represented a genuine threat and who didn't belong in their jail.

"A lot of people believe that an interrogator can just go in there and get information starting from scratch, without having information," said Lagouranis. "That's impossible—there's no way."

Interrogators were often hampered by an incomplete understanding of the country, the culture, and the political background. "Those of us who went to language training had a little bit of a window into Arab culture, but not much," said Lagouranis.

He described how detainees grew frustrated by their captors' lack of basic knowledge about Iraq, making it difficult to relay information to their questioners; some lacked a basic knowledge of the Ba'ath Party and local sectarian divisions.[8] Interrogators faced other systemic problems. For instance, they rarely heard back from the intelligence analysts reviewing their reports. Without such input, they were unable to build intelligence on detainees they had questioned.

"It would've been really helpful for me to know, after I filed a report, that everything that a [suspect] told me was bullshit. But it never came back. There was no feedback at all. Nothing," Lagouranis said. "Building a knowledge base would have been helpful—it would have just been helpful in honing my interrogation skills by knowing what I was doing was effective, and by knowing who was telling me the truth or who wasn't."

Campbell agreed. "[The] only time I'd ever get anything back, whether it was good or bad, was maybe if they had a couple of questions about [some] guy," he said. "It's like everything went into a vacuum."

Interrogators were overwhelmed by the volume of screenings, frustrated by their limited success, and unsure how to improve their results. The warrant officer at the Mosul base was also dissatisfied by their progress, perhaps because of pressure from his superiors.

"He didn't talk about pressure from above, but he certainly did talk about our need to get the intelligence—and better intelligence—from these guys," Lagouranis recalled. "And when they say 'intelligence,' a lot of that meant confessions."

Military interrogators faced contradictory expectations of what they were supposed to extract from their detainees. But their superiors' confusing orders and directives further compounded their problems.

Just before Campbell arrived in Mosul, he received a military directive from the command staff at Abu Ghraib. The directive was issued by Lieutenant General Ricardo S. Sanchez, the commander of coalition forces in Iraq from June 2003 to June 2004. Sanchez's directive, titled "Interrogation and Counter-Resistance Policy," authorized twenty-nine interrogation techniques for Iraq. Twelve of those techniques exceeded limits established by the Army Field Manual—and were informed by policy implemented at Guantanamo.[9] (In October 2003, Sanchez revised his memo to better comport with the Army Field Manual's guidelines.[10] Campbell is not certain which directive he received, but believes it was the first one, based on the page markings.) Not all intelligence units in Iraq were privy to that directive[11]; Campbell's colleagues, hadn't been aware of its existence until he showed it to them in Mosul.

"When I brought it up, they were like, 'Really? You're doing this?' " Campbell recalled. "They actually looked at it and said, "Wow, we could really use this.' "

The directive Lagouranis came across didn't spell out techniques, but appeared to present broad definitions of the parameters for coercion used in interrogations.[12] "The directive we received in Mosul gave us a sense of what was permissible and gave us some idea of what the limitations might be," he said. "It seemed to me to be rather open-ended and self-contradictory, so we really didn't have clear guidelines. We didn't get any ideas from the document. The techniques were out there and we knew about them."

Lagouranis and others on his team had met interrogators who had served in Afghanistan while they were at Fort Gordon, Georgia, before shipping out to Iraq. These veterans of the Afghan war described techniques they had used, for example, forcing detainees to hold various stress positions and exposing them to extreme temperatures.

Other methods were simple, but seemed excruciating. One involved tying detainees' hands behind their backs and placing a heavy weight on the handcuffs, pulling their arms downward, placing strain on their shoulder sockets.

In Mosul, the interrogation team decided to try some of those methods on detainees who seemed to have the most intelligence value and to be most resistant to normal questioning.

"We were targeting people that we thought would respond," said Lagouranis. "We would choose to use it on them according to whatever we got on their dossier."

And so they stepped up physical pressure. "It was a gradual progression, but part of that was just because of what sort of resources we had," he said. "We started using it [more] when things became available to us."

The plastic flex-cuffs that troops used to handcuff detainees were ubiquitous and easy to use for added pressure.

"You can just refuse to take those things off, and that's agonizing for them," said Lagouranis. "It gets extremely painful after a short time, and they'll start bleeding and stuff. And then if you start manipulating their arms—that's really painful for them."

When another four-person mobile interrogation team turned up at the base, they were able to expand their repertoire. The warrant officer was energized. "Okay. This is what we're going to do," he announced, according to Lagouranis. "We're going to start doing twenty-four-hour rotations on these guys, and we're going to start using sleep deprivation."

They got access to a steel shipping container and used it to expose detainees to cold and to induce hypothermia. Then dog handlers arrived, and they provoked the dogs into frenzied barking and snapping to frighten detainees.

And yet, Lagouranis maintained, none of the "enhanced" techniques seemed to produce useful intelligence beyond what they had learned through normal questioning. But the warrant officer pressed his staff to keep trying creative approaches.

"Just because you put some type of force on [a detainee] doesn't mean it's actually gonna work," said Campbell. "You're literally just trying something new and hopefully it works."

All of the interrogators at the Mosul base held thirty-minute meetings at the beginning and end of their twelve-hour shifts to brief each other about their interrogation sessions. They discussed the intelligence they had gleaned, what they had requested from intelligence analysts, and details about the latest batch of detainees brought in. They also discussed strategies. The warrant officer's approach was fairly consistent.

"If he wanted more information from somebody, or felt that somebody had information and they weren't breaking, his solution was to get rougher on them," said Lagouranis. "That was always his answer … every time."

On occasion, the warrant officer would transfer one interrogator's assigned detainee over to the incoming shift, just to keep up the pressure.

Interrogators kept fishing for other ideas, and sometimes they discussed what other military personnel were doing. For example, they looked to a group of special operations forces who jailed detainees at a separate facility on the base. Because special operations forces often work with greater autonomy and are often provided high-quality intelligence for their missions, their regular Army counterparts figured they must have solid intel on their detainees.

Lagouranis was able to learn a bit about these detainees through a corporal who worked as a guard for both detention facilities. The corporal told him about the sorts of things that occurred in the special operations forces' compound. They had a typical regimen, he recalled.

First, according to the corporal's account, the special operations forces stripped off detainees' clothing and doused them with ice-cold water. They piped loud music into the cells and switched on a strobe light. Then they took turns prodding the prisoners to keep them awake for hours. The corporal heard them call it "the disco," and told Lagouranis that the special operations forces puffed on cigars as they churned through this cycle of abuse all night, intermittently questioning their captives.

Eventually, some of the special operations forces' detainees were transferred to the regular interrogation facility at Mosul.

Campbell distinctly remembered one of them. "He was shivering," he recalled. "It was almost like as if someone had [just] took off all his clothes ... and kept him cold for a long time. I think it was cold at that time, so they probably just wet him down and kept him outside. He looked like he [became] hypothermic. I'm gonna be honest with you ... and he was famished. This guy looked like he'd been through hell. He was willing to talk to us about anything you wanted to talk about. He would have told us anything. Anything."

The former special operations forces prisoners also described to Lagouranis exactly what the corporal had told him about the regimen of abuse. But the detainees didn't get a reprieve. When the special operations forces released their detainees into Mosul's regular jail, the warrant officer believed they still possessed information that could be useful. Campbell said it seemed as if he reasoned, "If these guys did it, why can't we do it?"

"And so if we were going to go hard on them, we knew that we were going to have to at least match [the special operations forces] or go harder," said Lagouranis.

At first, they simply employed what they had already been doing—forcing detainees to kneel for hours, depriving them of sleep, and keeping them in cold shipping containers. But with two interrogation teams operating in back-to-back twelve-hour shifts, they had the flexibility to push the regimens longer. They provoked dogs to frighten detainees, blasted loud music into the shipping containers, and flashed a strobe light into their eyes. In the end, they replicated "the disco." But no one knew if their interrogation teams had any more success than the special operations forces.

"We were questioning people who had already been questioned by them—and questioned using [the same] harsh techniques," said Lagouranis. "We must have looked like idiots."

"They used to always tell us 'hearts and minds, hearts and minds,'" said Campbell, referring to his commanders' approach toward Iraqis. "And what do we do? We stick a dagger in both—and sometimes in their back."

From their bunker office, interrogators had to process two-page reports on each of their detainees. The forms included information on detainees' time and date of capture, their background—including age, religion, and tribe—and what interrogators produced from interrogation sessions. The warrant officer read their final reports, edited them, then filed them into an encrypted network. It was tedious work that involved formatting paperwork with arcane guidelines.

When the warrant officer wasn't processing interrogators' reports or holding meetings, he often napped or watched television and DVDs on a big-screen TV that occupied the office. There, Lagouranis and Campbell occasionally played cribbage and drank non-alcoholic beer. Sometimes they joined the warrant officer for smoke breaks and an occasional movie or TV show. It was a way to pass time and allay the boredom inherent in their routine.

At many military bases, troops had access to cheap DVDs including science fiction, crime dramas, and action movies. While watching DVDs with his superior, Lagouranis was struck not so much by the plots, but by the common themes of many scenes.

"I remember thinking at the time that it was remarkable how often interrogation scenes are in TV and movies," he said.

The dramas shared predictable elements. Heroes captured suspects who clearly had vital information. The clock was ticking. A bomb was set to explode or a lethal plan was about to be executed. So the captors turned the screws on a guilty captive: threats unnerved the villain, pressure sent the final blow—at last he cracked, providing critical information that led heroes to defuse the grave threat.

"I was extra-engaged by the interrogation scenes," admitted Lagouranis. "And I knew it was because I was looking for a cool response [from suspects]."

He and the other interrogators felt they were inadequately prepared for their work. After all, he only received the eighteen weeks' training at Fort Huachuca, had little to no experience in the field, and could rarely turn to experienced interrogators on other bases for advice. According to Campbell, "Tony was probably the only actual trained interrogator" on their team. "[The other team members] had a crash course ... I think we trained for about a week and a half, maybe two weeks at Abu Ghraib."

In the absence of further guidance, they sometimes watched for "cool responses" on the TV screen in order to understand what kind of pressure helped make suspects talk.

"I would've liked to have been taught by that person, but that person wasn't available," said Lagouranis, referring to the expert interrogators they watched in dramas. "So you sit around and you watch interrogators on TV."

He remembered how these fictional interrogators had a formulaic approach. "There's a way TV or movie interrogators break a prisoner, and that's by establishing a total power over the detainee until the detainee's will breaks," he observed. "It really never involves getting the detainee's guard down. It's always beating a detainee's guard down instead of finding the way around it. There are no smart interrogations on television."

In the course of watching these shows, Lagouranis began to wonder how Hollywood renditions of interrogations affected other intelligence workers. "None of us were complete idiots," he said. "We knew it was make-believe. But still, it affects you."

As Mosul's prisoner population steadily grew, commanders drew up plans to build additional interrogation booths and a larger detention facility to house more detainees. Lagouranis's warrant officer exchanged ideas with a captain and a platoon leader who were setting up the construction.

During one of the shift meetings, the three officers milled around the interrogators' office and discussed how best to design and build it. The widescreen TV glowed in the background as they talked. A thriller appeared on the screen, showing an interrogation scene. It depicted a detainee who was confined to a prison cell and overheard his captors electrocuting another prisoner in the cell beside him. Little by little, the torturers increased the voltage, intensifying the detainee's pain with more powerful electroshocks. The victim's screams steadily rose in pitch, and each shout rattled the isolated detainee as he envisioned the fate that awaited him.

But there was an interesting twist: the "electrocuted" detainee was actually on the interrogators' side—he was, in fact, faking the torture in order to scare the real detainee into believing he would suffer the same fate. And it worked: within a short spell, and without actually torturing the detainee, the suspect quickly revealed to his handlers the pressing information he possessed.

The scene ended, and the officers in the bunker office turned to each other. They suddenly had an idea that would help make the interrogations more effective in the new detention facility. It would be relatively simple to configure rooms to reproduce the same scenario. And they could also run other kinds of simulations to induce fear using this model. The officers didn't refer to the scene directly, but their description about how to set up a faux-torture scenario to induce fear was strikingly similar to what had just been shown on the office TV screen, Lagouranis said.

He and his fellow interrogators silently exchanged glances, disbelieving what they were hearing from their superior.

Campbell thought to himself, Are they really serious? Do they think some bullshit like that will work?

Lagouranis feared that a strategy of that kind was a form of psychological torture, something akin to mock executions, and wasn't legally permissible. The officers nodded in agreement, and the idea was ultimately dismissed. But the suggestion itself, and its fictional source of inspiration, seemed especially troubling—and revealing.

Perhaps it was an isolated incident, even a fluke. Or maybe it showed how myths and fiction had actually affected ideas about interrogation and torture during the war on terror.

★   ★   ★

Margaret Stock witnessed the atmosphere at her school change abruptly after the September 11 attacks. Her pupils weren't average college students who were suddenly confronted with the ugly realities of terrorism. Stock was, in fact, an associate professor of national security law at the oldest and most prestigious military school in America, the United States Military Academy at West Point, and her students were cadets slated to be officers.

Students in her classes suddenly took strong positions on legal and strategic issues following the attacks in New York and Washington.

"After 9/11, there was this sense that it was a new kind of war and that we needed to use new kinds of tactics [and] equipment," said Stock. "You'd hear, 'The paradigm is different from what we've been taught, and so we have to adjust. We have to be flexible in our thinking.' And I definitely heard that on the torture issue—that became hot quite rapidly."

As it did to most Americans, the spectacular brutality of the September 11 attacks stunned her students. These were also unconventional strikes, and the product of exceptional coordination. Yet Stock reminded her students that Japanese kamikazes employed similar tactics—piloting planes directly into targets—and that Japanese soldiers also beheaded prisoners. The terrorist experience wasn't new to Americans—with the Oklahoma City bombing and the 1993 terrorist attempt on the World Trade Center—nor were the enemy's tactics unprecedented, she insisted. Stock didn't set out to invalidate her students' fears about new threats that had emerged, but rather to put them into context before they argued that there was a "paradigm shift" that necessitated a new military stance.

Some of her students invoked scenes contained in movies such as *The Siege* to counter her position. *The Siege* is a 1998 film starring Denzel Washington, and it depicts similar terrorist attacks on civilians in New York and the government's subsequent reaction. The fictional government's responses include internment camps, widespread wiretapping, and even torture.

The torture scene is worth recapping, given how prescient it turned out to be. It involves Agent Anthony Hubbard, a counterterrorism FBI agent played by Denzel Washington; US Army Major General William Deveraux, a heavy-handed general who advocates torture, played by Bruce Willis; Colonel Hardwick, an Army intelligence officer linked to General Deveraux; and CIA Agent Sharon Bridger, played by Annette

Bening, an operative who works on Middle Eastern counterterrorism cases and who becomes an accomplice to Deveraux's torture. Then there's an Arab prisoner, Tariq Husseini, who has been arrested under the suspicion that he knows about "terrorist cells" that are poised to attack American civilians. Husseini is stripped naked, and while sitting in a tiled room overhears General Deveraux's rationale for torture and the tactics he and Bridger are considering:

GENERAL DEVERAUX: How much longer, do you think, before he gives up the other cells?

AGENT HUBBARD: He can't give up the other cells if he doesn't know where they are.

DEVERAUX: He knows.

HUBBARD: No, he doesn't. You said so yourself, Sharon, in the strategy meeting. One cell doesn't know where the other one is, right?

DEVERAUX: How long before he breaks, Sharon?

CIA AGENT BRIDGER: Well, at this rate, too long. The theater was hit nine hours after we took down the first cell.

DEVERAUX: So what other models do we have? Shaking?

BRIDGER: Won't work.

DEVERAUX: Works for the Israelis.

BRIDGER: Only in conjunction with sleep deprivation; it takes at least thirty-six hours.

DEVERAUX: We don't have thirty-six hours. Electric shock?

BRIDGER: The neurotransmitters will just shut down.

DEVERAUX: Water?

COLONEL HARDWICK: Palestinian Authority has produced good intel with water. Course, there's cutting. But it's extremely messy.

HUBBARD: Are you people insane? What are you talking about?

DEVERAUX: The time has come for one man to suffer to save hundreds of lives.

HUBBARD: One man. What about two, huh? How about six? How about public executions?

DEVERAUX: Feel free to leave whenever you like, Special Agent Hubbard.

HUBBARD: Come on, General. You lost men. I've lost men, but you can't do this. What if what they really want … What if they don't really want the Sheik, have you considered that? What if what they really want is for us to herd children into stadiums like we're doing? And put soldiers on the street and have Americans looking over their shoulders? Bend the law, shred the Constitution a little bit. Because if we torture him, General … we do that, and everything we have bled for and fought and died for is over. And they've won. They've already won.

One dimension of this scene represents reality: how ideas about torture, as well as the techniques, travel. Like Lagouranis's experience in Mosul and elsewhere, ideas are often traded through word of mouth. Troops chat about what has been done elsewhere ("Palestinian Authority has produced good intel with water"); what was supposedly effective (Deveraux: "Works for the Israelis." Bridger: "Only in conjunction with sleep deprivation; it takes at least thirty-six hours"); and how these techniques are often supported by pseudo-scientific language and beliefs (Deveraux: "Electric shock?" Bridger: "The neurotransmitters will just shut down").[13]

To its credit, *The Siege* is a cautionary tale about condoning and using internment and torture—even when US military and law enforcement personnel face imminent threats. Denzel Washington's FBI character becomes the hero, and Bruce Willis's General Deveraux turns out to be the villain.

That attitude shifted among Stock's West Point students. "Before 9/11, everybody thought Denzel Washington was a big hero," recalled Stock. "And then after 9/11, they [reasoned], 'No, Bruce Willis makes sense.' "

Jane Mayer's article on the television drama *24* was published on February 19, 2007, in the *New Yorker*. Mayer wrote about the producers of the show, their right-wing background, and the increasing prevalence of torture scenes in American television since September 11. The article also considered the impact of *24* on American culture and the military.

Shortly after the article came out, Stock met with fellow teachers during one of their regular, informal faculty meetings on campus. She gave her colleagues a pop quiz to see how many of them knew about Jack Bauer, the main character in *24* who played a prominent part in the show's torture scenes. Only a few instructors had heard about him, so she circulated Mayer's article to her colleagues and asked them to poll their students about Jack Bauer. To her surprise, all of their students seemed to know about Jack Bauer and frequently cited the counterterrorism tactics that he and the other characters employed in the TV thriller.

"They developed arguments based on what they [saw] on the show," said Stock. And the cadets weren't the only ones.

Author Philippe Sands discovered that Army Lieutenant Colonel Diane Beaver, the staff judge advocate at Guantanamo, had witnessed

24's impact on the base. "Bauer had many friends at Guantanamo Bay, Beaver said. 'He gave people lots of ideas … We saw it on cable [at the base] … people had already seen the first series, it was hugely popular.' She believes the show contributed to an environment in which those at Guantanamo were encouraged to see themselves as being on the frontline—and to go further than they otherwise might."[14]

Jack Bauer even seduced high US officials.

Speaking at a Canadian legal conference in June 2007, Supreme Court Justice Antonin Scalia challenged judges from North America and Europe about their views on torture and national security issues. He didn't cite any historical examples in which torture had been successfully employed during counterterrorism campaigns. Instead, he invoked Jack Bauer. Scalia even cited a particular season and key episode in which Jack Bauer tortures a suspect, who then quickly cracks under duress and provides vital information that prevents an attack against Los Angeles.

"Jack Bauer saved Los Angeles … He saved hundreds of thousands of lives," said Scalia. "Are you going to convict Jack Bauer? Is any jury going to convict Jack Bauer? I don't think so … So, the question is really whether we believe in these absolutes, and ought we believe in these absolutes."

Another American judge who endorsed *24* no longer weighed legal decisions in a courtroom, but he was managing real-world terrorist threats. This ex-judge also claimed that *24* accurately reflected the realities that his government agency faced. This former federal judge was Michael Chertoff, secretary of the Department of Homeland Security.

On June 23, 2006, the Heritage Foundation sponsored a discussion titled "*24* and America's Image in Fighting Terrorism: Fact, Fiction, or Does It Matter?" Rush Limbaugh moderated the panel, which included Chertoff; some of the show's writers, producers, and stars; and several right-wing pundits. Clarence Thomas and his wife were in the audience; it was a sellout crowd.

Chertoff spoke of his admiration for *24*, and the parallels he saw between the show and his own work.

"Typically, in the course of the show, although in a very condensed time period, the actors and the characters are presented with very difficult choices," he said. "Choices about whether to take drastic and even violent action against a threat, and weighing that against the consequence of not taking the action and the destruction that might otherwise ensue. In simple terms, whether it's the president in the show or Jack

Bauer or the other characters, they're always trying to make the best choice with a series of bad options, where there is no clear magic bullet to solve the problem, and you have to weigh the costs and benefits of a series of unpalatable alternatives. And I think people are attracted to that because, frankly, it reflects real life. That is what we do every day."[15]

Chertoff didn't explicitly endorse torture, but, like Scalia, he fed the perception that 24 reflected reality.

Margaret Stock was stunned by Chertoff's view. The show "is no way close to real life," she said. "I worked in counterterrorism, and 24 is so far off. And for somebody to even say that who's in a position of authority … is really scary. And yet, that's the head of Homeland Security saying that."

In addition to her legal background, Stock had extensive training in anti-terrorism and did various kinds of counterterrorism work for US forces in Japan as a Military Police officer.

"I did a lot of my work in a classified environment that actually looked a lot like the CTU [Counter Terrorist Unit] as depicted on 24," said Stock. "Except that our computers didn't work nearly as well as the computers work on TV, and we usually worked twelve-hour shifts instead of working twenty-four hours straight."

That work experience gave Stock a good insight into the various ways in which 24 is so improbable. "You have to think about why 24 is unrealistic," she said. "On that show, they always have full knowledge of everything …[and] whatever Jack Bauer is planning to do is going to turn out to be right."

In actuality, counterterrorism operations are quite a bit messier.

"One thing you'll learn a lot of times is that your initial perception of a situation is completely wrong," Stock explained.

Such misperceptions can result from chasing down false leads based on presumptions about crimes and suspects. And some misdirection is a product of the ungainly way in which government operations often work, as was summarized by the 9/11 Commission Report. Sleek computer systems like those depicted in 24 don't match the government's reality—the FBI's computer system, for example, has been in notorious disarray.[16] Intergovernmental cooperation has been slowed by bureaucratic infighting over turf and inefficiencies.[17] US intelligence operations are renowned for their shortage of translators, and so identifying suspects and sorting out information takes a lot longer in real life than it does in fiction.[18]

"Half of the time, you don't even understand what's going on because you're getting bad translations that don't make any sense," said Stock. "So you don't have perfect information. Ever. [And] your computer systems don't work perfectly."

Instead of focusing on harsh interrogation scenes, "Hollywood ought to be doing a show on how important it is [to know] foreign languages," she said.

Despite 24's popularity, Stock cautioned against focusing too narrowly on it as a unique representation of torture in popular media.

"24 is not the only one," she said, referring in particular to the show's use of torture. "It's just a concentrated dose of it."

There was, in fact, a dramatic rise in torture scenes in television shows and movies after September 11.[19] According to an article by the Associated Press, "Prior to 2001, the few torture scenes on prime-time TV usually had the shows' villains as the instigators ... In both 1996 and 1997, there were no prime-time TV scenes containing torture, according to the Parents Television Council, which keeps a programming database. In 2003, there were 228 such scenes, the PTC said. The count was over 100 in both 2004 and 2005. They found examples on *Alias*, *The Wire*, *Law & Order*, *The Shield*—even *Star Trek: Voyager*."[20]

According to Stock, her cadets would reference such scenes not just to argue for the use of torture, but also to make a case for exonerating those who had actually employed it in recent wartime situations. In her class, they often brought up the experience of Lieutenant Colonel Allen B. West.

West was a highly decorated officer who served in Iraq in 2003, where he was immediately confronted with lethal threats. "We experienced contact from hostile forces from the time we got there," he told the *New York Times*.[21]

Intelligence operatives had informed him that he was being targeted for assassination and that the men guarding him could fall prey to such attacks. At first he laughed off the reports. But within a day, he and his soldiers were ambushed. They were first struck by a roadside bomb, then engaged in a fierce firefight with insurgents.

West heard that a local police chief, Yehiya Kadoori Hamoodi, was involved in the attack, and he ordered his soldiers to capture him. Before twenty-four hours had past, they arrested the police chief, blindfolded him, and deposited him in their jail at the base.

Then West arrived. Hamoodi was relieved to see him, believing that the colonel would improve his treatment. But West brandished his pistol and pressed him for answers. Hamoodi insisted he didn't know anything about plots to kill West. The colonel still didn't believe him and threatened to shoot him. Yet Hamoodi continued to deny having any knowledge of a plot.

In response, West raised his pistol and fired a round near his head. Panicked and desperate to avoid getting shot, Hamoodi suddenly "admitted there would be attacks, and called out names."[22] US troops then stormed his home and searched for evidence that would corroborate his leads. But they failed to find anything, and whatever information Hamoodi provided turned out to be useless. The colonel succeeded in frightening Hoomadi into talking—he even got a confession out of him. But West plainly failed to obtain any worthwhile intelligence that would thwart attacks or locate insurgent suspects. After forty-five days, US troops released Hamoodi from custody.

Hamoodi has maintained his innocence and said he doesn't harbor ill will toward West. But he is still traumatized from the experience, and panics whenever he sees American troops on Iraqi streets.

West maintained that he "acted in the best interest for my soldiers and yes myself."[23] But his commanders were furious when they learned he had threatened a prisoner at gunpoint. He was charged with aggravated assault, fined five thousand dollars, and demoted.[24] West then submitted his resignation.

Back at West Point in Stock's class, "There was a great deal of discussion about this. Was this guy doing the right thing or not doing the right thing?" For Stock, there was no gray area: "It's crystal clear—you weren't allowed to do that kind of thing."

But many of her students strongly supported the colonel's actions. Even if he used questionable means—a mock execution—West did what he needed to do to protect his soldiers, they argued.

"And the argument they would use was *Rules of Engagement*," said Stock. "They'd cite that movie."

The film depicts Samuel L. Jackson as an Army officer who faces a similar choice in the heat of battle. In one scene, Jackson's character threatens to execute a Vietnamese officer in order to stave off an attack on American soldiers. And the play works. "The picture they have in their minds is very powerful," said Stock. "They saw a very emotional scene in the movie."

I told Stock how surprised I was to hear that West Point cadets would fall for such reasoning. Given the academy's strong reputation, surely most students there would have a more informed understanding of military events—both historical and fictional—and would therefore approach what they saw on the screen with more skepticism.

"Okay. Wait a minute. Hold on, hold on," she replied. "They're just like everybody else at any college in America."

Stock had a valid point: the mythology of torture wasn't particular to elite military academies. It has lurked in many corners of America, taking on many forms and exerting a widespread influence. But there is one powerful and ubiquitous story in particular that has been used to defend the supposed necessity of torture.

Hear the words "ticking bomb," and "torture" will soon follow. Those who have advocated the use of torture in interrogations have almost reflexively invoked the ticking bomb scenario to justify its use. But where does this incident actually come from? Is it grounded in a particular experience that demonstrated how a military or intelligence agency was compelled to take extreme measures? In short, does this example show how torture was successfully applied to thwart an attack?

Torture historian Darius Rejali, author of *Torture and Democracy*, has traced the roots of the first ticking bomb scenario to a French war correspondent and former paratrooper, Jean Lartéguy.

Lartéguy wrote a detailed account of a French paratrooper, Captain Philippe Esclavier, who fought against the Algerian resistance in the 1960s. The Algerian War, or Algerian War of Independence, was a bloody conflict marked by guerrilla warfare, hidden bombs that targeted civilians, and rampant torture.

Esclavier was a battle-tested warrior before he arrived in Algeria. He had fought against the Germans and Vietnamese, and was even captured and tortured by the Gestapo. His experiences seemed to make Esclavier the perfect man to ferret out and interrogate terrorists in Algeria.

In one instance, Esclavier learned that a dentist named Arouche had planted fifteen bombs in Algiers. When his men apprehended Arouche, they learned that the dentist's bombs were set to explode within hours. Esclavier was gripped by fear, terrified that Arouche's plot would claim many innocent lives.

"The bombs?" asked Esclavier.

But Arouche refused to answer. "No," he said. "I'm the only one who knows ... Your bomb disposal squads can spend all night searching the shops of Algiers, they won't find a thing. You can kill me, torture me, I'll die with pleasure in your hands because tomorrow ..."

"I could easily make you talk ..."

The dentist wasn't swayed. He silently watched the minutes tick away on the clock. Arouche needed only to bide his time until the bombs detonated.

"Arouche," said Esclavier. "I was tortured once myself. I know what it's like, and I know that one talks, for everyone talks in the end ..."

Still nothing.

Esclavier pondered what he should do. He first remembered his father's discussions about non-violence. But the urgency of the situation forced him to consider another tactic: he began describing how the Gestapo had tortured him years ago.

"It's not so much the beating-up that's hard to bear, Arouche," he said. "It's the waiting for it and not knowing what the pain will be like ...

"The German [interrogator] displayed no emotion, neither hatred nor pity, nor even a trace of interest. He actually told me: 'I don't think the information you've got will have the slightest effect on the eventual outcome of the war, whichever side wins, but what you'll suffer will mark you for the rest of your life.' "

And so, Esclavier reasoned that he had no choice but to torture his detainee to learn where he had planted the bombs. He inflicted demonstrable pain on the dentist that lasted for many grueling hours.

And it worked.

According to Lartéguy, "By the time the dentist was carried off on a stretcher, in the early hours of the morning, he had confessed everything; none of the fifteen bombs went off."

Esclavier sweated over how best to thwart a terrorist attack—it was a grueling moral dilemma. Arouche, the dentist, possessed crucial intelligence that was needed to defuse the bombs. Based on his own personal experience, Esclavier was certain that torture was effective and, with great reluctance, he decided to use it to save lives. Within hours, Arouche cracked under the pressure, and when that actionable intelligence led the French forces to the ticking bombs, Esclavier was vindicated.

There is just one problem with this story: it is a work of fiction. Lartéguy didn't describe an actual historical event. Instead, he wrote about an imaginary episode of ticking bombs and confession through torture in his novel *Les Centurions* (*The Centurions*).[25]

But the legend of the ticking bomb scenario lives on.

The fable of the ticking bomb is worrisome not just because it is based on a work of fiction, but because it has been validated and institutionalized: West Point cadets pointed to *Rules of Engagement* to defend the real-life use of mock executions. The former Secretary of Homeland Security told a packed audience that the fantasies in the television thriller *24* reflect "real life" counterterrorism situations. A Supreme Court Justice cited the same show to defend the use of torture to an international audience of judges. An interrogation team in Iraq gleaned ideas about coercive interrogation from scenes they saw on TV and in movies.

I often asked military intelligence personnel and human rights researchers if they were aware of other cases in which US military units were influenced by fictional scenes of torture, or even imitated some of the things they saw in the products of Hollywood during the questioning of detainees. Many said they heard about such situations, but few could point to any confirmed cases.

I pressed on to find other examples, because so many of my sources insisted that pop-culture references to torture greatly influenced commonly held ideas about interrogation. But perhaps this was the wrong way of looking at how fiction affected US forces. After all, in Lagouranis's experience the torture scenes that he and his fellow interrogators saw on TV and in movies ultimately didn't really influence the techniques they used. Instead, they learned about harsh techniques from other units by word of mouth and through imitating what special operations forces in Mosul had been doing.

But Lagouranis and other interrogators I met explained to me that Hollywood's interrogation scenes had an impact in other important ways. Namely, interrogators said they felt that in the absence of proper instruction and coaching, folklore and fiction stepped in. On TV shows and in movies they saw dramatic examples of effective interrogation using harsh techniques and torture. Referring to Hollywood's crack interrogators, Lagouranis recalled how he "would've liked to have been taught by that person, but that person wasn't available. So you sit around and you watch interrogators on TV." Even though they didn't reproduce specific techniques from Hollywood, those fictional interrogations fed the belief that harsh techniques were effective.

But there was at least one other case that seemed to echo the way troops did mimic the torture they saw on TV. It occurred, in fact, roughly at the same time that Lagouranis and his interrogators were abusing detainees in Mosul. It happened 124 miles away from Mosul, in Tikrit.

In July 2004 the Army Inspector General, Lieutenant General Paul T. Mikolashek, produced a report about detainee abuse in Iraq based on interviews with troops from the 4th Infantry Division, the 720th Military Police Battalion, and the 1st Infantry Division. Interviews conducted for the report cited various examples of abuse, including "many beatings ... after the detainees were zip-tied [cuffed] by some units in 4ID." But the publicly released report is so heavily redacted that where these troops tortured and abused detainees, and what kinds of techniques they used, remains unclear.

In what was perhaps the most arresting statement in the Mikolashek report, the CID documents revealed that officers "engaged in interrogations using techniques they literally remembered from the movies."

It turned out that Lagouranis's experience of being influenced by fictional torture wasn't an aberration. Myths and fiction not only informed ideas about torture, but were actually used in the field.

Chapter 6:
Crimes of Omission

F OR SOLDIERS WHO witnessed or participated in abuse, there was immense pressure to keep silent. Troops didn't want to betray each other. They didn't want to get themselves into trouble. Some might have feared that they wouldn't be believed. Others found their complaints dismissed and ignored by the people who were supposed to investigate such allegations.

Throughout the time that Tony Lagouranis worked as an interrogator in Iraq in 2004, he saw and participated in many cases of detainee abuse. Toward the end of his tour, he said he had become unhappy with what he was doing; he began to sympathize with the prisoners who had been hurt and resented the officers who encouraged or ordered harsh interrogations.

Eventually, he told me, he tried to do fewer interrogations while he counted down the remaining days of his tour. He said he reported the abuse four times, from three locations in Iraq. "In North Babel I put out at least two, maybe three reports that I wrote," he said. "They were just reports that I wrote on a Microsoft Word document and sent out through the chain of command."

Military personnel didn't reject his reports, but they didn't exactly welcome them, either.

"There was no resistance in putting these things forward, other than a clenched jaw," said Lagouranis. But when he filed them, "People would accept the abuse reports from me with a smile and promise it would be investigated, and then it probably would go into the garbage can. They felt that was the best way to get you off their back."

He detailed some of the abuses he saw in Mosul, including the torture linked to the special operations forces.

"I told them about some of the things I had seen coming out of the SEAL compound," he said, referring to the Navy's special operations forces unit, "including a guy that had been burned."

In fact, an agent from the Criminal Investigative Command (known as CID) had been pursuing leads regarding SEALs operating in the area and heard that they'd actually killed two detainees. (An earlier report on that case found the "investigation did not [yield] sufficient evidence to prove or disprove Mr. [redacted] allegation.")[1]

Lagouranis wasn't in the SEAL compound and never saw special operations forces interrogate anyone, but he told the CID agent about a "Corporal Crawford" who had witnessed abuses in the SEALs' facility. He even drew the agent pictures of the corporal's unit patch, a keystone for the Keystone State, and helped furnish him with further leads. "And he couldn't find the guy, which was absurd to me," said Lagouranis. A CID agent actually called on Lagouranis "not to ask me about anything that I had done, but just [because] I was an interrogator up in Mosul, and he was asking questions about special operations forces, which I found kind of amazing. It just showed me really how ineffectual these guys are and how powerless they are. He was showing me pictures of what he believed was where special operations forces did their interrogations and I was like, 'Well, why don't you just go up there and find out? Why are you asking me?' He kept bugging me; he kept calling my unit and asking via email to find this guy for him. I'm like, 'You find him. You're the goddamn investigator, you know? I gave you everything you need to know.' "

When Lagouranis returned home in 2005, he filed another report on detainee abuse to CID agents at Fort Gordon, near Augusta, Georgia, and refiled one of the reports he had sent from Iraq (which he found within CID's files at the base). But CID agents followed up with Lagouranis only after he described the abuse and torture he witnessed in a *Frontline* documentary broadcast on October 18, 2005. Shortly thereafter, he said, CID agents phoned him—about a year after he had filed his reports—and insisted he should have come to them first before going to the media. Lagouranis spelled out for them the procedures he went through to file his complaints.

Their response? "They said they didn't have the reports," he said.

A week after the *Frontline* episode aired, CID agents contacted Lagouranis and asked if they could pay him a visit at his house in Chicago. He obliged. Lagouranis said CID Special Agent Kerr

(Lagouranis can't recall the agent's first name) visited him in November 2005 and took a sworn statement from him.

"So you said all of this stuff on *Frontline*," the special agent said. "Why didn't you come tell us about it?"

"I did."

"Well, we ran your name through the computer, and we don't have any sworn statements from you."

"Okay, well, I'll do it again," said Lagouranis.

He gave various accounts of detainee abuse that were ordered, that he witnessed, and that he himself personally participated in. When they were finished, Lagouranis asked Kerr why CID didn't have any of the reports that he had filed both from Iraq and back in the US. "Well, the stuff in Iraq was all handwritten, and maybe it didn't get entered into the computers," the agent answered. That response didn't explain why CID wasn't aware of the statements he had made for agents at Fort Gordon or those he processed via computer and sent through the military's encrypted, internal Internet service.

"It doesn't make sense—everybody had SIPRNET," he said, referring to the military Internet. "They were running it everywhere ... it didn't matter where you were."

Nothing, it seemed, came of any of the reports he filed over and over again.

Huddled together in Balad, Iraq, months after the start of the war in 2003, part of Battalion 1-68 manned the hot, remote, windblown compound of Forward Operating Base Lion. But they did not work in a vacuum, cut off from any oversight. Some battalion officers were aware of the detainee operations that took place there.

In 2004, Major Bill Benson and Captain Sean Nowlan, operations and intelligence officers (respectively) attached to Battalion 1-68, produced a report detailing how Army personnel struggled to develop useful information. Their paper stated that more than 700 Iraqis passed through the detention facility at FOB Lion; some continued through the US military detention system and landed in Abu Ghraib prison. The authors did not detail the techniques used on the detainees, but their article obliquely mentioned the frustrations that intelligence officers faced while collecting information.

"Processing detainees in a short period of time (the standard is twenty-four hours) is a daunting task under any circumstance," the authors wrote. "With limited guidance and support from the brigade, the [task force] managed to develop effective, although resource-intensive, methods to collect information and develop exploitable intelligence."

These findings were not concealed in a redacted military report; they were published openly in the military's publicly available *Military Intelligence Professional Bulletin*. Some of the soldiers who worked in FOB Lion also relayed what had transpired in the base's detention facility.

Jonathan Millantz saw and took part in detainee abuse during his time at FOB Lion's jail. A native of western Pennsylvania, Millantz spoke in a low voice and often mumbled. He found it hard to describe what he had witnessed and what he himself participated in.

As a medic, he was responsible for checking detainees' vital signs in their makeshift jail. "My job was actually to do their blood pressure," he said. "And make sure we weren't killing them."

He remembered hearing officers say it was all right to break a detainee's arm if he touched any of the US troops, and he recalled how he and other soldiers pinned down prisoners while pouring water from five-gallon jugs into their mouths and noses.[2] Prisoners had been subjected to long nights of sleep deprivation, beatings, and mock executions.

Millantz routinely heard yelling and screaming, often witnessed men break down and cry, and saw prisoners soil themselves.[3] "There's plenty of stuff out there that hasn't been put on the media that would make Abu Ghraib look like Disneyland," he said. "I didn't think any of it was right at all. Then again, I couldn't say anything, because if I were to say something, then I would have been going against what we were supposed to be doing over there. There were plenty of people who wanted to report these acts of misconduct through a higher chain of command, but were discouraged by many high-ranking people."

Other soldiers in the unit were equally troubled by the abuses and said they puzzled over how to stop them. "A lot of the time I got sick to my stomach watching that stuff," said Millantz.

He himself tried to report it to his superiors, but was told that "if I made this stuff public, I would bring everyone down with me." A lieutenant colonel and a captain regularly observed prisoner abuse and overlooked it, he said.

"High-ranking officers saw these acts of misconduct and totally condoned it—West Point graduates," said Millantz. "It was beat into our brains the entire time we were there ... 'This is a company level operation. Do not talk about it. Do not tell anybody about this.' "

Millantz said his commanders rebutted his complaints about the abuse at FOB Lion's jail. "All my opinions were shouted down," he said. "I was told to mind my own business and do my own job, and don't make a scene. And the last thing you want to do is piss off a whole bunch of soldiers when you're deployed to a faraway country, because you might not come back."

The misconduct that Millantz and others described took place inside a secure US military holding facility in a secluded area of Iraq. The only people who knew what took place were the detainees, the soldiers who engaged in abuse, and the officers who ordered, encouraged, or over-looked it. Without reports, there would be no charges and no accountability; without action, the whole experience would remain unac-knowledged. And so, according to fellow troops, the abuse continued.

But Millantz did take some photographs of what went on, one of which he later showed to me. I passed it on to Daniel Keller, a friend of Millantz's and a tanker with Battalion 1-68 at the time. Keller had seen the picture before: it featured a soldier and an officer beaming smiles behind a detainee who was struggling to hold up a wooden board. Keller was struck by who was in the picture—beside the soldier and the detainee—and where it was taken.

"That's an LT standing next to him," he said. "I mean, that's an incriminating picture if I've ever seen one. That's an officer … that's an experienced first lieutenant."

The setting was also familiar to Keller: "This was the detainee shed, actually. A lot of them were interrogated right there, in that room, or in the adjacent cells until they got overcrowded."

Millantz told me he had other such pictures of detainee abuse, some of which were discarded by his mother. Keller had similar pictures as well.

"I had a picture of a detainee who I made sit on a concrete block for I don't know how long, on just the edge of his knees, on the edge of a concrete block," he recalled. "I smacked him around a little bit. I'd say horrible things to him and he had his eyes covered so he couldn't see anything … just horrible things were happening to him."

I asked Keller when the abuse finally ended.

"We were committed to detainee abuse to the end," said. "We even moved away from [FOB] Lion into another area, [and] right before we were getting ready to go … I abused [another] detainee on a concrete block. The time we moved to the tarmac"—that is, out of Iraq—"was the time the abuse ended."

*   *   *

Some of the troops from Battalion 1-68 squarely fingered the military intelligence section, or S2, for encouraging detainee abuse—especially when depriving prisoners of sleep.

"Somebody from S2 had to do that," said Sergeant Oral Lindsey, Adam Gray's tank commander. "I couldn't just go out and say, 'Hey man, I'm not gonna let these assholes sleep.' "

Keller echoed that account.

"The S2 did talk to us about that—you weren't allowed to let them sleep," he said. "If you let them sleep then they could get their will back, and they could resist longer. You had to keep them awake to keep their spirits broken. I mean it doesn't sound like much, but have you ever stayed awake for two, three days straight while in jail with people with guns in your own country? It's a pretty messed-up situation. It does a lot to your head."

Other soldiers relayed similar accounts, but did not assign all prisoner abuse to the battalion's S2.

During 2008 and 2009, my producer from American Radio Works, Michael Montgomery, and I contacted the Army nearly a dozen times and asked whether they investigated reports of abuse by troops from Battalion 1-68. The Army never responded.

On January 23, 2010, I was finally able to reach Battalion 1-68's former S2, Captain Sean Nowlan (who has since been promoted to major). We spoke about detainee operations for about forty-five minutes, and I asked him about the abuse that troops had relayed to us: whether he was aware of it, if any troops reported abuse to him, and if any military investigators followed up any complaints.

"I don't recall ever ordering anything like that," he said. "We didn't do that—that was definitely not a practice for us ... no one's ever come to me and said there was abuse. Never abuse. No one ever did that ... The battalion commander ... put orders out: nobody messes around with detainees. Nobody does anything to them."

Were there any lieutenants who were accused of abuse? What about the reports of tying prisoners in painful positions for hours, the forced exercises, the mock executions and water torture?

"If this was a frequent occurrence, I would be shocked," he said. "We gave them water, we gave them blankets. We made sure that they were clothed well ... The closest thing that ever would have been done to anything would have been yelling, or, I don't know what you define sleep deprivation as, but no. No sleep deprivation, no drowning. We had no water. No mock executions. No, none of that. Nobody was ever hurt."

Nowlan was quite definite. "We never had a single problem with the complaints [from] the local populace or anything," he said. "As a matter of fact, many of the detainees—they came back and they gave tremendous amounts of information because of how well we treated them. Very strange. But, it is what it is."

I later asked Benson (who was promoted to lieutenant colonel) if he ever heard reports of abuse. "I don't remember any complaining about it. Certainly no soldiers ever came to me and talked to me about it," he said. "If it ever happened, it would have been a one-time thing that somebody corrected ... There has never been a military investigation as far as I know of what went on in 1-68. And if there was, I can't imagine one happening without me knowing about it, and without me being questioned."

Human rights workers were critical of the problems with investigations into detainee abuse, both because of the lack of accountability and because overlooking mistreatment enabled it to continue in certain circumstances.

"You can't just think of abuse as something that a superior officer ordered. Often abuse is the product of the superior officer looking the other way," said John Sifton, the Asia advocacy director at Human Rights Watch (HRW). When he was a senior researcher on terrorism and counterterrorism with HRW, Sifton interviewed several soldiers and read military reports that illustrated cases in which troops were discouraged or ignored by their superiors when trying to report detainee abuse.[4] There were also cases in which soldiers felt threatened after coming forward with allegations of abuse. "Most troops don't report abuse because they think it's a waste of time—and they're right," said Sifton. "It's a waste of time to risk angering your fellow troops and your commanding officer ... You know that most likely your commanding officer is not going to listen to you, is not going to take any action to correct what is going on. So, for many people, that's what they were up against, and it's no surprise they didn't report what was going on. But some people did."

In 2008, the Associated Press investigated the way the military had generally handled whistleblowers in cases of alleged misconduct or wrongdoing. The AP found that "the Pentagon inspector general, the internal watchdog for the Defense Department, hardly ever sides with service members who complain that they were punished for reporting wrongdoing."

The AP report continues: "The inspector general's office rejected claims of retaliation and stood by the military in more than 90 percent of nearly 3,000 cases during the past six years. More than 73 percent were closed after only a preliminary review that relied on available documents and sources—often from the military itself—to determine whether a full inquiry was warranted."[5]

In some cases, military officials apparently discouraged reporting by arguing that any delay in submitting a complaint was a violation of the rules.

In May 2004 Scott Horton, an independent human rights attorney, met with several soldiers who had served at Abu Ghraib prison to review how the military was carrying out its investigation there. In the course of those discussions, Horton learned about meetings led by Major General George R. Fay, the investigating officer who was looking into detainee abuse by the Army's 205th Military Intelligence Brigade at Abu Ghraib.

As journalist Tara McKelvey notes in her book *Monstering*, "attorney [Scott] Horton and other critics of the administration have pointed out [that] Fay was also a financial supporter of the New Jersey Republican Party. Horton and others believed he was chosen for that reason."

Horton included his Abu Ghraib findings in a case filed by the Center for Constitutional Rights (CCR), which investigated the role of Secretary of Defense Donald Rumsfeld and other high-ranking Bush administration officials in the torture and abuse of detainees. According to the case file, "Fay held group meetings with soldiers in the presence of their group commanding officers. At these meetings, he reminded them that any soldier who had observed the abuse of detainees at Abu Ghraib and other sites and who had failed to report it contemporaneously was guilty of an infraction and could be brought up on charges. He stated that any noncommissioned officer who observed the abuse of detainees at Abu Ghraib and other sites and who failed to intervene or stop it was guilty of an infraction and could be brought up on charges."[6]

Some of the soldiers present at the meetings have said that Fay's warnings had a chilling effect for those who considered reporting abuse. Sergeant Samuel Provance and other soldiers corroborated the account for Horton. Provance, who served in 302nd Military Intelligence

Battalion, told Fay about the abuses he had witnessed at Abu Ghraib during the general's investigation. In February 2006, Provance testified before Congress about his three-hour interview with Fay, and how the general responded to him afterward.

Provance said that Fay told him "he would recommend administrative action against me for not reporting what I knew sooner than the investigation. He said if I had reported what I knew sooner, I could have actually prevented the scandal. I was stunned by his statements and by his attitude."

Provance spelled out for members of Congress the reasons why fellow troops felt uncomfortable about coming forward.

"When I made clear to my superiors that I was troubled about what had happened, I was told that the honor of my unit and the Army depended on either withholding the truth or outright lies," said Provance. "Everything I saw and observed at Abu Ghraib and in Iraq convinced me that if I filed a report [about the abuse], I wouldn't be listened to, that it would be covered up. I thought that the best case [scenario] was that I would be considered a troublemaker and ostracized, but that, potentially, I might even place my life in danger."[7]

To Horton and human rights workers, Provance's statement seemed to sum up the reasons why others didn't report the abuses that they had seen.

"It was perfectly reasonable to think that by reporting abuse you were putting yourself at risk," said Sifton, the human rights investigator. "Even if you weren't putting yourself physically at risk, you were putting yourself at professional risk."

Publication of the infamous Abu Ghraib photos was the catalyst that finally compelled Congress and the military to step up investigations into detainee abuse. But the scandal might not have gained traction if it hadn't been for one soldier: Joseph Darby.

Sergeant Darby served with the 372nd Military Police Company at Abu Ghraib. He had known some of the other MPs in his unit before they served together, including Lynndie England and Charles A. Graner, Jr.

Darby wanted to send pictures home to his family to give them a sense of his daily life in Iraq. He knew that Graner had been shooting lots of photos and asked to borrow some.

"Yeah Darb, hold on," said Graner, who then reached into his computer bag and handed Darby two compact disks with photos. The next day he riffled through the photos on his laptop.

"The first CD was, you know, normal stuff: places we'd been, Victory Palace, things like that," Darby told me. "But the second CD was 750 megabytes of prisoner abuse—an entire CD of nothing but prisoner abuse. I mean, there are pictures on that CD that I turned in that the public hasn't seen yet. And Graner had gigabytes of it."

Darby felt that the abuse documented in those pictures "violates everything I believe in, and it violates the very rules of war."[8] He tussled with what to do and asked one of his military mentors, a NCO, for guidance.

"When you go home and you wake up in the morning ... you [have to] look yourself in the mirror and know that you did the right thing every chance you had," the NCO told Darby.

And so, Darby anonymously dropped a copy of Graner's CD off at the military investigators' office at Abu Ghraib. Soon after, an investigation was launched. Darby tried to avoid contact with the accused soldiers and to disassociate himself from the investigation. Then, on April 28, 2004, news of the prisoner abuse scandal was publicly revealed. Nine days later, on May 7, Secretary of Defense Donald Rumsfeld testified before the Senate and House Armed Services Committees and praised "many who did their duty professionally ... First the soldier, Joseph Darby, who alerted the appropriate authorities that abuses of detainees were occurring. My thanks and appreciation to him for his courage and his values."

Darby was eating with friends at Camp Anaconda, sitting next to the TV, when Rumsfeld dropped his name. One of his friends flatly told him: "Dude, we need to get the fuck outta here."

At that time Darby was still an enlisted soldier serving a tour in Iraq, and pressured his commanders to protect him. "I had to raise hell to get out of the country," he said, recalling how he began to fear for his life. "There were a few people in the unit—Graner's friends and people who did not agree with me—who would have probably tried to do something," he said.

During his remaining nights in Iraq, he slept with a pistol under his pillow, the hammer cocked, his fingers gripping the handle. When a fellow soldier entered his tent, Darby nearly shot him.

"I don't know if I would have made it back ... if I wouldn't have gotten pulled from Iraq," he said.

Meanwhile, threats were leveled against his family back home in

Maryland; someone threw a Molotov cocktail at his house, just missing it.[9] When he was released from Iraq and returned to the US, government agents approached him about his safety.

"Where do you wanna go, son?" one of them asked.

"I want to go home."

"Well, the FBI and CID has done a threat assessment of your area, and we've come to the conclusion that you can't go home, and probably will never be able to go back to that area because of imminent threats to your life."

Soon after, Darby and his wife fled his hometown and entered into the military equivalent of the witness protection program.

"I came from a really patriotic small town," said Darby. "They didn't look at it as though these guys were doing wrong. They looked at it as though I was putting American soldiers in prison for Iraqis."

Today, Darby no longer lives under any kind of government protection, but he still safeguards his privacy and takes precautions to maintain his anonymity.

"No one where I live knows who I am," he said. "I have kids now. I worry about my family, so I try to limit my exposure as much as possible. I don't talk about to people [about Abu Ghraib]. I mean it's something that I'm proud I did. But it's too controversial to chance anything."

Officers encountered the same kind of obstacles when they tried to report other instances of abuse. Colonel Steven Kleinman was an Air Force reservist and intelligence officer with more than twenty years of interrogation experience. In September 2003 he was in Camp Cropper, near Baghdad, where he was part of a team tasked to oversee interrogations. Kleinman said he saw interrogators threaten detainees and abuse them through slapping, sleep deprivation, and forcing them to hold various stress positions.

"As an intelligence officer, as an officer, and certainly as an interrogator, I knew, wait a second: that's not an effective way of getting intelligence," Kleinman told me. "It's a good way of getting propaganda and false confessions; secondly, it's against the law; and thirdly, it was against my moral code."

He approached the interrogators involved and produced a written report about what he witnessed.

"I'll tell you what, it was a difficult part of my life," said Kleinman. "Just about all of my colleagues were in vehement disagreement, to the point where I was ostracized, set apart from everybody else. Nobody wanted to talk to me. A few threats were made to my life, even."

One day, after filing his report, Kleinman walked by the tent of a junior officer. The officer smiled at Kleinman as he sharpened a long knife.

"You should probably sleep lightly for the rest of my time in Iraq," he told Kleinman. It didn't take Kleinman long to realize what he meant—or to grasp what his report meant to his fellow service members.

"I was seen as coddling the terrorists," he said. "I was disrupting the Special Operations activities by my mindless adherence to the law." Other officers faced similar problems.

Captain Ian Fishback, a West Point graduate, said he routinely witnessed detainee abuse in Iraq between September 2003 and April 2004. He told his superiors about particular cases he witnessed at Camp Mercury, a forward operating base near Fallujah, including "death threats, beatings, broken bones ... exposure to elements, extreme forced physical exertion, hostage-taking, stripping, sleep deprivation and degrading treatment."[10]

He said he wasn't threatened, nor did military investigators discourage him from filing reports. But, like Tony Lagouranis, he felt his complaints were ignored.[11]

Fishback claims that he tried to report on abuse over the course of seventeen months, but was consistently met with discouragement and inaction from his superiors.[12] Finally, he approached Human Rights Watch, and senators John W. Warner of Virginia and John McCain of Arizona, both members of the Senate Armed Services Committee at the time. Then he went public, telling the *New York Times* he felt investigators seemed more concerned about tracking down soldiers who reported misconduct than following up on the actual accusations.[13] Fishback's experience showed both the difficulty of getting officers to pursue charges and the challenges of getting military investigators to act on them.

Stephen Lewis faced similar problems. Lewis was an acquaintance of Lagouranis and a fellow interrogator in the 513th Military Intelligence Brigade. Lewis served in Iraq at the same time as Lagouranis, though the two didn't work together.[14] Like Lagouranis, Lewis was frustrated by the military's follow-through on his reports about abuse, but sympathized with some of the challenges that investigators faced.

"I detailed in my reports [detainee] abuse," Lewis wrote me by email.

He listed various cases of abuse: "detainees being beaten, sodomized with a squeegee handle, locked in confined spaces like shipping containers in the heat, mock executions, degrading treatment while being naked, degrading treatment from females—playing on them being Muslim and so forth ...

"I filed maybe a dozen reports—probably a little more than that. CID didn't respond at all, really. They talked to me twice, I think, and never really followed up. I can't blame them—there were just too many reports, not enough CID [agents], and they didn't have enough power or resources to properly investigate anyway. I do not know if they actually went into the camps and questioned the detainees."

Susan Burke was unsurprised to learn about the problems soldiers had faced trying to report and investigate detainee abuse. Burke, along with the Center for Constitutional Rights (CCR), has represented 337 former detainees in a lawsuit against private military contractors who were involved in detainee abuse in Iraq.

In 2006, I met Burke and her colleague Jonathan Pyle at what was then her office in Philadelphia, a long, sun-soaked space with creaky wood floors and a sparse staff. She unloaded a cardboard box with hundreds of pages of email messages, letters, and other documents that related to exchanges she had with several military personnel. I scanned through some of the allegations that she and her staff were looking into:

INCIDENT NO. 1: A male was arrested on January 5, 2004, and released in June of 2004 ... He was taken to Mustansiriya where he was hung by his hands and feet and beat with a stick, kept nude for hours ... A female sodomized him with an artificial penis.

INCIDENT NO. 2: A female was arrested with her husband on September 4, 2003, in front of her two daughters ... While incarcerated, she was dragged on the ground and asked to pick up feces with her hands. When she stopped to vomit, she was threatened by American personnel that if she continued, she would be raped ... Her husband died in Abu Ghraib. She was photographed nude. She knows of six women who were tortured and raped, ages 16 to 60.

INCIDENT NO. 4: A male was arrested on November 23, 2003, and he died in early 2004 in Abu Ghraib. He was subjected to extreme conditions, including being hooded, stripped nude, and made to stand outside with cold water being poured on him in the winter months. His son (also incarcerated at the same time) witnessed his father's death and his physical conditions immediately before his death. The son pled for medical attention to no avail. The son was threatened with further punishment if he continued to plead for medical attention for his dying father.

Then I turned to the email letters that Burke sent to US military personnel over the course of several months:

October 23, 2004
… we represent those persons who have been abused in the prisons and detention centers across Iraq. We have filed a class action in San Diego seeking to recover from the two government contractors, Titan and CACI, alleged to have been involved in the abuses. We are most interested in working with you and others within the military who are acting in good faith to investigate fully and remedy the wrong that occurred … as the daughter of an Army Colonel (now retired), I am personally confident that many on active duty are as appalled as we are by the terrible abuses that occurred and unfortunately are still occurring. We are open to any suggestions you might have as to how to structure a sharing of information that helps to correct the problems.

September 28, 2005
We are trying to work out cost and other logistical details, but will make [our client] available for interview in either Kuwait or the United States.

Military personnel involved in investigating detainee abuse cases responded to Burke:

August 27, 2004
We will be interviewing and calling some detainees to testify in these cases …

August 28, 2004
We intend to interview the individuals identified in the CID file who were abused from OCT-JAN at Abu [Ghraib]. If you have additional clients who were abused or witnessed abuse during the above timeframe we would like to meet them.

For roughly two years, Burke wrote to military investigators as evidenced by copies of her letters. Along with the Center for Constitutional Rights, Burke tried to facilitate meetings between military investigators and victims and repeatedly offered investigators access to her clients—at her expense. She even tried to arrange meetings outside Iraq, in safer Middle Eastern countries, such as Jordan, Kuwait, and Turkey.

"We weren't saying, 'Go out in the streets of Baghdad and do it,' " said Burke. "We were going to bring the victims to do the interviews in safety."

According to Burke, as of the beginning of 2012, more than seven years after she had begun writing those letters, neither the Department of Justice nor US military investigators had interviewed any of her clients.

In 2005, the American Civil Liberties Union and Human Rights First filed a lawsuit on behalf of nine Iraqi men against Secretary of Defense Donald Rumsfeld, alleging that they were being tortured by US forces under his command. Lawyers for the suit say CID agents hadn't interviewed any of their clients as of 2009.

The United Nations Committee Against Torture reviewed the conduct of the US investigations and the limited number of officials and troops who have been prosecuted for abusing prisoners. In 2006 the UN agency issued a statement urging US authorities to eradicate torture and "promptly and thoroughly investigate and prosecute the perpetrators of those acts and punish them with the appropriate penalties."[15] In response, the State Department reported in 2006 that the military took action against 250 service personnel, producing 103 courts-martial and 89 convictions.

US officials often invoked such figures to show how vigilantly they have addressed these cases. But the numbers masked the military's incomplete investigations and anemic sentences for those found guilty.

A survey of the US military's investigations, conducted in 2006 by New York University's Center for Human Rights and Global Justice, Human Rights Watch, and Human Rights First, was detailed in a report titled "By the Numbers." The report found that out of 330 cases in which US military and civilian personnel allegedly abused or killed detainees after 2001, "only about half appear to have been properly investigated." It added that there were "numerous cases in which authorities failed to initiate investigations, delayed in initiating investigations (often adversely affecting their outcome), or failed to follow basic investigative techniques, including interviewing victims and witnesses and gathering physical evidence."

After the Abu Ghraib scandal broke, Bush administration officials and military commanders pledged they would aggressively root out abuse and punish those responsible for it. So why did a small Philadelphia legal office and a few nonprofit organizations need to pressure them for results?

After months of correspondence with the military, Burke finally secured a series of meetings with CID agents. In early June 2005, she and her investigator, Keith Rohman, flew to Kuwait and met two CID agents in a hotel. Burke and Rohman logged detailed notes of their meetings for an internal memo, which they shared with me.

According to Burke, the agents, Kenneth Dean and Julie Tyler, explained that they were part of a six-person task force investigating ninety to ninety-five cases of detainee abuse in Iraq—none of which pertained to the Abu Ghraib scandal. Burke said the agents told her that they lacked the resources to effectively manage their caseload. She recalled how agents Dean and Tyler described other grave challenges they faced: non-cooperation from a special operations unit accused of abuse, and problems securing physical evidence and medical records. Without information collected from these sources, and a lack of witnesses and corroboration—including abused detainees who had been released—they said they would have to close the cases.

Burke said she was shocked. Like others working on prisoner abuse cases, she thought a closed case reflected the results of exhaustive research by military investigators. "It doesn't," said Burke. "It means it's either been investigated until conclusion or it has run into a dead end, that people don't think it's worth pursuing.

"For instance, if there's difficulty finding soldiers in a unit, or it's an allegation that ends up being connected to CIA or Special Forces [special operations forces], it'll get closed because they don't have cooperation. They call it 'running into a brick wall.' So 'running into a brick wall' is enough to close a case."[16] (Christopher Grey, CID's Chief of Public Affairs, told me that cases are closed "when we complete all our leads, and are satisfied we've got a complete picture of everything that we need.")[17]

Burke was further stunned to learn that CID agents hadn't read the military reports on prisoner abuse that were available at the time, such as the Army's Taguba and Fay-Jones reports, and the International Red Cross report on detainee abuse.

"I just could not believe it," she told me. "This is the … Detainee Abuse Task Force. You're not very optimistic that much investigation was going to be done. This is why the American public only knows a fraction of these cases.

"It was very difficult to realize from meeting with the people who were charged with investigating abuses that they didn't view their top priority as getting to the bottom of the abuses. Rather, they viewed their top priority as making sure that they didn't place any additional burden on anyone in the military .... if the soldiers committed a criminal act, then they deserve to have the burden put on them."

Burke understood that the CID was overwhelmed and understaffed, but she also felt that the military failed to respond adequately to torture victims and their plight.

"We'd seen what their job was—to create a paper fig leaf," she said. "And then the administration would tout the number of cases that were investigated and closed. That's the thing that was so galling. The military portrayed itself as doing a good job by the sheer number of cases that it had investigated and closed. To most people, it sounds like it's a genuine investigation, right?"

I later spoke with Special Agent Julie Tyler, one of the CID agents who attended the meeting with Burke and Rohman. After leaving the military in 2007, she married, changed her name to Julie Kuykendall, and returned to college to become an art teacher in North Carolina. Kuykendall recalled the same meeting with Burke, but said that she and her fellow agents had earnestly tried to pursue every detainee abuse charge.

"I don't think there was a single unit that handled detainees in that country that didn't have an abuse complaint on someone in that unit," said Kuykendall. "You could look at a detainee the wrong way and [it was] 'Oh so and so hurt my feelings, so and so disrespected me.' And guess what? We'd get stuck investigating it. It was ridiculous, and we had to investigate every single complaint we got. Every single one. It didn't matter what was the complaint. It didn't matter how ludicrous it was."

Kuykendall sent me pictures of the T-shirts that she and her fellow CID agents of the Detainee Abuse Task Force wore while in Iraq. They were navy blue with yellow lettering. The back displayed an outline of Iraq with the names of the task force agents listed under US and Iraqi flags, and the words at the top read, "DETAINEE ABUSE TASK FORCE 2005 – 48th Military Police Detachment (CID) (FWD) AN UNKNOWN SUBJECT ASSAULTED AN UNKNOWN VICTIM, AT AN UKNOWN TIME AND LOCATION. INVESTIGATION

CONTINUES." The front of the shirt had an emblem of a CID badge, with a motto that read, "DO WHAT HAS TO BE DONE." For Kuykendall, the shirt exemplified the problems that agents faced in terms of fulfilling their mission while trying to chase down vague leads. In fact, she said, the statement on the back came from an actual case file in which a British soldier purportedly saw a detainee being chained to a wooden pallet, but couldn't identify where or when it occurred or who had been involved.

Kuykendall confirmed some of what Burke had recorded in their meeting, such as closing cases without medical or physical evidence.

"That was probably the one reason we used to close basically all of our cases," she said. I asked Kuykendall what CID investigators did when a detainee couldn't show medical evidence because the kind of torture or abuse used didn't leave any marks (e.g., water torture, forced standing and exercises, sleep deprivation, and the like).

"Then you still have nothing to prosecute it with. How are you going to prosecute that?" she asked. "That's not to say that they just swept them under a rug and tried to hide anything. That's not what happened. You prosecute what you can prosecute. We're not going to take a case to court just because it's detainee abuse."

Kuykendall said that she and her team would locate and interview detainees who were still jailed in US facilities across Iraq, but didn't pursue them after they had been released.

"We didn't have any way of finding any of these people," she said. "We'll close the case then because of a lack of being able to interview the victim. What are you going to do? There's no tracking people in that country. It's an impossibility."

I then asked Kuykendall about Burke's allegation that military investigators failed to interview any of her 337 clients.

"[It was] probably because their cases were already done—and more than likely they were interviewed," she answered. "I wouldn't take any of their words for granted."

But Kuykendall also acknowledged that sometimes military units and personnel interfered with their investigations. She pointed to special operations unit and CID agents who were both based out of Fort Bragg. The unit had been accused of detainee abuse, and so the DATF asked the CID agents who worked alongside them to conduct an investigation.

"When [the CID agents] would send the paperwork back, we wouldn't get the interrogators' real full names ... we would get their made-up, pseudonym names," she said. "They wouldn't get all the information they could get out of those people—it was obvious from our cases. We had that problem right there with only getting half-assed kinds of work from them. They were friends with [the special operations unit] … working with them closely. I just think they did the minimum of what they had to do, and that was it … Pretty much every case we had with that group … all went the same way. We wouldn't get information. We had to close them because there just wasn't enough information to go forward."

Human rights workers found that investigations linked to special operations forces often faced additional obstacles.[18] But Kuykendall remembered that average soldiers often "weren't gonna rat on their buddy … no matter what," and so without corroborating testimony, CID agents would have to close cases. It didn't surprise her to hear of cases in which troops reporting abuse felt discouraged, ignored, and even threatened at times.

"I have no doubt about that happening at all," she said. "These commanders are not going to want to have CID all up in their unit asking about detainee abuse. I wouldn't want any part of my unit investigated for that. Who would?"

In the end, how many cases did Kuykendall recalled actually advanced to a court martial hearing, known as an Article 32?

"As far as I remember, not a single one," she said. "I would've remembered if one of our cases went to an Article 32."

Even after the Bush administration left office, the belief that the military had fully investigated detainee abuse cases still prevailed.

During President Barack Obama's 2008 presidential campaign, he often stated that "Americans don't torture," and promised accountability for those Americans who had. He moved shortly after his inauguration to set a deadline for closing the prison at Guantanamo, and seven months later his attorney general, Eric Holder, reopened some detainee abuse investigations connected to CIA personnel, reversing a Bush administration decision.

In May 2009, the Obama administration halted the release of additional photos showing detainee abuse by military and intelligence personnel. Obama warned such images would stoke anti-American hatred and possibly prompt attacks on US forces overseas. The president apparently assumed that military investigators had already looked into the allegations of abuse connected to those photos, saying, "Individuals who violated standards of behavior in these photos have been investigated and held accountable. There is no debate as to whether what is reflected in those photos is wrong, and nothing has been concealed to absolve perpetrators of crimes."

Obama's assertion that wrongdoers had been held accountable seemed questionable, whether one took Kuykendall's or Burke's perspective on the management of past detainee abuse investigations. For the few cases that were prosecuted, most of those convicted avoided severe punishment. "By the Numbers," the 2006 report by human rights organizations, found, "Of the hundreds of personnel implicated in detainee abuse, only ten people have been sentenced to a year or more in prison."

The many problems with reporting and investigating detainee abuse came as no surprise to Tony Lagouranis. Military investigators had failed to contact the head of his interrogation team, Shawn Campbell, after Lagouranis lodged his complaints. And he, like others, was frustrated to hear that cases had been closed without anyone being found accountable. "It really is incredibly damaging closing [a] case," he said, "because media will get ahold of that and say, 'Well, these things were investigated and they were found to be unsubstantiated.' "

He pointed to the military's response after he appeared on the MSNBC program *Hardball with Chris Matthews* on January 17, 2006, where he detailed his experiences with prisoner abuse, including one incident with a Marine Unit. The Marines sent MSNBC a statement saying, "The allegations were later referred to the Naval Criminal Investigative Service to ensure the matter was thoroughly investigated … [One] allegation was unsubstantiated, while the remaining two incidents—including the one brought to the command's attention by Lagouranis—are still under investigation."[19]

"That's incredibly damaging, and it's ridiculous, because I know it wasn't investigated," Lagouranis told me. "In fact, in response to what I reported on in the Marines [case], it wasn't until 2005 [or 2006] that somebody came and talked to me."

He said he asked the NCIS agents, who conduct investigations in the Navy and Marine Corps, "So has anybody tried to talk to anybody? Have there been any investigations about this in the past two years?"

"There hadn't been any investigations in like two years," they told Lagouranis, according to his account.

"Well, good luck finding these detainees now. Or anybody from this unit. You're not getting anything on this. It's not going to happen."

Chapter 7:
Silent Suffering

AFTER SWEATING OUT eleven months of armed service from April 2003–March 2004, the soldiers of Battalion 1-68 rotated back home. They departed the white hot plains of the Iraqi landscape, returning to the coarse, arid buffs surrounding Fort Carson, Colorado. From there, various members of Battalion 1-68 either headed home or signed up for further military service. Sergeant Oral Lindsey hoped to join the Cavalry Scouts and attend sniper school, but the Army couldn't find a slot for him and so he retired. Daniel Keller went back to California and eventually attended college in San Diego. Jonathan Millantz said he was suffering from debilitating post-traumatic stress disorder and applied for a medical discharge. The military approved it, and he soon returned home to Greensburg, Pennsylvania. After Adam Gray visited his family in Wisconsin and California, he traveled to Fort Wainwright, Alaska, where he underwent training to operate new armored vehicles known as Strykers.

Though they were far from the violence of the Sunni Triangle, many of Battalion 1-68's soldiers struggled with their return home. Tony Sandoval drank heavily. He also gained weight, his high blood pressure shot up, and a low-level depression ate away at him.

"My stress was incredibly high," remembered Sandoval. "Things weren't funny, sweets weren't sweet any more."

Like other veterans I met, Sandoval also struggled to overcome the defensive impulses he developed in Iraq. Troops called it "hypervigilance," and it was tough to turn it off after they returned home. It was unnerving to hear Fourth of July fireworks because they reminded the vets of exploding bombs. It was even hard to adapt to driving in the US. In Iraq, troops dodged attacks and IEDs when they drove out on patrol. Back home, veterans told me how they recoiled when their vehicles hit a pothole, became edgy whenever they were stuck in traffic, and had difficulty controlling the impulse to drive aggressively. They were often anxious in large crowds, and many of them suffered from nightmares and insomnia.

For Keller, that pattern of behavior evoked familiar images of "Vietnam vets on TV ... waking up and sweating and screaming. They went through much more intense stuff than I did. But a lot of the guys I've talked to ... share one commonality of not being able to sleep."

Some abused drugs and alcohol, in what they called "self-medicating."

"I drank a hell of a lot, absurd amounts," Keller recalled. "It's not like you go to the bar and get drunk and puke ... frat boy kind of stuff, which is bad enough on its own. You drink and you drink and you drink, and all of a sudden you think about putting yourself out by drinking. That's the self-medication I was doing—when you actually try to drink yourself to death."

Keller, like other veterans, also struggled to control his anger.

"I had to actually actively control myself if I felt my temper rising," he said. "I had to kind of hold myself back, and sometimes people would have to physically hold me back."

Adam Stevenson could relate to that kind of hypervigilance. He said he was edgy and wanted to be armed whenever he went out. He also had periodic nightmares. Like other vets, he suffered from post-traumatic stress, but he had difficulty pinpointing the source of it.

After his tour ended in 2004, Stevenson went back to school to channel some of his military experience into law enforcement work. He applied to a sheriff's department in Riverside County, California, and went through their battery of exams. But Stevenson abruptly lost interest when they told him that part of his job would involve work in their jail.

"Never mind," he told them. "I hate working with detainees."

It was a great disappointment, since he had been looking forward to a law enforcement career. But he simply couldn't do work that reminded him of his experiences handling prisoners.

"It's not for me—I don't want to work in a jail," he said. "I have zero desire."

I met several members of Battalion 1-68 who were still grappling with memories of their time in Iraq. Most of the interviews I conducted with those soldiers started out upbeat, with vets recalling warm memories of their camaraderie, how they enjoyed working on tanks, traveling through the Iraqi countryside, and interacting with children. But many of them would grow subdued as we talked about their violent encounters in Iraq. They would become especially quiet as they discussed detainee treatment. Their eyes would drop, and many would simply shut down.

Those who were traumatized by experiences in Iraq described individual wartime events, and mulled over the violence they encountered. Some of the soldiers I interviewed had referenced their collective experience with detainee abuse as being especially painful and damaging.

Adam Stevenson reflected on how confusing it was to fight against Iraqi insurgents one minute and guard them the next.

"It was the duality of it—going from one edge of the sword to the other," he said. "That's what would mess with you the most. You're treating these people like numbers and cattle—you're corralling them into an area."

By overseeing them, Stevenson also began to better understand them.

"You've got these guys in the jail and you're talking to them ... treating them nicely," he said. "Sometimes I [went] back at night and [thought], 'Damn, I could've just been talking to a guy that just killed somebody for no reason.' You're flip-flopping all the time."

The empathy that Stevenson felt for detainees also made it difficult for him to soften them up. "It's really hard to want to add stress on somebody ... because you don't always hate people," he explained. "I never once hated anybody. You feel bad for them too, because they're in a caged room."

Daniel Keller and others reflected on what they had done in Balad. "It sort of slowly started happening," he said. "You get this big, looming crap feeling. I think a lot of it was because I was pretty unhappy with myself, and I started figuring that out."

Their sweeps gathered up large batches of prisoners, often for seemingly arbitrary reasons, and most of them were eventually freed. For some troops, in retrospect, it didn't seem rational to abuse and torture prisoners. Back in Iraq, some soldiers griped to their superiors about abusing prisoners; others ignored and resisted orders, or just followed them halfheartedly. Some of the most abusive soldiers later admitted they began hating the torture the most, and it became a festering secret that they would take back home with them. Yet few felt comfortable sharing their experiences with the military's mental health professionals.

I asked Jonathan Millantz if he ever approached any therapists at FOB Lion (or another base) for counseling.

"There wasn't a detainee torture mental health specialist on the base," he said as he laughed about the possibility. "There was barely a PTSD clinic on the base."

The stigma attached to detainee abuse and torture made it hard for troops I met to seek treatment. But some veterans also admitted to me that they were reluctant to get help because they feared prosecution.

In 2006, the Department of Defense (DoD) issued a directive that instructed "Any health care personnel who in the course of a treatment relationship or in any other way observes or suspects a possible violation of [detainee protocol] ... for the protection of detainees shall report those circumstances to the chain of command."

Bob Ireland, the program director for mental health policy at the DoD, told me that the military would help any service member with a psychological problem. But he also acknowledged that because military medical personnel were required to report cases of prisoner abuse that they heard about, that could have discouraged soldiers from seeking help for abuse-related trauma.

"The service member who is suffering [over detainee abuse] is confronted with that issue," said Ireland. "It doesn't block their getting treatment, irrespective of the environment they'd find themselves in as a result. But that is a burden ... [when] you get yourself in these situations."

Perhaps because of such fears of recrimination, and the stigma attached to torture, it has been difficult for soldiers to openly discuss their involvement in detainee abuse and torture. That partly explains why there are so few studies that have been able to examine how torture traumatizes the person who commits it. Such documented accounts with primary sources are indeed rare, but those that do exist have proved to be illuminating. For instance, there have been select studies on Brazilian, French (serving in Algeria), and Greek torturers during the twentieth century, chiefly conducted by academics.[1] Other medical studies have touched upon the ways in which American soldiers have been affected by prisoner abuse.

In 1983, the US Congress set up the National Vietnam Veterans Readjustment Study (NVVRS) to research PTSD and other psychological problems that Vietnam veterans suffered as a result of the war. In so doing, the study also documented the psychological damage to veterans who engaged in torture.

The NVVRS included four years of research and 3,016 interviews. The researchers found a strong correlation between increased exposure to combat and psychological trauma. But the report also found that "abusive violence had the strongest correlation with PTSD" for Vietnam veterans. This abusive violence included, but wasn't exclusive to, the "degree of involvement in torturing, wounding, or killing hostages or POWs."[2]

"We can go into long philosophical discussions of torture—Is it effective? Is it justifiable?—but the one thing the research has shown is that ... it's not good for the people doing it," said Dr. Richard Kulka, the chief author of the study.

Kulka said the research turned up another interesting fact: "In general, most people are not going in there predisposed to do these things."

That is, military personnel who commit abuses during war were not necessarily abusive people beforehand.

"There was speculation at the time that said, 'Look, people who participate in abusive violence in Vietnam are probably people who were abused at home—they were abused as children, etc.,' " said Kulka. "That wasn't a very strong relationship at all. In fact, I think it was an insignificant relationship in our data. In general, most people are not going in there predisposed to do these things, and therefore it can have a very significant effect on them."

David Foy, a professor of psychology at Pepperdine University and a research consultant for the National Center for PTSD, researched cases of veterans affected by prisoner abuse during the war on terror.

"We know that participating in experiences or events beyond what are normally expected—where civilians are killed, for example—contributes to the development of PTSD," said Foy. "But we also know that doing things in the context of war zone duty that involves activities that ... challenge someone's sense of moral correctness, even if it's required for survival or if they're ordered to do it, leaves them with an altered sense of correctness about themselves. That's what we would call a 'moral conflict,' or more generally an inner conflict, that may be connected to PTSD. So, there's the mental health consequence ... but then there's the spiritual injury or moral injury."

Across the board, all of the therapists and social scientists I interviewed agreed that soldiers who had been traumatized by committing abusive

violence needed to get help quickly. The longer troops kept their experiences buried, these professionals maintained, the more deeply
entrenched the symptoms of PTSD would become.

Not everyone who has mistreated prisoners is psychologically traumatized. Studies on abuse-related trauma show that guilt is the key factor in
determining the extent to which troops are psychologically affected by
their experience with torture.[3] Daniel Keller echoed that feeling when
he described how his wartime experiences affected him.

"There's a lot of stuff that you're not supposed to do that you do over
there and ... of course it raises the morality issues," said Keller. "A lot of
your emotional ramifications come from these feelings of guilt."

Like many others in the battalion who suffered from insomnia, he was
forced to meditate during many sleepless nights on what he had done in
Iraq. "That's when you really start thinking about it," Keller said.
"You're there alone at night in bed, staring at the ceiling, and you're
thinking about all the bad stuff you did. And that's kind of how it hits
you."

Keller conceded his feelings of guilt weren't rooted in any kind of
empathy for those he had tortured. "I kind of wish it was," he said. "But
at the same time I'm happy it's not, because I think that would just make
things worse."

There was another kind of touchstone that compelled him to reflect
on the "bad stuff" he was involved in. In movies and media portrayals,
he noticed, torture and harsh interrogation weren't glamorized as heroic
acts against terrorist suspects. In fact, the shows he watched condemned
such behaviour.

"It's always shown as a bad thing; the bad guy's doing it, and the bad
guy is always portrayed as this ugly person," said Keller. "So, you're
seeing how in effect everybody else sees you, and eventually you just
can't escape that. And you start seeing yourself that way."

On April 28, 2004, the Abu Ghraib scandal broke, and fiction turned
into reality. Most media outlets that displayed those infamous photos
blurred out parts of the pictures that exposed nudity and other unsavory
features. But the images were nonetheless clear: American soldiers were
plainly involved in torture.

"It was like having an opportunity to be there watching myself do it,"
said Keller. "And that is pretty God-awful, to actually have to come to
terms visually with what you're doing. It's no longer just watching

somebody in the movie do it … No, you're watching somebody really doing it in real life—and this time … they're wearing the same uniform. It is just more of the same."

I asked Keller if his trauma would have been any less severe if he could subtract torturing prisoners from his overall combat experience in Iraq.

"If I hadn't actually hurt anybody, I'd be sitting pretty—I'd be happy as could be," he said.

He further reflected on my question, and then he unloaded.

"I wouldn't have any problems. I wouldn't be on fucking medication. I wouldn't be sitting here doing an interview because I wouldn't know anything, and I would be fucking living life out there. I would be done with fucking school because I wouldn't have had three fucking years where I self-medicated, fucking drinking myself to death over this dumb shit until I realized that it was okay to get help because I'm not an asshole … You would see a fucking professional sitting in front of you that is earning a great paycheck and living life the way he wants, has plenty of time to himself, done with college.

"My violence robbed me."

It was the first time I had heard him so agitated.

"You sound very resentful," I said.

"I am," he answered. "The terrible things that I did … and I'm still paying the price for it."

The soldiers with Battalion 1-68 weren't the only ones traumatized by torture. There were also the victims of their abuse, and those who were tortured by other US forces, whose stories have gone largely untold.

There are myths about torture's general effectiveness, and the particular techniques that "work." There is also misinformation about the costs of seemingly mild forms of torture. Many of the techniques that US forces have used during the war on terror are referred to as "torture lite," suggesting that such practices seldom rise to the level of "severe pain or suffering"—the legal threshold according to the Bybee memo.[4] Such turns of phrase also make these techniques sound comparatively gentler than other forms of torture, and makes the idea of using torture more palatable. Most of the abusive techniques that were approved by US officials and generally used by US forces left few marks. Nevertheless, these "lite" techniques still caused grave damage to their victims. Some of Iraq's physicians and psychiatrists understood this quite intimately.

Dr. Maytham Alyasiry had worked as a psychiatrist since 1997, mostly in the Department of Psychiatry at the Baghdad Medical College. After the fall of Saddam Hussein's regime in 2003, he helped assemble one of the first facilities in the country to offer physical and mental health treatment for torture victims.

Along with assistance from Iraqi expats, a small group of Iraqis rented two buildings, furnished them, and secured three psychiatrists, two psychologists, a general practitioner, a nurse, and support staff. The clinic was named the Center for Psychosocial Health Iraq.[5]

"But ... in our publications and in our meetings we spoke about it and said 'this center is for survivors of torture,' " said Dr. Shatha Besarani, an Iraqi exile who worked as a gynecologist in the United Kingdom and who helped form the clinic. Besarani explained that the clinic was careful to distance itself from any explicit references to torture.

"From the beginning we were a center for survivors of torture," she said. "The only one thing was, we didn't make it clear in Arabic ... because we didn't want to be a target for the militants."

For years, physical punishment and abuse in Iraq was routine, but it was dangerous to discuss it openly. Even though the Center was disguised under its oblique name, hundreds of clients poured into its cramped rooms when they first opened, seeking help. According to medical staff, they served victims from Saddam's rule (the largest sample), those who were tortured in Iran as prisoners of war during the Iran–Iraq war, Iraqis who had been tortured during the Gulf War, and, finally, those who had been tortured during the latest conflict with the coalition forces. There were fairly common symptoms that most patients shared, including post-traumatic stress, depression, insomnia, appetite loss, and body weight fluctuations.

"These features are shared by all the victims," said Alyasiry. "It is not different for the patients if you are tortured by whatever system. If it was Saddam or the Americans it is all the same—it's the trauma, and this is the result of the trauma."

Likewise, he said, most patients also exhibited "exaggerated reflexes in terms of anxiety and trauma" and often avoided certain police stations or security areas—regardless of whether they were manned by Iraqi or foreign forces.

Alyasiry detailed the various ways in which Saddam's forces brutally tortured Iraqis, and described the chambers where women were raped in prison.

"They used many, many types of torture," he said. "They were professionals. Not like the ones at Abu Ghraib.

He and his colleagues admitted that the overwhelming number of torture victims who visited the clinic had been tortured under Saddam and that the regime's style of torture was different than others. "With Saddam the main torture was a physical torture," said Alyasiry. "Now it's different. They [coalition forces] avoid inflicting wounds or making scars on the body of the victims.

"Saddam was not afraid to be in the media or to be unpopular with Iraqis, doing physical or psychological torture to those who faced him politically. The Americans avoid these acts of torture, like leaving marks, because everyone is watching ... so they will avoid giv[ing] a bad picture about what they are doing in Iraq. These types of torture are inflicting more problems on patients even if they don't leave marks that they can show others [to prove] that they faced torture."

In 2008, Physicians for Human Rights (PHR) published a study titled *Broken Laws, Broken Lives: Medical Evidence of Torture by US Personnel and Its Impact*, detailing the mental and physical damage caused by the techniques that US forces had used—including "torture lite" and techniques that didn't leave marks.[6]

In Baghdad, the clinic's staff saw how this damage would sometimes manifest itself. Some signs were not outwardly obvious, such as renal failure from forced standing. Many victims suffered from chronic fatigue, made worse by the aches and pains resulting from hours spent in stress positions. Former prisoners wanted to sleep all the time, but they were plagued by nightmares. And detainees who had been sexually humiliated were filled with shame.

"Sexual harassment or sexual abuse is something that is not accepted morally and religiously in Iraq," said Alyasiry. "So those patients [who were] sexually abused during torture will not speak about their experiences ... They will say that they were tortured but they will avoid saying that they were abused sexually or were forced to do things that were humiliating to them—especially when they are speaking about sexual issues."

The number of torture victims swelled as violence blazed in "postwar" Iraq. Brutality emerged from all sides. Religious and ethnic militias, paramilitary death squads, and insurgents (sometimes dressed as police) were all involved in extrajudicial killings and, to varying degrees, torture. But during 2006, the Center actually saw fewer patients. Violent attacks in Baghdad made it perilous for patients to brave the streets to seek care at the clinic.

"Many of the clients were calling on the phone and [saying] that they couldn't come to the Center because of the insecure situation," said Alyasiry, remembering the sharp spike in violence during 2005–2006. "But those [of us] who were working with NGO organizations were more prone to danger than the others—especially those who were speaking about torture."

The clinic's funds slowly dried up, yet most of the staff stayed on during its last six months. In 2006, the clinic finally shuttered its doors; victims of tortures had to look elsewhere for sanctuary.

Violence continued to engulf Iraq years after the war began in 2003, forcing Iraqis to flee their country by the thousands. Refugees found safe havens in Jordan, Syria, Turkey, and elsewhere. It was sometimes difficult to arrange interviews with Iraqis in their own country while the war raged on. The exodus of Iraqi refugees provided an opportunity, borne of tragedy, to track and speak with those who were incarcerated and interrogated by US forces.

In Jordan, I talked with Philadelphia lawyer Susan Burke's best-known client, Haj Ali Shalal Qaissi. In June 2005, I met Qaissi in a dingy hotel lobby in Amman, and over the course of several interviews, he cradled his left hand and quietly, dispassionately described his experience at Abu Ghraib.

Qaissi told me that before the war, he lived in a quiet Baghdad suburb. He was a *mukhtar*, or community leader, whose neighbors sought him out for advice or to settle local disputes, and he often stayed at his local mosque during the day.

Qaissi enjoyed a genial rapport with the coalition forces, even though he never supported their intervention in his country. Insurgent attacks against those forces intensified soon after the invasion, and in the fall of 2003, coalition forces launched Operation Iron Horse, one of many military campaigns that targeted insurgents and anyone considered sympathetic to them. On October 13, 2003, two military vehicles pulled up to Qaissi's mosque. In front of a crowd of bystanders, soldiers cuffed and hooded Qaissi, and carted him away.

They first took him to Al Amaria, an old Iraqi military base in Baghdad. The next day, American troops deposited him at the Abu Ghraib prison.

Soldiers took fingerprints and eye scans, spread his arms and legs apart, and thoroughly searched his body. Then they deposited Qaissi inside the tent encampment just outside the main prison building. One hot, tedious day blurred into the next, and he spent a full month waiting to talk with his captors.

Finally, American interrogators summoned him.

"Are you a terrorist?" they asked.

He denied it.

"We have good information you hate the coalition forces—that you're working against them."

He showed them that his hand was so damaged from an old injury—trauma caused by an antique rifle that misfired when he shot it off during a traditional Iraqi wedding—that it was impossible for him to grip a weapon. Finally they asked, "Where is Osama bin Laden?"

"In Afghanistan," he answered.

How do you know?

"I read it in the newspaper."

The questions went on for days, then weeks. Between interrogation sessions, Qaissi was hooded and deposited in a cell. Eventually, American guards transferred Qaissi to the prison's "hard site," where Saddam's police had tortured and executed inmates. A young group of GIs clad in beige fatigues encircled Qaissi, cut his plastic flex cuffs, and ordered him to strip.

They must be joking, he thought. Nudity is unbearably shameful in the Middle East. These Americans must understand. I cannot.

When he would not undress, they threatened him, then kicked and punched him so hard he fell to the floor. Eventually he stood upright and removed his clothes with quivering hands. The soldiers cuffed his wrists behind him, fastened leg restraints around his ankles, and ordered Qaissi up a flight of stairs. He had to crawl on his knees and chin as the guards laughed. Qaissi heard voices screaming in the background.

Help me! Help me!

When he reached the top stair, soldiers suspended him by his wrists from overhead pipes and repeatedly poured ice-cold water on him. Sometimes they urinated on him.

He remained hooded throughout the night, and translators repeatedly woke him and peppered him with questions. One night turned into several days. Qaissi could vaguely identify the time through the Muslim calls for prayer that divided the day.

"You must help us to help you," a translator told him. "Work with us, answer our questions. Give us the names of all the people that are dangerous to us. We'll fix your hand if you help us. We'll try to make your hand work again. American doctors are good."

But Qaissi pleaded that he simply could not help them even if he wanted to.

"I don't know anyone. How can I name people that I don't know or know anything about?"

And so the questions continued, coupled with regular dousings with cold water and beatings with a car antenna. While he was hanging by his wrists from the overhead pipe, they forced a rifle barrel into his rectum.

"Give us some names," a translator said. "Help us. If you don't help us, we'll kill you. We'll send you to Guantanamo, and your life will be worth less than a dog."

When they finally cut him down, he could barely move his arms or walk. But the questions continued, along with more attempts to break him psychologically.

Troops kept Qaissi from sleeping by blasting the David Gray pop song "Babylon" inches from his head for twelve straight hours. Qaissi couldn't hear after the music stopped, but the song continued to ring in his ears.

He was forced to stand for hours cuffed in various painful positions. While hooded, he was told to keep his arms extended as an interrogator curled wire around his fingers. The questions came again: Where are the weapons of mass destruction? Who are the insurgents? Where is Osama bin Laden?

Qaissi insisted he didn't know. Burning pain shot through his body, and he fell flat on the floor—he said he was stunned with electric shocks. The soldiers picked him back up, and he was made to assume the same position. He could hear laughter and cameras clicking. His eyes burned. The shocks had caused him to clench down on his tongue and it was bleeding.

Qaissi said he was shocked three more times, and then it stopped. He slumped onto the concrete floor, and his hood was taken off. A soldier approached with a menacing look and stepped on Qaissi's deformed hand. He stomped on it again, pressing harder until Qaissi finally passed out from the pain.

Once the Abu Ghraib photos surfaced, Qaissi was able to identify that soldier as Specialist Charles Graner, one of the prison's Army reservists who was later to face charges for abusing detainees.

After the electric shocks, the guards dressed Qaissi in a red prison uniform. Photos taken by US troops at Abu Ghraib show Qaissi in his red jumpsuit with "the claw" scrawled on his back in thick black letters, along with close-up images of his damaged hand. But finally being clothed offered little comfort to Qaissi. Under Saddam, inmates were given the red uniform to wear when they were slated for execution. Qaissi spent weeks fearing that his uniform signified his own death sentence.

But it did not.

Qaissi was returned to the same outdoor tent where his captivity at Abu Ghraib began. He had lost considerable weight and looked pale. He had a blank stare and barely spoke; when he did, he talked in whispers.

Bassam Akram Marouji was an inmate at Abu Ghraib and befriended Qaissi when the two were confined to the outdoor prison tent. Before the US invasion, Marouji worked as one of Saddam Hussein's butlers. American troops assumed that his proximity to Saddam meant he likely possessed valuable intelligence, and they captured Marouji several months into the occupation. Marouji told me they beat him and administered electric shocks during his interrogation.[7] He required weeks to recuperate. The experience left him physically and emotionally shattered, and he convalesced on a cot within Abu Ghraib's tented encampment.

When Qaissi was returned to the prison tent, Marouji noticed how his friend's demeanor had changed after his stay in the prison's hard site. Qaissi had scars and moved listlessly. Marouji tended to Qaissi: he helped him into the showers, filled his water bottles, and brought him meals. From Qaissi's demeanor, Marouji had a sense of what his fellow inmate had been through—Marouji had exhibited the same symptoms while recovering from his own interrogation.

Today, Qaissi lives in Amman, Jordan, where he heads the Association of Victims of American Occupation Prisons. He meets with local human rights activists, collects testimonies from victims, and lectures about his experience. Qaissi said the detainees he talks with resent not only the abuse and torture themselves but also the way American authorities largely ignored their testimonies after the fact. They're frustrated, he added, with the scant redress for US torture, represented by limited courts-martial and few serious sentences, mostly for low-ranking soldiers.

Qaissi has been interviewed by television and newspapers about his experience. He's been the subject of controversy over whether he was or was not the man in the most notorious Abu Ghraib photo, the hooded man on the box with wires attached to his hands. Qaissi's business card includes this image. In March 2006, the *New York Times* profiled Qaissi and described him as the figure in that photo. But the internet news magazine *Salon* cited military reports to the effect that the hooded man was actually another detainee. The *Times* investigated and wrote a lengthy retraction, saying the man in the photo was not Qaissi.

"Whether he was forced to stand on a box and photographed is not clear," conceded the *Times*, "but evidence suggests that he adopted the identity of the iconic man on the box, the very symbol of Abu Ghraib, well after he left the prison."

Qaissi and his lawyer, Susan Burke, both said that whether or not he is the man in the famous photo, he was treated similarly. There is no doubt, in any case, that he was in fact imprisoned at Abu Ghraib. He's featured in various photos from the prison, with "the claw" penned on the back of his jumpsuit. Photos clearly show his broken hand.

Still, his story illustrates how difficult it is to substantiate detainees' claims of abuse. Corroboration is difficult to come by. According to Burke and many human rights groups, military investigators failed to interview the detainees they represented, including Qaissi himself. Burke and others wrote to the military, repeatedly offering to make these detainees available, but investigators never spoke with them. So stories that might corroborate Qaissi's were never gathered.

Forensic evidence is equally hard to find.

Burke put me in touch with Dr. Thomas Fasy, an associate professor of pathology at the Mount Sinai School of Medicine, who was part of a delegation of 150 doctors and scientists who had been hired to assess health and environmental issues in post-war Iraq. He traveled back and forth between New York and Baghdad, and even Amman, Jordan, where he met Qaissi in 2005. He examined Qaissi to see if doctors could do anything further to repair his damaged hand. I asked Fasy to provide some insight into what else happened to Qaissi, based on his examination.

"Can you tell if Qaissi was electrocuted?" I asked.

Fasy said that an Army doctor did treat Qaissi for a bleeding tongue, ostensibly caused when he bit on it during the electroshocks. But Fasy said he couldn't provide a definitive answer. Torture experts consider electroshock a stealthy technique, because it leaves few marks on the epidermis, and any subcutaneous evidence (damage under the skin) often disappears in a matter of weeks. That is often why many torturers use electricity.

After the *Times* printed its retraction, I wanted to ask Qaissi himself about the controversy over whether he was the hooded man, so I asked an Arabic-speaking colleague to call him for his reaction. Qaissi became very emotional, my colleague said.

To Qaissi, the focus on this question seemed like a way of turning attention away from his claims of abuse, a way of silencing him.

Burke agreed with Qaissi's position.

"People don't really want to … hear it from the perspective of the victim," she said. "The victims don't want a blue ribbon commission that sits around and comes up with another report. They want criminal prosecutions, and they want the people who raped them and beat them and subjected them to electric shocks—they want those people to go to prison.

"Think about what you'd want if you were treated like that. You'd like the actual perpetrators. And that's the real reason why the military does not want to hear these stories from the victims now. It changes the tone of the debate when you hear these people."

To Qaissi, issues like the identity of the man in the photograph were ultimately immaterial. What mattered to Qaissi, and to most of the other detainees I interviewed, was the US government's response to his claims, as well as the reaction to the Abu Ghraib scandal and other similar cases. I rarely met a detainee who had received an apology, or any acknowledgement at all, for the harsh treatment he had endured during US captivity.

In 2005, Iraqi refugees poured into the Syrian Arab Republic, because the state granted relaxed entry to fellow Arabs more readily than Jordan did. That year, the Syrian government and the United Nations High Commissioner for Refugees (UNHCR) estimated that roughly 700,000 Iraqi refugees were living in Syria.[8]

Like most foreign correspondents, I needed a translator to help me track down and interview detainees while I was in Syria. I turned to Laila Tomeh, a local woman who had worked with the International Organization for Migration and therefore had connections with Iraqi refugees living in Syria.

Although it was easy to locate former detainees, our meetings still had to be arranged somewhat surreptitiously, since I arrived shortly after

John Bolton, the US ambassador to the United Nations, and other neoconservatives called for "regime change" in Syria. Tomeh and my colleagues insisted that I proceed cautiously and not stir up attention, since foreign agents sometimes claimed they, too, worked as journalists. Asking questions about torture, even if it wasn't about Syrian torture victims, would also arouse suspicion.

Tomeh was a member of the Syrian Orthodox church, so she also had contacts within the local Christian community. She knew about an Iraqi parish priest, Father Sarmad Yousef, a thirty-year-old Chaldean Catholic who had recently fled his country and taken over at Damascus's Saint Theresa's Church. The modest-sized church was wedged between old ashen-colored buildings in the Christian quarter of the historic city, known as Bab Touma. At that time, it served 2,000 Iraqi families—most of whom were very recent refugees—who feared persecution against Christians back home as their country became inflamed in ethnic and religious infighting. Fanatics were targeting women who didn't cover their heads with scarves and bombing Christian shops that sold alcohol.

Tomeh thought Father Yousef would be sympathetic to our project, and arranged an appointment. One muggy summer morning, we went to his air-conditioned office, which was decorated with paintings of Saint Theresa, the patron saint of the church, tenderly clutching bouquets of crimson roses. He carefully shut the door and took a seat behind his desk.

Tomeh described the project we were working on: we were looking for former detainees from US detention facilities to investigate any common themes that had not yet been fully explored. Father Yousef listened patiently. Then he unbuttoned his collar, wove his fingers together in front of his mouth, and nodded.

"So that's what we're looking for," said Tomeh, breaking into English.

Father Yousef leaned forward and adjusted his oval glasses, then began describing how he actively backed the coalition forces when they toppled Saddam. He helped organize meetings between Americans and sheiks to resolve community concerns; he condemned Shi'ite leader Muqtada al-Sadr's forces when they fought with the US military in Najaf during 2004; and he helped the police capture neighborhood criminals. All of this came with grave risks; Father Yousef barely avoided getting shot during two drive-by attacks, and his name was circulated on a "death list." But his support for the coalition forces still didn't waver.

He had certainly heard rumors that the Americans were rough with their prisoners. And he also heard some accounts of detainees being forced to undress, but it wasn't exactly clear to him what was happening.

And then the Abu Ghraib torture scandal emerged.

"This Abu Ghraib," said Father Yousef, as he lowered his eyes and gently shook his head. "Before that, Iraqis loved Americans. Before that they were eating with them, chatting with them, playing with them in the streets, going to church. Directly after that—those photos, that scandal—directly destroyed the dignity of Iraqis."

Father Yousef witnessed an increase in violence in his Baghdad neighborhood, al-Baladiat, following the scandal. Americans simply did not understand how deeply the sexual abuse had humiliated and infuriated Iraqis, as well as most Arabs, regardless of their creed, said Father Yousef. He heard about former detainees who were too ashamed to face their communities, and even some who avoided their families, because of how they had been debased and exposed in the photos, even if their faces had been blurred.

American Catholic soldiers continued to come by to pray at Father Yousef's Baghdad church, Saint Pathion. But following the scandal, he refused to let them inside.

"I was one of the first who refused to see the Americans who came to see me," he said. "The relationship between the American Army and the Iraqis just ended." Father Yousef said he no longer engaged with US personnel; he didn't invite them into his home, he didn't greet them in the street, and he didn't hold any more meetings with them.

Tomeh and I absorbed his account in stunned silence. We expected that he would be an ally, perhaps in part because of our similar religious backgrounds, and recommend other interviewees who could lend their voice to our project. But he politely demurred.

What good would it really do? he asked. Iraqi torture victims generally didn't want to revisit their trauma, and Americans didn't seem to sympathize with what they had experienced, or so it seemed to him. It therefore didn't seem reasonable to Father Yousef to trouble former detainees about their ordeal. Tomeh and I thanked him for his time and departed.

As we strolled down the cobblestone streets just outside the church, we meditated on our meeting. Here was a Catholic priest who was not only sympathetic but who had put himself in harm's way by publicly supporting coalition forces and their rebuilding efforts. US forces never arrested or threatened him—in fact, they embraced him. But he was so repulsed by the Abu Ghraib scandal that he shunned US forces and refused to help them further. Moreover, he didn't feel that Americans would really be so moved by hearing detainees' accounts that it would result in meaningful change.

Just being an average news consumer and an Iraqi citizen, Father Yousef was deeply affected by "that scandal" and the US response to it. Tomeh and I wondered about the Iraqis who supported coalition forces and yet had been detained and interrogated, and whether it affected their alliance with Americans, just as it had Father Yousef.

Trying to find former detainees in Jordan and Syria proved difficult. The International Red Cross does not reveal the names of detainees because of the agreements it maintains with host nations. But I located a non-profit organization in Iraq that had successfully tracked down and interviewed some of them, and they agreed to help us. Ironically, it turned out to be another Christian connection. The Christian Peacemaker Team (CPT) gladly facilitated contact with their sources. They suggested we meet Najeeb Abbas Shami, a Shi'ite leader who was once exiled during the Shi'ite *intifada*—an uprising aimed at toppling Saddam in 1991. Saddam's forces crushed that revolution, claiming about 100,000 lives.[9] Like many other Shi'ites in the region, Shami desperately wanted Saddam and his regime overthrown. He still lived in Karbala. He agreed to be interviewed, and traveled from Iraq to Damascus to see us.

Shami greeted us warmly at the entrance of a rustic hotel in the predominantly Shi'ite neighborhood of Sayeda Zeinab. He was a congenial, middle-aged man who dressed smartly in a suit and tie and gesticulated elegantly as he talked. During our interview, he smoked cigarette after cigarette in a black cigarette holder, and inhaled deeply on long drags of smoke.

Shami told us he was a city councilor in Karbala and an emissary for coalition forces, aiding the rebuilding efforts there. Months after US troops entered Baghdad, insurgent violence began to swell in Karbala province. Shami was asked to help manage local security and provided coalition forces with intelligence about local Ba'athists. US troops relied on local help and information, but Shami said many informants provided them with faulty intelligence just so they could settle private scores and collect bounty from the US military.

Because of his stature within the community, Shami was also asked to resolve land disputes between various Iraqi tribes. On May 15, 2003, he was summoned to the governor's office to update officials about the progress he had made in settling such disputes. Upon his arrival, two plainclothes American intelligence agents approached him.

"Brown and David," Shami said, speaking in English.

They had a few questions for him, and asked Shami to follow them to a parking lot. Once there, Brown and David frisked him and forced his hands behind his back. "Where are you taking me?" he asked them.

Shami was brought to the detention facility at Camp Lima and interrogated by three soldiers. The agents said they had documents incriminating Shami but declined to show them to him. The agents insisted that these papers, along with witness testimony they collected, conclusively proved that he was an Islamic militant, a spy, and a Ba'athist.

Shami laughed and told them that their accusations were ludicrous. An Islamic militant *and* a Ba'athist?

"Who says this?" Shami asked them. He reminded them of the enmity between Islamic militants and secular Ba'athists.

They told him that a local governmental official had accused him. Shami was familiar with the man they named—someone Shami had reported to the governor's office for embezzlement. To Shami, this suggested that the informant reported on him to the American troops in order to settle a score. But the agents who detained Shami didn't believe his explanation and threatened to imprison him indefinitely if he didn't disclose information about insurgent groups with which he was allegedly involved.

"I really don't know about them," he pleaded.

Brown became impatient with Shami's denials. Still Shami insisted that he didn't know anything about insurgent members and that he was set up.

Brown signaled a group of soldiers, who abruptly grabbed Shami, forced him to lie on his stomach, and tightly cuffed his wrists behind his back. Though Shami's English was limited, he understood that Brown instructed the soldiers to withhold food for forty-eight hours and give him plenty of "roughing up."

"Have a party with him," Brown told the soldiers.

And they complied.

Within his Damascus hotel room, Shami pantomimed the kinds of stress positions they forced him to hold. He described how soldiers pushed him face down on a cement floor and stepped on his head, some-times even kicking it. They set him upright, taped toys to his head (such as stuffed animals), and took trophy photographs of him. They withheld food, as instructed. At one point, Shami requested water. A soldier pulled down his pants and placed his penis in front of Shami's face.

"Drink this," he said.

He then pulled down Shami's pants to expose him and repeatedly yelled, "Feekie, feekie!" They beat him, pointed guns at his head, and told him he was being sent to Guantanamo.

Shami paused in his recollections and broke down in tears.

After several weeks of captivity, Shami was eventually cleared of any wrongdoing or links to insurgent groups and released. Days later, a mili-tary commander entered his house and re-arrested him in front of his family. The US forces shuttled him between bases and eventually sent him to Abu Ghraib, where he was questioned further. He became severely depressed and was exposed to prolonged bouts of heat in the prison camp, which exacerbated his cardiac angina.

"Help me! Help me!" he cried. "I'm a sick man."

According to Shami, it seemed to him that guards believed he was whining about his imprisonment. Shami's health worsened, and he suf-fered multiple heart attacks and a stroke. Abu Ghraib's medical staff did come to his rescue in these cases, and Shami was struck by the kindness of one American doctor in particular, whom he remembers as "Dr. Jasy."

"Where was your family during all of this? How were they respond-ing to your detention?" I asked.

"Please don't ask such questions," he said, breaking down again. "I feel too much pain to answer."

His family was, in fact, trying to locate him. Shami's son went to Abu Ghraib where he pleaded to see his father. American troops at the prison refused him access, and told him lawyers and humanitarian organizations were also forbidden inside the prison.

Shami grew desperate, and refused food and medicine to protest his treatment and publicize his condition. He held a high status in one of Karbala's venerated tribes and was a well-known and respected leader. In due course, word spread about Shami's treatment, and it provoked Karbala's citizens to demonstrate for his release.

Even *60 Minutes* got wind of what happened to Shami. A CBS crew visited Abu Ghraib, where they questioned Brigadier General Janis

Karpinski about Shami's arrest and protracted detention.[10] With cameras rolling, Karpinski declared that the prison's conditions had far improved since Saddam's time and that no prisoners were being held without charge.

"I mean, there's nobody being held for no reason," said Karpinski, looking somewhat defensive. "There's foundation or … charges for all of our prisoners."

She further insisted detainees were charged after an initial seventy-two-hour processing period. The interviewer countered that Shami had been incarcerated for more than a month. The *60 Minutes* crew continued to press Karpinski and followed her into the prisoner's computer room, where they asked her to look up Shami's record. She found his record and asked the *60 Minutes* crew to shut off their cameras. Karpinski admitted to the reporter off-camera that it was true: Shami had been detained beyond the normal processing period without being charged. But she added that he was a "suspect of crimes against the coalition." His detention would therefore stand.

Protests over Shami's imprisonment continued, and the *60 Minutes* report embarrassed the Army. Officials at Abu Ghraib couldn't justify holding him there any longer; the military couldn't produce evidence to establish that he was "an Islamic militant, a spy, and a Ba'athist." If he died during his hunger strike, or from complications from his heart condition, Shami could become a martyr—his name might become a rallying cry for those denouncing the coalition forces. On December 28, 2003, officials at Abu Ghraib finally freed him—about seven months after he was captured.

Some may argue that Shami's experience represents detainee abuse rather than torture. Perhaps his account shows how little these semantics really matter for victims and communities. Regardless of how one defines his experience, it highlights how the denigration of prisoners didn't just discredit US troops; it quite possibly further imperiled them by fostering resentment among ordinary Iraqis. By wrongly arresting, re-arresting, and abusing a popular figure in the Karbala community, American troops fueled a cause célèbre and alienated their allies. They publicly humiliated an important tribal leader, which reverberated far beyond the city of Karbala.

Although Shami was deeply embittered by his ordeal, he emphatically praised Dr. Jasy and other Americans who came to his aid. And even after his harrowing experience, Shami still pinned hope on cooperation with American forces. He, too, wanted to quash the insurgents and help repair his damaged country.

Yet Shami could not let go of his anger against the agents who arrested him and the soldiers who abused him. He resented how his family suffered when they saw US forces arrest him in his home, and how they wept as he was once more carted away for unknown reasons, unsure whether they would see him again. Shami cried in shame as he recalled how American soldiers sexually humiliated him. It was, he said, the most upsetting part of his experience.[11]

Shami reflected on that day—that moment—in his room in Damascus. At the end of our interview he muttered something in Arabic. Tomeh did not translate, and a stone-cold silence filled the room as her face turned ashen.

"What did he say, Laila?" I asked.

"He's asking for revenge from God," she said.

We waited until he finished dabbing away his tears and regained his composure.

It took a day and a half to interview Shami about his experience, and we were all drained by the end of it. Tomeh and I finally rose to leave, and he escorted us out into the street where we exchanged farewells. Shami touched my arm tenderly and said something to me in Arabic. Tomeh smiled.

"He said, 'You are like one of the prophets, doing work for humanity,' " she said.

I was flattered, but embarrassed. I felt compelled to apologize for what he had endured at the hands of the US military.

During my time in Syria in summer 2005, I met Rami Khalid Mousa, a tall, slight Iraqi Chaldean Catholic with short-cropped hair and dark, darting eyes. He agreed to speak with me, but only on the condition that we meet in a private home. I agreed and made arrangements to get together at a fellow journalist's apartment.

Mousa asked me about my background and where I lived in the States. He had met several Americans and quickly befriended them. Mousa and his friends had enthusiastically supported the US invasion and occupation of Iraq, and cheered the Americans on when they entered Baghdad. But they grew nervous about the changes: violence quickly swelled, and the economy and infrastructure, already in bad shape, soon worsened. Jobs were scarce, he explained, and work with the Americans and their private military companies was lucrative. That's why he took a job with one of them. "It was not the best work, but it was a job," he explained.

Mousa also helped do interpretation for interrogations. "American soldiers trusted me, and they liked me because my job was to help them with the prisoners," he said.

I gently prodded him about how the process worked, what sorts of questions they asked. Did they use any force?

"Oh, Josh ..." said Mousa, laughing uncomfortably and shifting his legs in the chair. The unspoken answer was yes. "I will tell you another time—when I know you better, brother."

"Okay, tell me about your average workday."

Mousa admitted that he found many aspects of the work disagreeable, and even told his American colleagues he regarded them as "occupiers."

"What else would you be?" he said he asked them. He admitted to protesting against the coalition forces when they used excessive force against Iraqi civilians. And, like other Iraqis, he was distressed by Abu Ghraib, and saw how it inflamed anger against his employer—the Americans.

"My friends from America they told me, 'We are not like the soldiers in Abu Ghraib. Don't believe we are all the same [like] those people in the scandal. Not all Americans are bad.'"

Mosua heard them out, but now felt he needed to take extra precautions outside of the office in order to avoid any negative attention he attracted through the nature of his work. Mousa left his house at varying times, just to break up any kind of routine that could be tracked. He would contact a coworker and arrange to be picked up at a nearby location—changing the destination each time—so that they could drive to work together without being noticed. Soon after coalition forces arrived in Iraq, the number of civilian kidnappings increased dramatically. Kidnappers often targeted anyone suspected of having even moderate wealth. As the war dragged on, many who worked with the Americans suffered worse fates.

"They started to kill interpreters," said Mousa. "Especially in 2004 ... they killed interpreters every day."

His family began to worry about his associations with foreign soldiers.

"My mother she was angry—she was afraid—because they started to kill the people who are working with the Americans," said Mousa. "She told me many times to quit this job. But I told her, 'If I quit from this job, what will I do for work?' " He was, after all, his family's main breadwinner.

Mousa and his coworker, a middle-aged Shi'ite man he scarcely knew, usually left together after they finished their shifts. As with their morning commute each day, they mixed up their route home to avoid any kind of discernible routine. But during one rainy afternoon commute, Mousa's friend noticed that a black Opel had been following them. He told Mousa to remain calm.

"Maybe they will pass," he said. "Or maybe they are looking for someone else."

But the Opel pulled up beside them and the window was lowered. Mousa's coworker was prepared. He grabbed his pistol and opened fire on the Opel. Its occupants returned fire, and bullets poured into their vehicle.

Mousa's colleague recoiled, slumped forward over the steering wheel, and crashed their vehicle. Surveying the damage, Mousa realized that both of them had been injured. At least the Opel drove off, he thought. He prodded his coworker, but the man was unresponsive—he had been killed. The black Opel returned, and their attackers peered into the vehicle to be sure they had killed them both. Mousa pretended to be dead.

At last the Opel departed, and Mousa quietly got out of his vehicle. But as soon as he stood upright, he buckled over in pain. He had been shot in the stomach.

A crowd gathered, and Mousa pleaded for help. No one responded. Some, he assumed, feared they could also be targeted for helping him.

"Please," he implored. "Just take me to the hospital. I won't tell anyone you helped me."

But onlookers just watched Mousa bleed. He felt they were unsympathetic to him and he sensed they suspected he worked with the coalition forces. A lot of Iraqis worked on the US bases nearby, and translators were particularly likely to be singled out by the insurgents.

At last, someone came forward and pointed to a car. Mousa staggered toward its rear door and limped inside. He lost a considerable amount of blood and nearly went into shock. But the driver delivered him to a hospital in time to save Mousa's life.

Mousa passed me a few photographs of himself in the hospital, with layers of gauze wrapped around his torso. Then he lifted up his shirt to reveal his scar, still pink and fresh. "I am very, very lucky," he said. "And

I will never work for the Americans again, no matter how much they pay me. It is too dangerous—I would be killed."

Mousa later found out that the man who drove him to the hospital was shot and killed.

I didn't know if Mousa was specifically targeted because he helped interrogate prisoners, or if it was the mere association with coalition forces that endangered him and his colleague. It was clear, though, that just mentioning "how they used force" during interrogation made Mousa nervous. In Damascus, I tried to interview Mousa's friends who also worked as interpreters for US interrogations in Iraq. They corroborated Mousa's account but were too afraid to talk about their own experiences helping Americans conduct interrogations.

As the Iraq war raged during that period, violent groups lashed out against Iraqis who helped American forces and their allies.[12] Many of those vulnerable Iraqis said they felt betrayed when the US and its allies failed to provide enough support to protect them when they put their lives on the line—especially when they were supporting coalition forces in security and military matters.[13] Virtually all of the Iraqis I met in the Middle East during 2005 told me that the US involvement with detainee abuse further inflamed anger against both the Americans and those who helped them. As Father Yousef said, it was "the scandal"—Abu Ghraib—that sparked a wave of outrage and hostility toward Americans, along with anyone who seemed to be associated with them.[14]

Kirk Johnson, director of the List Project, a nonprofit that has helped resettle Iraqis who were imperiled due to their affiliation with the US, also saw Abu Ghraib as a watershed moment.

"What Abu Ghraib certainly did was change the rules of the game very quickly," said Johnson. "The Iraqis who joined [the Americans] with pure altruism and pure hope for the future Iraq, [suddenly] they were sort of cornered—they were now grouped in with what was seen as an increasingly unjust and immoral occupation at that point."

From Johnson's perspective, Abu Ghraib amplified the dangers for Iraqis who worked with US forces and contractors.

The accounts of Rami Khalid Mousa, Najeeb Abbas Shami, and Father Sarmad Yousef are tragic stories about the effects of detainee abuse and torture. They also reveal dimensions of torture that have been largely ignored by those who have advocated "harsh interrogation." So far, most of the debate about the efficacy of torture—that is, if torture "works"—has centered on whether it is an effective tool for eliciting actionable intelligence from detainees. That debate will likely rage on for years to come. Yet those on both sides of the argument seem to over-look one fundamental dimension of policing and counterterrorism campaigns. Research has shown that police, security and paramilitary forces heavily rely on public cooperation to provide them with intelligence for investigating and prosecuting a wide variety of cases.[15] Therefore debates about whether torture "works" have to include accounts from people like the men I met in the Middle East, whose experiences showed not only the plight of torture victims, but also how torture actually endangered Americans by alienating valuable allies and inciting anger against US forces—in some cases from those who had earlier been their closest friends and supporters.[16]

Detainee abuse also provoked violent responses aimed at US troops, according to some military officials. Alberto Mora, the former Navy general counsel who helped quash the Pentagon memo for harsh inter-rogation at Guantanamo, testified before the Senate Armed Services Committee on June 17, 2008. He discussed the treatment of detainees in US custody, and argued that "there is little or no moral distinction between cruelty and torture, for cruelty can be as effective as torture in savaging human flesh and spirit and in violating human dignity. Our efforts should be focused not merely on banning torture, but on banning cruelty."

Mora's position was that the US engagement in "cruelty and torture" also endangered Americans.

"[T]here are serving US flag-rank officers who maintain that the first and second identifiable causes of US combat deaths in Iraq—as judged by their effectiveness in recruiting insurgent fighters into combat—are, respectively, the symbols of Abu Ghraib and Guantanamo," Mora said. "The net effect of this policy of cruelty has been to weaken our defenses, not to strengthen them, and has been greatly contrary to our national interest."

Over time, it became increasingly difficult to locate and interview former detainees in the Middle East. My translators and I quickly exhausted the list of former detainees that we had pieced together from human rights workers, local refugees, and others. In June 2005, I trav-eled north to Aleppo, Syria's second-largest city, where one of my translators had arranged interviews for me with various former detainees. But one by one, each of them suddenly declined to meet and talk with me. My translator called them all from Damascus, trying to change their minds; she insisted that I would speak to them only for a short while and do everything in my power to avoid attracting attention. But she failed to convince anyone.

I knew a young shopkeeper in Aleppo who spoke flawless English and claimed he wrote reports about human rights abuses in Syria for Amnesty International. He agreed to help me speak to some of the local human rights activists and translate interviews if anyone agreed to speak with me.

Together, we snaked through the interlacing alleys of Aleppo's vaulted-covered marketplace, past the shops displaying freshly butchered meats, burlap bags overflowing with pistachios, and pyramid-shaped mounds of spices that perfumed the air. Aleppo boasts a population of 1.5 million, and vies with Damascus for being the oldest continuously functioning city in the world. Beyond its charm, Aleppo had become a haven—or stopover—for those crossing between Syria and Iraq, some of whom had been involved in insurgent activity, and it was therefore heavily monitored by the secret police, or Mokhaberat.

My companion and I located a local human rights activist who worked away from the marketplace, in a shabby, poorly lit office, and we implored him to reach out to find anyone who would agree to describe his experiences of being detained and interrogated. Again, nothing came of it.

Eventually, however, we were able to find an Aleppo businessman who had been captured by US forces in Iraq. Ali Said, a forty-eight-year-old of stout build, with orange hair and a thick mustache, managed an import-export business that required him to travel back and forth to Iraq. During one such trip to Tikrit in February 2004, he was pulled over by US forces at a checkpoint on the road that linked Baghdad to Mosul. Said had been carrying a wad of American dollars, which soldiers might have deemed suspicious, perhaps believing that the large amount of cash was meant for insurgents, and they arrested him.

He was held for eleven days, then questioned for four days. Said detailed a familiar litany of abuse during his detention and interrogation. His head was covered with a burlap bag and his wrists bound. Soldiers blasted loud music (country and western, he said) all night to keep him from falling asleep. Menacing dogs were commanded to bark and lunge at him and other detainees. During interrogation, Said's captors slapped him and beat his thighs with something like a riding crop, he said. Blows were interspersed with questions: Why are you in Iraq? What were you doing with so much cash? What organization are you supporting with the money? The sessions went on for about four hours, he estimated.

He was eventually sent to Abu Ghraib, where he went through biometric exams that calculated his height and weight, and logged his thumbprints and retinal scans. He was then deposited into one of the outdoor tents. Said wasn't the only foreign businessman being held there for suspicious activity—he also encountered a Jordanian and an Egyptian, two Moroccans, a student from Saudi Arabia, and a cluster of fellow Syrians.

After several months, American forces released him, and he returned home to Aleppo. Said wiped away tears after he finished describing what had happened to him. I asked him if there had been any lingering effects of his internment. He answered that the bruises on his legs, caused by strikes with an object similar to a riding crop, hadn't healed for six months, and that the Syrian security forces were suspicious about why US forces detained and questioned him.

"Until this moment, local security forces still watch me," he said. "They even questioned me four months after I returned."

We wrapped up our interview, thanked each other, warmly shook hands, and my companion and I departed. I didn't know it at the time, but it was the last interview I would be able to conduct in Syria.

The following afternoon I returned to my Aleppo translator's shop, where we sat on stacks of Persian carpets, sipped tea, and waited for any remaining sources to return our calls. The shopkeeper's brother glanced out the store's window, turned to me and asked sharply, "Why are the Mokhaberat following you? What have you done?"

I was jolted and suddenly felt flushed. I asked how he knew I was being tailed.

"Of course I know. Everyone knows that they're the local Mokhaberat," he said, gesturing toward two mustached figures who stood idly beside Aleppo's citadel, just outside the shop.

I worried about how much they knew about my sources and affairs. I needed to contact my translator and others, so I excused myself and swiftly returned to my hotel. Before going up to my room, I peered into the front office, where I noticed a clerk speaking nervously to someone in Arabic and flipping through a passport—my passport, it turned out. I politely removed it from his hands and returned to my room, where I called one of my translators.

"Leave Aleppo and return to Damascus," she instructed. "Immediately."

I didn't yet know what had happened, but I followed her instructions. The day after my return I met her in a Damascene café, and she reported that the Mokhaberat had paid a visit to Ali Said and threatened to imprison him if he spoke to another journalist. My Aleppo translator might also have aroused suspicion by visiting the office of a local human rights worker who was almost certainly under surveillance. Perhaps he was even an informer and used his identity as a cover.

Days later, a fellow journalist pulled me aside and asked me to shut off my phone. The Mokhaberat had paid her a visit too, and "requested" that she report to their office for questioning. She complied and took a friend to provide support. The Mokhaberat officials were polite, and very curious about this "young American journalist" with whom she had been associating. My stomach sank. I had endangered Ali Said by interviewing him; then Syrian security officials questioned my friend and colleague because of my work. I suddenly began to notice shady figures lurking behind me in the Damascus streets.

"Once you're being followed you're always being followed, even if you're not being followed," a friend there once told me.

I grew paranoid, quickly packed my bags, and left Syria for Beirut. I was able to get away without incident.

While seeking out former detainees in Jordan and Syria proved to be difficult, it was especially dangerous to locate and interview them in Iraq. Marla Ruzicka, the founder of Campaign for Innocent Victims in Conflict (CIVIC), routinely dealt with civilians who had been victimized by US attacks (accidental or otherwise) and often helped journalists like me contact former detainees. In April 2005, she was traveling to the Baghdad airport when a roadside bomb exploded, killing her and an Iraqi colleague. In November 2005, members of the Christian Peacemaker Team (CPT), who put me in touch with Qaissi and Shami, were kidnapped in Iraq. Days later, Tom Fox, one of the four members and a Quaker peace activist, was shot in the head and chest, and killed.[17] The other three hostages were eventually freed through a coalition forces military operation in March 2006.[18]

I understood the frustration that detainees, their lawyers, and human rights workers felt about the lack of follow-through with military investigations into abuse and torture. Yet I also grew to appreciate how hard it was to pursue detainees through official channels and investigate their cases. It highlighted the bravery of those who reported on these cases independently, like Ruzicka and the CPT members. They faced grave risks when they sought out victims in the field, and some of them paid the ultimate price for their service. The war and political tensions in the region made it increasingly difficult to pursue detainees. If human rights groups were unable to research and document their accounts, it would be more difficult for them to fully determine the pervasiveness of US torture, as well as how and where it had taken place. And so, abused detainees have had to wait for redress and for someone to take responsibility for what they suffered.

The abuses at Abu Ghraib, and some of the other revelations of US torture, drew international shock and outrage. But they have also provided a source of inspiration to some foreign police and military forces.

Egypt has earned a notorious reputation for torturing prisoners. Even though the US has been its strong ally for decades, the State Department (along with international human rights bodies) has routinely criticized its government for grave human rights abuses. Gamal Tajeldeen Hassan, a lawyer who has directed the Sawasya Center for Human Rights and Anti-Discrimination, learned the feebleness of such criticisms during the Iraq war.

In 2004, Hassan noticed a new pattern in detainee abuse cases in Egypt. Security forces and interrogators continued to employ beatings and electroshock torture, but prisoners began to tell him that torturers were also subjecting prisoners to sexual humiliation, and had coupled this abuse with new threats. According to Hassan, Egyptian torturers referred to these new techniques as "the Abu Ghraib."

As he put it, "Torturers here seem now to compare their methods to what happened in Iraq and say, 'Hey, there are more things that we need to try.' And now they try the most horrendous kinds of torture."[19]

Dr. Aida Seif El Dawla saw the same patterns emerge in her work. Dawla has run the only torture treatment center in Egypt since 1993,[20] and, like Hassan, she has heard about the ways in which local torturers have added more sexual degradation to their interrogation routines. According to Dawla, Egyptian forces now invoke Abu Ghraib during interrogations in order to instill fear in their detainees.

"The language"—the threats—"was definitely there after Abu Ghraib," she said. "Things like, 'We'll make you think you're in Abu

Ghraib' or 'Do you want an Abu Ghraib from the front or the back?' It was all about sexual torture. And we kept hearing stories about sexual torture." Sometimes, she said, Egyptian forces also threatened to take photos.

"The Abu Ghraib" began surfacing in other countries as well. In 2009, Slovakian police photographed and videotaped their prisoners— young Roma boys—being attacked by dogs and sexually humiliated.

When news broke of the incident, "police inspectors were poring over tapes depicting their colleagues humiliating Roma children in scenes reminiscent of mistreatment at Baghdad's Abu Ghraib jail."[21] Police shot about half a dozen videos showing Roma children being forced to strip naked, kiss each other, then strike each other.[22]

International human rights groups have also found more cases of military and security forces using various kinds of water torture against detainees. In 2009, Scotland Yard accused London's Metropolitan police of using "waterboarding" against a group of accused drug traffickers.[23]

The American use of torture during the war on terror did not just affect the nation's image in the world community. It diminished the moral authority of the US, and therein its capacity to criticize other nations. Worse, it unwittingly inspired, perhaps even encouraged, explorations into new methods of torture in other countries.

While it may have been more difficult to locate former detainees from Iraq who could describe their experience with US detainee abuse, it became progressively easier to locate victims of "the Abu Ghraib" from Egypt and elsewhere around the world.

Abu Ghraib became more than just a "prisoner abuse scandal." It became a devastating international symbol, and even a set of techniques that other security forces borrowed to torture detainees. That replication of torture techniques reminded me of Haj Ali Shalal Qaissi's statement that he was forced to stand on top of a box, arms extended, and threatened with electric shocks. It turned out that this set of techniques also had a history—it was, in fact, known as "the Vietnam."[24]

Chapter 8:
Confronting Torture's Legacy

ON FEBRUARY 24, 2007, I hopped into a silver Toyota Corolla and traveled toward the Hindu Kush Mountains with Noorrullah, a slight Pashtun kid in his early twenties. He was the younger brother of one of my Afghan friends, and with his gelled hair, designer jeans, leather jacket, and hip sunglasses, he could have easily passed as an American teenager. He was intimately familiar with the roads that connected Kabul with the Bagram Air Base, many of which remain somewhat perilous.

Noorrullah gingerly navigated Kabul's busy streets as I tried to make conversation. He spoke English very well, which had helped him secure work on Bagram with Kellogg, Brown & Root, a US construction and engineering company that was once a subsidiary of Halliburton. Noorrullah told me that the pay was decent, but travel to and from the base meant a two-hour commute each day. We climbed a wide expanse of snow-covered mountains. The highway narrowed and Noorrullah decelerated, skirting small fruit stands and markets on either side of the road. He then veered right and sped up rapidly, bottoming out the car as he braked hard, dipped into a deep pothole, then sped onward.

"Is there a problem?" I asked, wondering if this constituted normal driving in Afghanistan.

"There are many bandits on this road," he replied.

Noorrullah pointed to a burned-out truck by the side of the road. That was where US forces attacked a group of Taliban as they tried to escape from Kabul during the first wave of attacks in late 2001, he said. Talk of the Taliban led Noorrullah to remember a good friend who also worked for American contractors. It was about a year ago, he said, that the Taliban abducted his friend and decapitated him.

"I've seen the video," Noorrullah said, referring to the tape the abductors released. He shook his head in disgust. Like many Afghans, he was weary of the war and frustrated by its slow successes, and made it clear to me how much he wanted to leave Afghanistan.

"Anywhere overseas," he said. "Maybe Europe." Yet he seemed conflicted about the prospect of departing. Despite his newfound American dress and swagger, Noorrullah was still irrevocably connected to Afghanistan and had very close family in Kabul. If his country could find peace and normality, he and his friends might not be so eager to abandon their homeland, he explained.

We finally arrived in Bagram, roughly forty miles north of Kabul, and were slowed by the traffic and pedestrians crowding its main road. Noorrullah turned into a parking lot, got out of the car, and straightened his jeans. I threw my black shawl-like *patu* around my shoulders and joked that I was the Afghan and he was the American.

Afghans guarded the first of Bagram's gates, while the second one had American sentries. The US soldiers in the second station requested IDs and questioned us about why we were there. I told them I was meeting an American on the base who worked for a private contractor.

Torin Nelson and I had traded occasional emails and phone messages for about a year before we met in Afghanistan. Nelson had served as a military interrogator in Europe before September 11, then had first-hand experience at Guantanamo and Abu Ghraib prison in Iraq. But his work in Iraq had badly damaged his career. Nelson explained he had been through a lot after the fallout from the revelations of torture at Abu Ghraib, in which he had played a part, and was skittish about any further media attention. His concerns were well founded: three years after the scandal broke, he still had difficulty securing work as an interrogator. When we met, he wasn't even engaged in military training or analysis—he was working in Bagram's post office.

He had to proceed with caution, he said, if he was to have any chance of climbing out of his predicament.

"Let me think it over and get back to you," said Nelson.

Our meeting lasted less than an hour and didn't include an interview. We shook hands and parted. Nelson turned and walked back to Bagram's post office, and Noorrullah drove me back to Kabul. I had to wait for Nelson's answer.

Three days passed before I returned to Helmand province. Vice President Dick Cheney made an unscheduled, unannounced visit to the Bagram Air Base on February 27, 2007. But the Taliban had learned of his presence, and a suicide bomber struck the outer perimeter of Bagram's first gate. Cheney was safely sitting in his room inside the base, but the explosion killed twenty-three people.[1] The bomb went off just where Nelson and I had been talking three days earlier. Exactly one month later, a suicide bomber blew himself up near where I was working in Helmand, killing himself and five policemen.

Thankfully, I never fell victim to any attacks during my stay in Afghanistan. But the violence that flared up around me demonstrated how urgently the Afghan government, the US, and its NATO allies needed capable forces and quality intelligence to combat the Taliban and al Qaeda.

I thought about Torin Nelson. Here was an experienced interrogator who ended up working in a mailroom. How did this come to pass?

By July 2007, both Nelson and I had returned from Afghanistan, but he was already getting ready for another job in Bagram, so I scrambled to meet him at Fort Benning, Georgia. We met at the base's shopping mall and spent several dinners together unpacking his story.

Nelson had attended the University of Utah but dropped out shortly after his father died in 1988. He took up odd jobs, traveled across the country with friends, and roamed around the Pacific Northwest. After he got back to Salt Lake City, he saw a TV military recruiting ad showing US forces rappelling from helicopters, foraging through the woods, and engaging in heroic feats. He went to an Army recruiter's office the next morning, and said that he was interested in military intelligence work. The recruiters showed him videotapes of the various kinds of military intelligence jobs they offered, including interrogation.

"And it just clicked," said Nelson.

He was twenty-three years old at the time and already proficient in German. The recruiter suggested that he take a language proficiency test. If he did well on the aptitude test, he could move to Monterey, California, live on the beach, and learn a foreign language while he was getting paid. Nelson was sold.

In 1993, Nelson began a year-long course in Russian at the Defense Language Institute. Two years earlier, the Soviet Union had broken up, and US soldiers were now able to study in Russia. He traveled there in 1994 for a fifty-week course to solidify his proficiency. Afterward, Nelson went to Fort Huachuca in Arizona for interrogation training and was immediately struck by his instructors' professionalism. They described the various psychological approaches that interrogators employed to engage detainees and elicit information from them. They also reinforced the Law of War and the Geneva Conventions, which every soldier had to abide by.

Huachuca's instructors showed trainees gruesome slides of US troops who had used field telephones to electrocute their Vietnamese prisoners. Instructors sternly warned them that the soldiers who were involved in such torture were identified and severely prosecuted.

"They were showing it as an example of people who weren't interrogators," said Nelson. "The assumption was that *real* interrogators don't do that."

He learned the sixteen standard approaches used by Army interrogators. Some went by shorthand names like "Love of Family," "We Know All," and "Mutt and Jeff"—commonly known as "Good Cop, Bad Cop." Instructors explained that the various techniques should be used to fit the profile of the person being interrogated. And the instructors emphasized common sense: Ask direct questions. Remember, soldiers that have just been captured are shocked from being pulled off the battlefield. They're often disoriented and frightened, so they're especially happy when they're getting treated well, and good treatment might warm them up to talking with you, so always try that.

"We were always told, 'Look, we're just teaching you enough to be able to have you pass the test … Don't think that you're by any means anywhere close to being an actual real interrogator just because you went to a schoolhouse,' " recalled Nelson.

More than anything else, Nelson said, his skills truly developed while he was working with seasoned interrogators in the field. Most of his early work remains classified, he said, but he openly described how his mentors prepared for and executed interrogations. They were carrying out intelligence operations in Eastern Europe during the early 1990s, and diligently studied the region and its people. "They intimately knew that area, and so I was able to really learn that cultural awareness was very crucial," said Nelson. "I learned about confidence *through* cultural awareness. I just started to read books like crazy, watching movies, [local] television programs."

Even though the Cold War and the war on terror are vastly different, Nelson insisted that there are "certain similarities." For instance, understanding the people who are being questioned—their history, language, and cultural nuances—enabled interrogators to establish a rapport.

"You really need to know who your enemy is first, before you go into the [interrogation] booth," he said.

Nelson also observed that experienced interrogators often obtained the best information just through casual conversation. "You can definitely convey an attitude or thought in such a way that the guy really has no clue what you're after," he said. "And basically, [the detainee thinks,] 'I know this guy is interrogating me, but I don't think I gave him any information.' "

Nelson worked as an Army interrogator from 1996 to 1997, as part of a Force Protection Team that was tasked with gathering information for peacekeeping operations in Bosnia. When his assignment ended, he joined the National Guard, and taught interrogation to members of his guard unit in Salt Lake City. Nelson also helped translate documents related to American prisoners of war and soldiers missing in action during both world wars. In the course of his work, he stumbled upon a book about interrogation work during World War II. He read it cover to cover, and the book had a big impact on him. It articulated precisely what he intuitively understood already.

The book profiled a World War II veteran whose models greatly influenced professional interrogators. He wasn't an American or with the Allied Forces, but was actually a German Luftwaffe (Air Force) officer named Hanns-Joachim Gottlob Scharff, commonly known as Hanns Scharff.

I heard many other interrogators reference Scharff, who has been called a "master interrogator," and they pointed to his approach as a paragon of effective interrogation.

"Scharff and his colleagues, his cohorts, his mentors, did things so well," said Nelson. "And it's overlooked because the stereotypical German intelligence officer that you see in the movies is portrayed as being in the dark room with the dark seat, smoking, and brandishing something like his gun and flailing it until you tell him what he wants to hear."

The way in which Scharff conducted his interrogations couldn't have been more different.

Scharff told the people working under him, "There are but a few of us who have not yet felt the burden of this war. In almost every family somebody was wounded or lost or killed, but never let a prisoner of war feel it!"[2]

In the introduction of Raymond F. Toliver's book *The Interrogator: The Story of Hans Joachim Scharff*, a friend of Scharff's wrote, "He methodically and deliberately treated his prisoners with dignity. Nevertheless, while so doing, he did not neglect the wartime purpose of the interrogator's task."

By some accounts, Scharff didn't even raise his voice while questioning prisoners. His adversaries admitted that Scharff enjoyed tremendous success by gently gleaning information from his captives, and said he never used physical coercion to get it.

On the surface, using Scharff's methods seemed to be a tall order in the heat of battle. But it was also very effective. Because of his reputation, the US Air Force invited Scharff to the US to lecture about his techniques after World War II.

What was Scharff's formula for success? In short, it involved a combination of language proficiency; relaxed, casual conversation over the course of several weeks if time permitted; and above all other things, empathy.

On a clear autumn morning in 2001, Nelson dropped his wife off at work. He was listening to National Public Radio as he drove home when an abrupt news bulletin announced that a plane had hit the first tower of the World Trade Center.

Back at home watching television, he saw the second plane crash into the south tower and absorbed the rest of the day's news. After a while, Nelson went outside to sit on his front porch, and looked up at the sky. His house was just under an approach path for planes landing at Salt Lake City International Airport. The silence was unsettling.

"It was just shocking," he recalled. "There were no contrails in the sky, no sound of planes flying overhead. Just quiet, very quiet. And then I was pretty much certain that I would be called up not long after that."

Nelson's National Guard unit was activated in late 2001. He was told that he was going to Afghanistan as an alternate on an interrogation team. Everyone else from his unit was deployed, but he had to stay behind and wait. A few months later, in the summer of 2002, he got the call: he was being sent to Guantanamo Bay.

During that time, Guantanamo's detention and interrogation program was still being developed. Interrogators had their hands full. Nelson estimates that they worked six days a week for about ten to twelve hours a day.

He was responsible for roughly forty detainees and devoted most of his time to preparation. Nelson had a methodical, organized approach.

He spent one or two days reviewing a detainee's capture notes and reading previous reports. He diligently combed through every detail that he could find about the prisoner, including the location and circumstances of his arrest, the people he was captured with, and the "pocket litter"—the items found on him at the time of capture. After sifting through all of this information, Nelson developed a strategy and compiled a list of pertinent questions. Finally, he met the detainee with an interpreter to do an initial assessment, and to see whether the prisoner matched the profile that Nelson had created. Then he left the interrogation booth and reviewed his observations.

Nelson only started to seriously interrogate a detainee after he had completed every step of this process. He typically questioned detainees for no more than a half hour to two hours a day.

"Anything more than two hours and the conversation starts to bog down," he said. If interrogations were successful, he wrote reports and sent them on to command.

"We were getting good information—especially at first," said Nelson. "I personally knew a number of interrogators who were getting excellent information that was very important."

By late 2002, Nelson's tour at Guantanamo was winding down. He and his colleagues told me they had produced quality intelligence through their interrogations, but they also knew that others weren't satisfied with some of the reports they had filed.

"We were continuing to get good information," said Nelson. "Unfortunately, it wasn't the type of information people were looking for, like linking al Qaeda with Saddam Hussein and weapons of mass destruction in Iraq, and chemical weapons training for Saddam's agents … or an Al Qaeda guy [connected to] Iraqi agents. And so people were saying, 'It's not good intelligence.' "

Interrogation policies and Guantanamo's stewardship shifted in late 2002; Major General Geoffrey D. Miller became the new base commander, replacing Major General Michael Dunlavey.

According to those who worked at Guantanamo during the change in leadership, the atmosphere at the base changed noticeably as soon as Miller took command. Order and discipline were sternly enforced. Troops were instructed to say "Honor bound, defend freedom" to each other whenever they exchanged a salute.

Miller had a background in artillery but lacked experience in intelligence or interrogation.[3] When he arrived at Guantanamo, he said he had "never before" witnessed an interrogation.[4]

Soon after Miller's arrival, he reorganized the base's structure and the joint task forces that were charged with intelligence operations. And, like some others involved with Guantanamo's operations, Miller seemed to believe in an unconventional approach to dealing with the base's "enemy combatants."

"I think of Guantanamo as the interrogation battle lab in the war against terror," Miller boasted to a journalist.[5] His attitude toward interrogation seemed to echo what other military and political figures had expressed.

Nelson was on his way out of Guantanamo before Miller started experimenting in his "battle lab." But he sensed what was looming. "We didn't need to experiment," said Nelson. "If I had stayed there longer, I think my experience, my memory of GTMO, probably wouldn't have been as good."

His experience also challenged certain stock conceptions about Guantanamo. Nelson worked on Joint Task Force 170 (JTF-170)—the task force assigned to collect actionable intelligence (i.e., vital information about attacks and tactics)—from August 2002 to late February 2003. In fact, he worked at Guantanamo during the period in which select interrogators received lessons from Survival, Evasion, Resistance and Escape (SERE) instructors on techniques, and when others had been implicated in abuse and torture. Nelson had favorable impressions of Dunlavey as "just a really nice guy [who was] genuinely concerned [about] the safety of the troops and … the integrity of the mission," while he described Miller as "General Patton on steroids." Nelson's account illustrated the perils of portraying particular people and units simplistically in order to understand their role and accountability. Yet many news stories have taken that approach to explaining detainee abuse and have assigned blame accordingly—that is, through attributing Abu Ghraib torture chiefly to Army reservists Lynndie England and Charles Graner, the so-called "few bad apples."

Nelson continued as an interrogator during the war on terror, and he began to realize how expectations, in Guantanamo and elsewhere in other war theaters, affected the work he was doing.

"It's something that I saw over and over again with less experienced interrogators," he said. Nelson noticed how many of them went into interrogation booths "and right away they think of it as a tactical environment where they've only got the guy for forty-eight hours, and so they've got to get on detainees right away. They don't have time to do any of that unnecessary planning and prep with going through all the documents and checking all the records and crosschecking to see if there were any affiliations to the people that we already have in custody or captured previously."

Nelson saw another disturbing pattern of behavior that he felt was probably fostered by TV and movies: interrogators kept on seeking confessions.

Although it might seem counterintuitive, confessions can be very deceptive. A detainee's admissions can mislead interrogators into believing they have the right suspect and are pursuing the right line of questioning, even if they're completely off course.

"They figure if the guy confesses to actually supporting al Qaeda or the Taliban … then that means that the person is actually broken, that they can just extract all the information they want to from him," said Nelson.

I had met other military interrogators who likewise worried that these ideas about extracted confessions became especially problematic in counterinsurgency wars, where suspects' identities are uncertain. Colonel Steven Kleinman was one such interrogator; he worked for the Air Force for many years and provided congressional testimony about the problematic expectations of interrogation. Kleinman often explained that interrogators actually try to work counterintuitively by *not* seeking a confession, even hearing refutations, in order to expand their understanding of a situation beyond what they already know. "Confession is not the Holy Grail that it is in law enforcement," said Kleinman. "Speaking specifically from an intelligence perspective, in really very few cases would a confession be really of any value. For the most part, I'm more interested in what the person knows through direct access— what they've seen, what they've heard, what they know to be true. And then, later on, I [might] find out exactly … their involvement with something."

"You could have a guy who never admits to doing anything against American forces, but still gives a lot of … valuable information," Nelson said.

Yet not every detainee talks. Sometimes particular detainees would shut down and refuse to cooperate with interrogators. "That was their way of trying to show you who was boss," said Nelson.

But interrogators saw such behavior as a challenge and puzzled over how best to get uncooperative detainees to respond. "I tried to get them talking about whatever they wanted to talk about," said Nelson, "and then steer or manipulate the conversation to … elicit some information."

He would introduce topics like travel, history, Koranic and Biblical ideas.

"They would tell me about Mohammed, all these sorts of things," he recalled. "Sometimes one of those little things would trigger a response."

As for the most defiant detainees who clammed up, Nelson had a more straightforward approach. "Generally I wouldn't even bother with those guys," he said. "I'd go back to people I'm feeling closer to, and [who were] being productive at that time."

Since individuals involved in a terrorist organization don't work in isolation from one another, interrogators simply pursued leads from those who were more forthcoming.

"There is a cooperative association between like-minded individuals who are working together for some sort of purpose," said Nelson, explaining that this applied even to "high-value" detainees—that is, senior al Qaeda leaders who had been questioned in secret CIA facilities. If one member of the group didn't cooperate, interrogators often just moved on to someone else who would.

"It's like going to a bar and trying to pick up a girl," explained Nelson. "If you think that there's only one girl that you can pick up, and think she's not going to like you, chances are you're pretty much going to strike out every time you go to the bar. But if you realize that, 'Hey, there's this one girl that I tried and she didn't really respond. I'll just go on to the next one.' "

After Nelson's tour in Guantanamo ended, he linked up with a military intelligence brigade and flew to Kuwait in April 2003 to prepare for the Iraq war. But after two and half months of waiting, their commander rotated the unit back to the States.

Nelson returned home to Salt Lake City, where he struggled to find work. He ended up at a truck dealership, handling business-to-business transactions.

"It was a far cry from interrogations," he said.

Around that time, a friend from Guantanamo contacted him. Nelson's friend heard that private military contractors were desperately trying to fill slots for interrogators and other military specialists to go to Iraq.

Nelson decided to look into it and was surprised by what he found. "I just realized, 'Wow, this opens up a whole new world to me,' " he said. "I've been doing it for years in uniform, but as a civilian you get paid more, you get a lot more respect [and] you also get to actually do the job!"

In October 2003, he signed on with Consolidated Analysis Centers, Inc. (commonly known as CACI), a defense contractor that had been hired to do intelligence work for the US military in Iraq. Once he was hired, CACI dispatched him to Iraq. He was to face one of his most challenging career assignments: working at Abu Ghraib prison.

To Nelson, the prison seemed like a troubling environment right from the start. The main compound had been heavily attacked with mortar fire just before he arrived, claiming the lives of both soldiers and detainees. CACI's administrative office appeared to be in complete disarray. Intelligence workers had trouble getting basic information on prisoners before they interrogated them.

"There was a great deal of confusion on the part of almost everyone involved; [nobody] knew who they were working for and what the overall mission was," Nelson recalled. Of military commanders, he said, "They were really focused on just going after Saddam Hussein's people, and they thought that was the entirety of the insurgency. They weren't looking at all the other factors."

He and other contractors worked seven days straight, fifteen or more hours a day, in a dangerous and disorderly work environment. Nelson observed that his peers' work experience and skills were uneven, and those disparities, along with the other challenges they faced, manifested themselves in ways that he had never before seen.

During one of his first meetings with Abu Ghraib's interrogators, Nelson batted around ideas on strategy and described some of his experiences at Guantanamo. But the room fell silent, and some of his colleagues rolled their eyes. "Did I say something wrong?" he asked.

They told him that other veterans of Guantanamo came through the base months earlier, dressing down the staff and dictating how their system should be revamped. The Abu Ghraib staff resented it. The friction between competing interrogators worried Nelson, and he soon saw other troubling things. At first, it was just the sheer number of detainees. Nelson and his colleagues felt that US forces took a scattershot approach to hauling in Iraqis, and picked up suspects on thin or questionable evidence. Some interrogators grew impatient, and seemed frustrated with sorting out detainees and with the slow progress of gathering intelligence. During meals and casual meetings, Nelson overheard some of them venting and discussing the ways they remedied their problems.

"It was the end of December or beginning of January when I really started to get suspicious about it," said Nelson. "They were talking about other interrogations [and] the techniques that they were using."

In January 2004, Nelson interrogated an Iraqi general who "was actually very nice, very cooperative, and very talkative all the time." The general mentioned an earlier interrogation session with a different American.

"He described this episode where he was accosted by the interrogator, [and] showed me a bruise on his arm," said Nelson. The bruise was over six inches long. Nelson also noticed that his detainee had a bump on his forehead just above his left eye, and the general explained that it was caused by being grabbed and thrown against a wall.

Nelson realized that some detainees exaggerated stories about abuse in order to gain sympathy. So he consulted a military intelligence analyst whom he worked with at the prison. "Do you know anything about this?" he asked.

The analyst did. He had worked as a guard one day when the prison was short-staffed, and personally witnessed interrogators mistreating detainees.

"[He] saw a contract interrogator throw a sixty-plus-year-old Iraqi general from the back of either a truck or a Humvee," said Nelson. "The Iraqi general was bound with cuffs and leg irons and had a sandbag over his head, so he could not save himself or see what was coming. Then the contract interrogator grabbed the detainee by the left arm and dragged him across a field of gravel … to the interrogation booth, where he then threw the old man into the booth and disappeared from view."

Nelson was shocked and distressed. He wondered how pervasive such treatment was.

At Abu Ghraib's offices, Nelson combed through interrogators' files to learn how detainees were being mistreated.

"I was going through the report work that these other interrogators had been writing up, following their interrogations to see if there were any leads or clues as to what they were doing," he said.

Nelson read one report in which an interrogator described an evasive detainee—"I don't believe that this guy is telling the truth," the report stated. According to this document, the prisoner was put in solitary confinement for thirty days. Nelson came across records of other questionable acts. For example, he read about one young interrogator who argued that all the prisoners had to be broken, and a female interrogator who tried to humiliate a prisoner sexually by forcing him to strip.

Nelson found other interrogators at Abu Ghraib who were troubled by the abuses and corroborated the detainees' accounts. It became clear that a pattern was emerging in Abu Ghraib, and Nelson felt compelled to report it. At that time, he heard that an Army general named Antonio Taguba had been summoned to investigate some of the abuses at the prison. Investigators asked all prison staff to come forward with anything that they saw or heard about. Most declined. But Nelson agreed to talk.

He met with General Taguba's investigators for two hours on January 21, 2004, and provided them with a sworn statement about the abuses he had learned of. Because the investigators had promised confidentiality, Nelson felt at liberty to share the information he had. But somehow word spread about his testimony.

One morning, Nelson bumped into a friend on his way to the mess hall for breakfast.

"Hey, what's going on?" he asked. But the colleague completely ignored him and walked on. Nelson was puzzled but continued toward the mess hall. Along the way he ran into another friend, who pulled him aside. "What's the deal?" he asked Nelson. "Did you rat on these guys? That's what everybody is talking about."

Nelson instantly knew it meant trouble and tried to play dumb. "What are you talking about?" he replied.

"Well, a lot of people are upset about it and are saying a lot of harsh things about you."

Later that day, Nelson encountered one of the interrogators he had told the investigators about. "You better watch your back around me," he said. "You're a dead man to me."

The interrogator turned his back and walked away.

Nelson's remaining friends told him that colleagues had leveled threats against him as well. "I didn't really know how legitimate they were," he said. "It just became a really hostile working environment."

One of Nelson's friends and colleagues, Sammy Villela, described how others behaved after Nelson met with CID investigators. "Once the word got out that he had talked to CID," said Villela, "there were people that said, 'Oh, that guy is a rat … He is talking to CID about all the shit that he thinks he knows about.' I never heard anyone say, 'He needs to watch his back, somebody's going to take him down,' anything like that … But he was definitely a black sheep. I mean he was eating alone. He [really] was on his own."

Nelson quit and quickly left the country.

Shortly after his stint at Abu Ghraib, Nelson accepted a job in Afghanistan helping special operations forces secure proper translation and other resources with a contractor known as Worldwide Language Resources.

"I left Abu G and I never wanted to mention the word Abu G again," he said. "I'd done my service, I'd gotten burned … I just wanted to continue with my life and call it good."

Then, in April 2004, the Abu Ghraib photos splashed across the news. Taguba's report became public knowledge, and an unredacted version of the report was released on the Internet. It contained Nelson's statement and cited some of the personnel he reported on. But Nelson wasn't aware of this for days, until his sister emailed him and asked, "What's going on? Why are you mentioned in this report?" His email inbox was soon flooded with media requests for interviews.

"I was very surprised," said Nelson. "My involvement got blown out of proportion. I was a very small piece of the overall investigation."

Nelson feared the publicity would endanger his current job in Afghanistan. "I loved my job and I was doing real good," said Nelson. "Everybody liked me, and I would have stayed there for years … if the freaking Taguba report hadn't been put out on the Internet."

He worried that his association with the Taguba report could compromise the secrecy of his mission. His employers also realized that the constant interview requests from news organizations did draw too much attention, and eventually they asked Nelson to leave Afghanistan. He complied. "But if I hadn't quit, they probably would have fired me," said Nelson.

After he left his job in Afghanistan, his friends were supportive and tried to help him secure work with other military contractors. David R. Irvine, a retired Army brigadier general and former interrogation instructor, wrote a letter of recommendation for Nelson: "If I were commanding an interrogation unit, he is exactly the person I would want as a supervisor and mentor for every interrogator assigned to that unit. I have absolute confidence that he would give me unvarnished information, that he would set and maintain a rigorous standard of lawful operation for himself and those he would direct."[6]

Irvine's recommendation helped, but only fleetingly, it seemed.

On October 1, 2005, Nelson arrived at the airport in Bishkek, Kyrgyzstan, and was scheduled to fly on to Afghanistan to work as an interrogator for another private military contractor, SYTEX, Inc. He checked his email as his plane refueled. A message flashed on his screen: "I must inform you that your contract has been terminated by the client. Do not go to Bagram, Afghanistan."

Nelson was stunned.

He replied to the email and asked for an explanation. After flying to Incirlik Air Base in Turkey, Nelson finally heard back from his project manager:

"The decision was based on your association with the high-profile issues surrounding Abu [Ghraib] ... I have expressed concern about employing anyone who was involved in any way with the Abu [Ghraib] incident."

Because of his short stint in Iraq, Nelson found it difficult to secure steady work as an interrogator. "I was hired a couple of times for Afghanistan," he explained. "Since then, I was hired once for Iraq, but then got fired ... [It has] been off and on, back and forth, getting hired, getting fired, getting hired, fired."

Nelson saw a clear pattern: he had been blacklisted because of his association with Abu Ghraib, especially since he volunteered to report on the abuse. Employers told him that there was no blacklisting policy that kept him from work. But his colleagues disagreed.

"That is absolutely true, that impact to his employment," said Sammy Villela. "It's bullshit. I thought he was an effective interrogator. You know he went in there, he used the rapport building. He took a little more time than the others—and he was a little more patient and that's the sign of experience. [H]e was effective and it's a shame ... It is a shame because we do need guys like him."

Villela also faced employment problems because of his association with Abu Ghraib, even though he hadn't been involved in whistleblowing or abuse or implicated in anything controversial. Employers became skittish about hiring him when he admitted being at the prison in 2004.

"And I tell you what, it made me run from interrogations. I'll never do that again," said Villela. "I won't subject myself to that ... just seeing how that you can be guilty by association over an event like that. ... I am still looking for bad guys and trying to keep everybody safe. But in terms of going in a booth and conducting an interrogation as part of [the Department of Defense]. No. Won't do it."

Like other American soldiers and officers I had met, Nelson tried to confront detainee abuse and torture before it became corrosive. He dutifully reported the abuses at Abu Ghraib, just as other US military personnel had done elsewhere in Iraq. But their efforts came at great cost to them personally and sometimes upended their careers. A number of officers and civilian officials had also quit the military after the prisoner abuse scandals during the war on terror, including some of the most prominent figures who spoke out against the way harsh interrogation had been approved in Washington and then used in Guantanamo. Several of them wanted to get jobs in the private sector: Alberto Mora, once the Navy's top lawyer, left the Pentagon to work for Wal-Mart and the Mars candy company, and Dr. Michael Gelles, the chief psychologist for the Naval Criminal Investigative Service, began working at Deloitte Consulting.

Britt Mallow, Mark Fallon, and Tim James, senior members of the Criminal Investigative Task Force, left the military but continued doing security and interrogation work. Even though Mallow and James were proud of their service, including their time at Guantanamo, they could not escape the legacy of the detainee abuse that took place there.

"If you were involved in any detainee operations, you say the word 'detainee,' and the very first word out of everyone else's mouth is, well, 'abuse,' " said Mallow. "I got disgusted with an awful lot of things that took place."

After his retirement from the military, Mallow worked for several national security contract firms. James took a job instructing law enforcement personnel in Kentucky. Part of his curriculum involved teaching interrogation. He tried to impart rapport-building approaches and discourage the temptation to use any kind of coercive interrogation. James taught his students that interrogation involved thorough, dispassionate work—even when working on emotionally charged cases, such as those involving child molestation. He taught many effective ways to question sources and carry out investigations. James also explained the pitfalls of coercive interrogation, and how it actually hampered police work. His students heard him out, and seemed receptive to his lessons. But whenever James mentioned his work at Guantanamo, his students recoiled.

"They look at me to this day [and say], 'Oh, you were one of those people down there abusing people,' " said James. "It just tainted everything that we tried to do."

That attitude seemed to be shared by family and friends, including his mother.

"When I came back from GTMO, she heard of the good things," said James. "She was probably happy with the fact that I've been down there, trying to contribute."

But that changed once the abuses were revealed.

"Now the only thing she knows is what she sees on TV about GTMO and all that," said James. "She doesn't know the difference between the task forces, [and] she's probably wondering what kind of mess I was in. It's just bad."

Nelson attempted to erase that stigma in his own way.

He networked with colleagues for years to set up an organization for fellow intelligence workers. Nelson hoped such an organization would allow them to trade ideas about their work, including approaches to effective, non-coercive interrogation. Their aim was not only to correct the legacy of US torture, but to ensure that US forces could successfully fight against future terrorist attacks.

"You need to instill in the leadership—military and civilian—that we are playing by the rules. These rules are strict [and] they're more effective," said Nelson. "This is just the better way to do it. It may seem hard right now, and it may seem like we're tying our hands behind our back. But in the long run, we're going to win. That's what real leadership by example is."

But leading by example, by using and promoting non-coercive interrogation, was only part of the solution. Nelson maintained that leadership also meant sharply discouraging "harsh techniques," "torture lite," and anything resembling detainee abuse.

"Fifty years from now, how are people going to look at us?" asked Nelson. "We will be painted with this big broad brush, and it will hurt us so severely in the overall war that long-term we'll be taking two steps back for every one step forward."

It reminded me of the images we have retained from the Vietnam war, which were highlighted by Nelson's instructors at Fort Huachuca as examples of tactical and moral failure.

Even after leaving office, former Bush administration officials boasted that harsh interrogations saved American lives—without offering concrete, verifiable examples to support such claims. Yet the use of torture has created an abundance of images that hurt the standing of the US in the eyes of the world and has frequently sabotaged efforts to defend against terrorism.[7]

Meanwhile, the fallout from torture during the war on terror continues, both overseas and at home.

Chapter 9:
Homecoming

O N MARCH 15, 2008, I attended a large gathering of veterans in the Washington, DC, area. There I met Don Dzagulones, an Army interrogator who served in the Vietnam war. Because of his background, I thought Dzagulones might have some special insight into US experiences with interrogation and torture—both during the Vietnam war as well as the war on terror.

Dzagulones had a normal upbringing: his family was Polish Catholic, he hailed from Detroit, and his father was a World War II veteran. As a draftee, he was selected to undergo specialized interrogation training for conventional warfare in Fort Meade, Maryland. After Dzagulones arrived in Vietnam in January 1969, he quickly realized that interrogations were managed haphazardly in the field.

He was sent to Vietnam as part of the American Division's 11th Infantry Brigade—the same brigade that was involved in the My Lai massacre one year before Dzagulones's arrival. Because he worked as an interrogator, Dzagulones wasn't personally involved in bloody combat operations. He did, however, see fellow soldiers and officers routinely employ extreme violence. In fact, during one of the first interrogations that he witnessed, Dzagulones saw mid-level officers poking a prisoner's wounds while medical staff stood in the background. And he observed how MPs and officers looked the other way when interrogators abused prisoners. It seemed to signal to Dzagulones that such abuse was permissible, even encouraged at times.

Interrogators didn't employ a considered strategy or use a standardized set of coercive techniques.

"A lot of what we did was trial-and-error experiment—it was nothing formalized," he said. "I did a lot of experimentation."

Sometimes troops beat their prisoners, and even asked MPs to help rough them up. At times, they dehydrated prisoners by feeding them salty crackers and peanut butter while withholding water. Troops often hooded detainees as a way of "keeping them off balance, keeping them disoriented so they're more likely to break down and talk," said Dzagulones.

Once Dzagulones added an extra dimension to that disorientation: he hooded detainees and loaded them onto a helicopter, took them on a half-hour flight, landed at the very same base, and told them they were on American soil. Many of their Vietnamese prisoners were poor, uneducated rural villagers who didn't know much about the US, and so they believed their captors. And they quivered with fear.

Yet Dzagulones's interrogations rarely produced vital information, and he seldom found detainees who had actionable intelligence. But he would willingly ratchet up the pressure if he suspected that one of them had any information about where American prisoners of war were being held by the Viet Cong.

"There's no limit to what I would do," he said. "I would've gone to the ends of earth to gain information and get those guys out."

Once he had a suspect who he believed actually possessed such information. When soldiers patted down the prisoner, Dzagulones saw that he had a razor blade taped to the inside of his leg. It seemed to prove that he was a Viet Cong sympathizer who was prepared for enemy capture. The prisoner refused to talk. And so, Dzagulones kept his prisoner dehydrated, and had MPs prevent him from getting any sleep. Then he turned to other techniques.

Dzagulones recalled how other interrogators casually discussed the techniques they had used in the field: sometimes they put bamboo slivers up detainees' fingernails and used the power generated by field telephones to electrocute prisoners.

"Ideas about torture come from folklore, oral tradition, and experimentation," explained Dzagulones. And he, too, replicated the techniques he learned from such sources. Even though he interrogated the Vietnamese detainee for three days, and increased the electrical voltage during several sessions, he still wasn't able to elicit any information from him.

"The ends do not justify the means by any stretch," he said. "But it's all your sense of perception."

I asked Dzagulones if he engaged in torture. No, he replied. "It's that fine line between coercion and torture. Maybe that's just a rationalization so that I could live with what was going on."

Dzagulones eventually tired of abusing prisoners in Vietnam, and during the end of his tour he refused to do any more interrogations. It was even tougher for him to reckon with what he had done when he returned home to Detroit.

"I didn't go out during the day, I walked around at night … solitary walks, hours and hours at night," said Dzagulones. "That was my re-adjustment coming home."

He bounced from job to job, abused drugs, and felt he led "a pretty meaningless existence." Dzagulones's friends thought he might channel his feelings about the war through local political actions, and invited him to a gathering at Detroit's Old Mariners' Church. The meeting turned out to be an antiwar teach-in where fellow veterans openly described some of the everyday violence that occurred in Vietnam, including bombing hamlets with napalm and abusing Vietnamese civilians. At first, Dzagulones was stunned to hear the public outcry.

"All of a sudden, it's an offense against humanity," he said. "This is shit that you live with for a year and it becomes routine—it's part of your life. You come back to the world, and it's criminal. So where does that put you?"

Dzagulones was forced to reflect on that question and measure his own culpability.

"That's one of the things you have to resolve for yourself individu-ally," he mused. "You have to determine to what degree you're responsible for these things."

But not everyone was traumatized by the same experiences or felt compelled to reflect on what they had done in Vietnam.

"I've met a lot of guys who were totally unaffected," said Dzagulones. "I can't understand how anyone could've gone through that experience without being affected … It diminishes your humanity, and I'm trying to atone."

In 1971, one of Dzagulones's former officers approached him about public tribunals that Vietnam veterans were putting together. They called it "Winter Soldier." Veterans were stepping forward to talk about what they had done. Many felt that ordinary troops were taking the fall for widespread US abuses, and often referenced the case of Lieutenant William Calley, the Army officer found guilty of ordering the My Lai massacre. Even Dzagulones said that My Lai, "while extreme, was not exceptional." Calley's case compelled Dzagulones to publicly testify about prisoner abuse; he wanted to help expose the pervasiveness of such violence in Vietnam, and to reckon with how he had contributed to it. Still, Dzagulones emphasized that high-level political and military officials were, by extension, also responsible. "It goes all the way up the chain of command," he insisted.

Yet Dzagulones still grappled with his personal culpability; he never admitted to using "torture," though he referred to himself as a "war criminal."

"When you're attacked, you have to respond," he said. "But other circumstances, like prisoner abuse for example, you have a choice … I think you're probably more affected by wanton acts of violence than responding to violence."

He didn't shy away from his own involvement in those acts of violence, but he pointed to the situation that he and fellow soldiers had been placed in, and how it affected them long after the war.

"My concern at this point in my life, being sixty years old, is that future generations don't view me as being some kind of crazy monster— somebody that was out of hand," he said. "I was part of the machine, part of the process. I often wonder about people I was with, fellow interrogators, where they are emotionally and mentally. I'd imagine they're in the same place I am—except they're not vocal about it."

Dzagulones saw the current generation of US soldiers being caught up in "part of the machine, part of the process" and helped stand up for them. When I first met him in March 2008, he and his son were volunteering at another Winter Soldier event, this one sponsored by Iraq Veterans Against the War (IVAW).

Dzagulones and his son, Adam (who had not served in the military), explained that they were there to "honor the warrior not the war." Together, over the course of three days, they listened to dozens of veterans deliver emotional testimony about their experiences. The wars in Afghanistan and Iraq were surely different from Vietnam—their purposes, peoples, and military strategies were markedly dissimilar—as were the veterans' testimonies. Yet young and old veterans saw parallel experiences: both felt betrayed by government policies, were remorseful about the abuses that occurred in combat, and reflected on the legacy of their experiences—both on soldiers and their victims.

"I was on the verge of tears all the time," remembered Dzagulones. "It was about hearing that tremendous pain being experienced again. All of those kids were my sons … There's just a sadness—a sadness that won't go away. It's going to be a sadness that people are going to carry throughout their whole, entire life."

Even though Dzagulones's experiences were rooted in Vietnam, his story seemed to mirror similar patterns found in the war on terror. In Vietnam, Dzagulones found that abuse wasn't necessarily a product of top-down policy decisions, but was facilitated by the absence of leadership when commanders simply looked the other way. And yet, soldiers like Calley took the blame while senior officials were never held accountable. Dzagulones and fellow veterans examined their role in abusive violence as they encountered media coverage, movies, and public discussions by fellow veterans of what they had done. Over time, they began to realize how they were haunted by their involvement in prisoner abuse and torture.

"When I think about Vietnam, sure we were shelled many times, and I experienced terror many times. That's not what bothers me," said Dzagulones. "It's being put in a position where you have a disproportionate amount of power. How you employ that or don't employ it is what you have to come to grips with as you age [and] face the end of the line."

Over several years of reporting, I was able to piece together what happened to Sergeant Adam Gray and those he served with in Battalion 1-68. They explained how their mission changed over time, how they went from being tankers to serving as troops who performed raids and oversaw detentions. They confirmed many of the abuses that Adam had revealed to his mother, Cindy Chavez, and further described the circumstances that led them to abuse and torture detainees.

Since Adam's death, his mother has fought her own kind of battle overcoming and understanding her son's demise. Cindy maintains that it is a mistake to talk about closure. The tragedy is now simply a part of her.

"That doesn't go away—that's life altering," she said. "You will never be that same human being ever again. Ever."

That indelible experience profoundly changed her personal outlook. "It makes you smarter as much as age does," said Cindy. "You're wiser. You're more compassionate to what's going on around you."

Cindy and Roy never want to forget their family tragedy, even if it were possible. Over holidays, they include Adam's name on presents and cards that they give to friends and family. Roy puts out a special Christmas tree each year that memorializes Adam. His name is engraved on the license plates of Roy's truck, along with stickers that read:

"Sergeant Adam James Gray—The Bomber. You're our hero—3/20/80–8/20/04."

"You never want to forget … when it's in your blood and heart, when you love someone," said Roy.

At their home in Tehachapi, California, Adam's room remains untouched. Army photos, medals, and decorations festoon a tall wooden dresser, and a commendation letter signed by President Bush hangs on a wall.

Roy maintains that he and Cindy were never very political, but whenever they "pick up the paper [and] I see a soldier die, it breaks my heart. I see parents and they don't even know the tip of the iceberg."

The war encroaches on their lives whenever they hear about friends and relatives whose children are in Iraq and Afghanistan, and whenever their hometown is draped in flags during national holidays. Questions about Adam continue to plague Cindy. She and Roy puzzle over how his death was ruled "accidental" by military investigators, even though they better understand why he turned to alcohol and drugs to escape his pain.

"What do you do when your life sucks? You cope … whatever you can do to get through the problem," said Roy. "We're men. We're supposed to be tough. Then we find a breaking point. In that case, accidents happen. I don't think Adam had a death wish."

Cindy still wonders why the military didn't do more to intervene with Adam after his first suicide attempt three weeks before his death, and why they didn't inquire further into what had troubled him so much in Iraq. Her son had told her about the shooting incident that claimed a child's life and the detainee abuse he participated in. But she never fathomed how deeply troubled he was. She had only an incomplete sense of what happened to her son and others in his unit. For Cindy, the mysteries of Adam's death can be traced back to Iraq. Her feelings are echoed in the pages of the military's psychological autopsy and are shared with many of Adam's friends and fellow soldiers.

On May 28, 2008, I returned to Tehachapi with Michael Montgomery, my co-producer from American Radio Works, to tell her what we had learned from Adam's fellow unit members. Cindy knew that Adam had been thinking a lot about the abuses he committed in the jail at FOB Lion. But she didn't know how pervasive the abuse was and how it affected other troops in his unit.

"Cindy, you know we have spoken to about a dozen of the people in his unit, and it's true about what Adam said about torturing detainees—that did happen," I said. "But it's also true he wasn't the only one. Plenty of guys were doing it in the unit. And it's clear that many of them are deeply troubled because of it."

"I can't even imagine how you couldn't be," she replied. "When Adam was telling me the story and it was graphic … I [said,] 'I can't even listen to this. It's just too crazy' … How can you bend people's minds like that—it's so insane. And then shoot you back in the States and say, 'Hey, go be a family man.' So many ways of wrong.

"How does one come out of that and become a normal person? They live it and relive it and relive it. To me the government has robbed them blind of a big chunk of their soul because they were instructed to do something that was inhumane. I think that is so wrong."

She paused.

"Does it matter that other guys told us what they did to detainees?" I asked.

"It makes a difference because it's not just Adam," said Cindy. "There are another thousand, ten thousand people carrying that with them—that burden. And that can never be erased. Nobody can do things like that to people without some reflection at some time. You're born with a soul, and then they take it and they restructure it. And that soul is telling you, 'this is wrong.' "

In the course of investigating Adam Gray's life and death, I met several members of Battalion 1-68. Some had served at the jail at FOB Lion; others had been stationed at bases nearby.

Not everyone agreed to speak with me about Adam and Battalion 1-68's involvement in detainee abuse. Some told me they were skittish about revisiting their experience—in part because they feared recriminations by the military, even after they had been discharged. Others declined to talk because they didn't want to stir up painful memories.

Most of the veterans I spoke to who had served in Iraq and Afghanistan said they were traumatized by the war in some way. It was clear that discussing their experiences was difficult for most of them. One veteran granted me a long interview but wouldn't meet with me again afterward. After months of unreturned phone calls, he sent me a text message: "Can't do it. Can't talk about Iraq any more—too painful. Can't …"

Not everyone was traumatized by the same experiences, and different soldiers referenced disparate wartime events. Some said that the greatest source of guilt and anxiety centered on their experience with abusing and torturing detainees. Daniel Keller, one of the tankers with Battalion 1-68, took a kind of comfort in knowing that detainee abuse wasn't uncommon.

"I'm glad that it wasn't just me, that it wasn't isolated," said Keller. "I know that sounds bad but really I'm just happy to know that I'm not crazy. I'm glad to see that when other people get put in a situation where they're around people who might have [abused detainees] that they're just as merciless as I was."

Keller was one of the soldiers I met who felt that his involvement with detainee abuse wounded him irrevocably.

"None of us were like this before," he said. "No one thought about dragging people through concertina wire or beating them or sandbagging them or strangling them or anything like that ... before this."

Keller struggled for years to undo the pain that those experiences had caused. He tried to get help overcoming his post-traumatic stress disorder through a controversial therapy known as Eye Movement Desensitization Reprocessing (EMDR). This therapy involves concentrating on a traumatic experience and verbally describing the memory while a therapist instructs the patient to move his or her eyes from side to side. For Keller, the therapy helped erase certain painful memories. Over time, it was harder for him to remember how he blasted loud music in prisoners' ears, and how detainees desperately gasped for air as he held them down and poured gallons of water into their mouths and noses.

"I can't picture what actually happened," he said, "[but] I can sort of picture other people doing it."

Keller recognized that he wouldn't be able to fully expunge those painful memories and that he had to try to make peace with his past, to whatever extent possible.

"I don't think I'll ever be done coming to terms with it for the rest of my life," he said. "I am just going to learn how to be a better person and live with what I have done."

Not everyone had been able to reconcile themselves to painful wartime memories. Some veterans were reluctant to seek help. Keller was aware that wartime trauma led many Vietnam veterans to suicide, and he saw those same patterns emerge among Iraq war veterans. But he hadn't known any soldier personally who had taken his own life or died of a drug overdose.

"And then all of a sudden, here's a guy that I know doing it," said Keller, referring to Adam Gray. "Someone that I would hang out with, somebody that I would drink with."

Keller and Jonathan Millantz were two of Adam's Army buddies who wanted me to assure his mother that he wasn't the only soldier involved in detainee abuse. They also wanted me to emphasize to Cindy that the experience was a source of shame for them as well. It forced many others in Battalion 1-68 to grapple with the same haunting memories.

"I really have sympathy for his mother and family," said Millantz. "I know what he was going through. You get all that built up inside, all that anger and frustration and all those memories. Hate really is baggage and it will destroy you and it will bring you down ... I can see how that played a major part in his unfortunate death."

Millantz was the first person who told me about Adam Gray. On May 3, 2006, after Millantz learned that I had been reporting on soldiers' stories of Iraq, he phoned me to talk about what had distressed him and others. At first he was cagey about identifying the unit he belonged to and didn't want to name individual soldiers or officers. When we first spoke, Millantz downplayed his involvement in abuse, and said he chiefly monitored detainees' health as a combat medic.

"I don't care if you use my name," he said at the time. "But I'm not going to release any information about anyone else's name or anything like that."

Eventually he decided to share more about Battalion 1-68 and his role in abusing detainees. Millantz sympathized with what Adam went through, and he knew Adam's mother was searching for answers. And so, he urged me to get a better sense of what happened to all of them. It was important to Millantz that I understood that he and his unit weren't rogue soldiers acting out sadistic impulses. He also wanted me to recognize how traumatic the experience had been for them.

"A lot of people look at Adam Gray's story and say people who commit suicide are cowards or they don't have, in the army lingo, 'intestinal fortitude,' 'the hoorah' or whatever," said Millantz. "It's exactly the opposite. Adam was the most gung-ho soldier I ever met in my entire life—the first guy to kick down a door.

"Obviously he suffered deeply from what he saw. He wasn't a coward or a bad guy. He was just a guy who was put in a position ... I think anyone who was put in a position that he was [in] or any of the other soldiers [were in] would have done the same thing."

Millantz stressed, just as Cindy had, that to "expect these guys just to turn off the switches is unrealistic—human beings are not like that."

He referred to Adam's death as a "suicide" and hoped that publicly sharing it would help other veterans who underwent similar experiences. Even though they had very different backgrounds, and sharply divergent opinions on the war and the military, Millantz deeply empathized with Adam.

"I think he hated who he was when he was there," he said. "I think a lot of the problems Adam had [were because] he couldn't deal with what he had done. And I still have trouble with that. It haunts me every day, and it's something I'll never get away from."

I had no idea how prescient those words were for Millantz.

Jonathan Millantz applied for a discharge from the Army because of PTSD and other, physical problems. His medical evaluation showed that "he reported thoughts of hopelessness in regard to ever feeling 'normal' again." In June 2005, the military granted his discharge. But the events in Iraq continued to trouble him well after he returned home, and Millantz kept consuming news about the war. He learned more about how it was planned and executed, and the strategic decisions that claimed so many Iraqi and American lives. He found friends and fellow veterans who shared the same perspective on the war, and together they channeled their anger through antiwar activism. Millantz joined Iraq Veterans Against the War and marched in protests across the country. He told me about attending one large rally in Manhattan where he was out front, heading a parade of protestors, hearing cheers from throngs— and jeers from disapproving passers-by, including fellow veterans.

"A guy from the American Legion came up and called me a traitor," Millantz recalled. "I guess I can understand where he's coming from, but he didn't see the same things that I saw."

Millantz's friends weren't surprised that he took a stand against the war. Many of them believed he was prompted to speak out specifically because of his experiences working in the jail at FOB Lion.

"Jon wanted to speak out against detainee abuse. He had been involved in enough [detainee abuse] where I'm confident to say it had wrecked a significant portion of his life," said Keller. "[That] explains why after he came back he went on such a large personal crusade against it."

After exchanging calls and emails with Millantz for several months, I finally met him at his mother's house in Greensburg, Pennsylvania, on January 2, 2007. He invited me into the living room, where he leaned back in a chair and lit up one cigarette after the other. His eyes were sullen, his face was pale and gaunt. Once again, he was very guarded about what he would discuss. In fact, he didn't want to talk about detainee abuse at all. His mother, Linda Johnson, sat in the adjoining room and quietly smoked cigarettes while Millantz described some of the things that he witnessed in Iraq. After our interview was over, she chided him about revealing what she called "war crimes" and warned that admitting anything else could lead to charges.

His mother later told me what she was thinking: "Oh, you are going to get into so much trouble and this is going to follow you—this is going to stay with you and you might regret this. You sacrificed enough and have been through enough. I don't want to see you ruin the rest of your life."

But Millantz pressed on. He wanted the public to know what happened to him and his unit in Iraq, and how it damaged him and other soldiers.

"Everybody came back with problems," he said. At the time, Millantz also felt lucky that he had the support of family and friends, and was able to handle his post-war stress.

"I consider myself very fortunate," he said. "I have friends [who] committed suicide when [they] got back. I know people who had guns pulled out of their mouth. I know people who can't get out of bed every day without being on fifteen different types of medication [from] the VA."

I didn't expect to hear from Millantz for a while after our interview, considering how guarded he was at the time. But he phoned me three days later, just as I was preparing to leave for a trip to Afghanistan. Millantz sounded distraught. He mumbled incoherently and finally explained that he had just returned from the hospital, where he had been recovering from an overdose—an overdose, he said, that had been brought on by unearthing harrowing memories during our interview.

"You process all this information, you talk about it, you have it all on the back burner and you bring it all to the front," Millantz told me. "You do an interview and it's still out on the front burner ... it's hard to deal with."

I knew that Millantz would revisit disturbing memories during our interview. But I had no idea it would cause him so much suffering and even compel him to attempt suicide. I spent the remaining hours before my flight trying to encourage him to seek help and support. Although Millantz had survived the overdose, he no longer felt more fortunate, and separate from, the veterans he once viewed as being irretrievably damaged. He had, in fact, become one of them.

Millantz and I kept in touch periodically by email while I was overseas. After six months, I returned home. But back in the States, I had constant difficulty trying to reach him. Millantz didn't answer his cell phone for weeks at a time, and his number would often go out of service. Some of his friends told me he had gone off the radar. But he eventually revealed to me the reason for his erratic behavior.

"I got addicted to painkillers and just pretty much ruined my life," he said. "It was painkillers and anything that would give me the euphoric effect that I used to have all the time before I went into the Army ... I think the drugs were just a way to kill the pain."

Millantz dropped out of college and fell into serious debt. Then he developed seizures. Once, he suffered a grand mal seizure while driving and caused a car accident. Not surprisingly, it led to the revocation of his driver's license and seriously curtailed his mobility. Throughout the time we knew each other, he went through dramatic undulations—highs of positive energy followed by spiraling despair—and went in and out of treatment at the local VA hospital. Over the years, he vacillated between withdrawing and reaching out; sometimes he called to check in and update me about his life, then he wouldn't return my calls for months.

I wanted to be sure that Millantz was doing well. I also wanted learn more about what happened to Battalion 1-68 and, by extension, what happened to Adam Gray. But Millantz wasn't in any condition to talk for a long time. Nearly a year and half after our first meeting in Greensburg, he decided he was finally ready to revisit his wartime experiences, and invited me to meet with him in person once again.

"I was reluctant to do this interview," he admitted when we first got together again. "I've been thinking about this for a while because I don't like talking about it. It's very hard, and I had a breakdown last time, afterwards."

But Millantz maintained it was still important for him to unload some of the experiences that he had bottled up for years. I remained concerned about how he would fare after discussing his experiences again, and wanted to be sure he wouldn't suffer another breakdown. He promised he would be fine, and that he'd periodically check in with me and others.

"Actually, I have people I can talk to more, this time," he said.

And so, he continued to share his stories about Iraq with me. He discussed the tension he often faced as a combat medic, helping the wounded and then being called upon to join combat operations. And he kept revisiting how he monitored detainees who were abused and tortured inside of FOB Lion's jail.

"Keeping a person alive while doing these so called 'interrogation techniques' … definitely burns an image in your brain that you'll never forget," he said.

Over time, Millantz cautiously admitted that he wasn't only tending to detainees as a medic but was abusing them as well. He, too, forced detainees to hold heavy boards for hours, and even helped pin them down as fellow troops poured water into their mouths and noses.

"I don't care who you are—if you're drowning you're going to resist, and you're going to fight back," said Millantz. "So we were holding them when this happened."

He said he was wracked by guilt and often agonized over those experiences.

"I was contemplating suicide—I couldn't believe what I did," he said. "It's very tough when you have a conscience that is filled with atrocities [and] you know what you did to people. I went to confession, I went to counseling. I still can't forgive myself for what I did to those poor people … It's been hard over the years coming to terms with what actually happened over there. I don't know if I'll ever have closure."

After our second meeting in Greensburg, I frequently called Millantz and his mother to make sure he didn't unravel and overdose again. He repeatedly assured me that he was fine and had been seeking more support from friends. He insisted that there was something cathartic about talking through his experiences again. Months later, I paid him another visit, and he seemed even better. He had put on weight and looked healthier. Millantz openly told me about the counseling groups he attended, and said he was determined to go back to school. At first, he hoped to become a physician's assistant, but he later decided to study psychology in order to help fellow veterans.

In late 2008, Millantz called to tell me he had suffered another setback: he discovered he had brain lesions caused by a concussion from a roadside bomb in Iraq. He said the lesions caused his seizures and had led to a minor stroke. He feared he would need surgery.

We talked again in late March 2009. Even though Millantz was still struggling with his medical condition, he sounded upbeat and positive, determined to overcome his problems and forge ahead.

"I'm still a soldier and always will be," he said. "I'm soldiering on, and I'm not going to give up."

In May 2009, nearly three years after my first in-person meeting with Millantz, I visited his family and friends in Greensburg. His mother, Linda Johnson, greeted me warmly. She wanted to share happy memories of her son and took out some old photographs that, she felt, showed "the soul of a person who wanted so much to be good and bring happiness."

Johnson shuffled through a stack of pictures showing Millantz as a toddler in their old house, going to the zoo with his family, and playing in their backyard as a small boy.

"We planted garden vegetables," she said, pointing to a photo. "Jonathan, he was so proud of himself ... and he would take the tomatoes to church and give them away. He cried at the end of the season when they all died. I told him, 'They'll come back next year, honey.' "

She also had photographs of Millantz as a clean-cut recruit who had just finished basic training, and a few pictures of him as a young soldier in Iraq. Her daughter, Roslyn Millantz, joined us one afternoon in her mother's living room and recalled how her brother sent her money when he was in the military. Roslyn and her mother downplayed Millantz's explanation that his military service was partly a response to the September 11 attacks. Instead, they felt he joined the Army mainly to get direction and self-discipline. They also felt, as did many of Millantz's friends, that he took great pride in his work as a medic. They recalled that his warmest memories of Iraq were his interactions with the children there.

"He loved children, and he would give them his food rations and buy them things," his mother recalled. It reminded me of the same warm memories that Cindy Chavez had of her son Adam. But Iraq also stirred up unhappy memories for both of them.

"He felt bad about causing the women and children terror when he would come into their houses," said Johnson. "They would pound on the houses at night and tell them all to get on the floor … The women and children were terrified, and he felt terrible about that."

His mother went on to describe Millantz's physical problems: how he suffered from a concussion, and had cysts on his brain that affected his sleep patterns, which in turn led him to abuse sleeping pills and other drugs. "He started taking pain medication for his different injuries, and then getting addicted to pain medication and eventually [he] moved on to harder stuff," she said. "It was just a downhill spiral. As much as I loved him and tried to stop it, I couldn't … unfortunately the call of drugs was too strong."

Once, she gave her son $400 for a Christmas present, and he used the money to buy heroin. He injected it with a dirty needle and contracted an infection. Millantz also discovered he had Hepatitis C, which required treatment with prescription drugs. One of the drugs that the local VA prescribed for him was interferon, which, according to his mother, "has a bad side effect, which often causes suicide."

From that point on, Millantz instructed his mother to give him only small amounts of money so that he wouldn't be able to purchase drugs. Yet he still suffered from sleeplessness, and continued to take medication for it, rendering him increasingly addicted to sleeping pills. When he was able to finally fall asleep, he often had nightmares. Millantz told his family that his nightmares featured his unit's nighttime raids and often contained images of him choking people.

"That's not my brother—that's not what he was all about," said Roslyn Millantz. "He thought he was going to be helping his country, not hurting people."

I asked Millantz's mother and sister about the sorts of memories he talked about as his struggles worsened.

"Horrible things," answered Roslyn. "They would have to torture people."

"Don't talk about that," said her mother, curtly.

"I wasn't aware I wasn't allowed to bring that up," said Roslyn. "Sorry. I didn't know …"

Days later, I asked Roslyn about their exchange.

"Why should I have to shut up about that?" she asked. "I want it to be known. I want everybody to know what happened over there."

Roslyn felt her mother chiefly focused on Millantz's physical problems to explain his decline.

"She wants people to see the medical side of things," said Roslyn.

"She wants it to be blamed on the medical, that he was sick all the time. Well, there was more to the story than just the medical … There's the dark parts you don't see."

When I visited Millantz in August 2008, he wanted to show me some of his own photos that featured the detainee abuse he had described to me. Just before I arrived in Greensburg, his mother stumbled across a stack of them and recoiled. She thumbed through pictures of detainees hanging from the bars of a jail and a soldier pointing his gun at a prisoner. His mother felt that the photos "sent off evil energy" and threw them away.

"I didn't realize that they were ever going to be useful for anything," she told me. "I just thought that they were a horrible reminder of the horrible things he went through."

Johnson purged other artifacts from his room that might have reminded him of the war and decorated his walls with pictures of sun-soaked mountain landscapes and religious icons in order to "try everything I could to bring him peace," she said.

Millantz and I understood his mother's position; she was simply trying to protect her son. Yet he was still determined to locate the photographs for me in order to validate his account of what happened. Together, we spent several hours rummaging through garbage bags in their garage trying to locate them. But we weren't able to salvage anything.

The following day, we stopped by a house near Greensburg that belonged to Millantz's friend John Hutton. Hutton had a number of photos and letters that Millantz sent him from Iraq. After the news about Abu Ghraib broke, Millantz urged his friend to keep the photos under wraps for him. Hutton assured him that he stored the photos and letters in a locked box, and Millantz could pick them up whenever he desired.

When we visited Hutton, he gave Millantz the few remaining photos that he had. One of them featured Millantz posing with a lieutenant as a detainee was forced to hold up a heavy wooden board. The two troops smiled broadly, while the prisoner's face showed a pained expression and sweat soaked through his white shirt. The back of the photo read: "That stupid son of a bitch. We eventually let him go. He's been holding that board for 45 minutes. Notice the sweat stains on his man dress. Hard luck?" Millantz told me that the prisoner's wrist eventually snapped from the exertion. The photos also came with a letter Millantz wrote on December 20, 2003:

Hutton,

What up Dawg? ... We tortured the shit out of some prisoners. It was funny as fuck. We put sandbags over their heads, and broke their thumbs. By accident of course. They killed two American Warrant Officers. We burn[ed] them with cigarettes. We mind fuck[ed them] by waking them up at all hours of the night. So how are you? ...

Peace,

Millantz

I visited Hutton at his house nine months later, and he reflected on his friend's photos and letters.

"At the time I'm sure everybody was doing it, and they were having a good time messing around with these prisoners," said Hutton. "But once he got back and the reality, laying there at night thinking about it, it got to him. I know it got to him. One night he came over here, he broke down ... Obviously he was having issues with it."

One of Millantz's friends from Iraq, Michael Blake, remembered how Millantz coyly revealed the photos to him.

"I remember him showing me some of the photos—of him making a prisoner smile while they were hurting him," said Blake. "It's just such a strange thing because it's almost like pornography in a way—it's almost like a secret. Like, 'Do you wanna see these pictures? Do you wanna see what we did?' Like it's a secret thing [that's] not to be talked about or discussed."

Blake knew other soldiers who had similar photos and videos. Like Millantz, he also joined IVAW and vigorously spoke out against the Iraq war. Sometimes veterans kept such photos to expose abuses in Iraq and Afghanistan. Others held onto them as trophy pictures and revealed them with embarrassed timidity. Blake was interested to see what Millantz had documented, since they served alongside each other in Iraq. Even though they both served with Battalion 1-68, they served on separate neighboring bases. Blake was stationed at Camp Anaconda, five miles away, and regularly provided food and supplies to FOB Lion. But he had no idea what his fellow soldiers were doing inside their makeshift jail until Millantz showed him the photos.

"Right there in that tiny little jail, right near the little gate ... that I drove through every single day, some fucked-up shit went down," said Blake. "I didn't even know what was going on in there. But they were hurting people, and they lost their humanity when they were doing it. And Johnny lost his humanity and his compassion when he was doing it.

"I know it never left Johnny—it never left his thoughts, it never left his nightmares. Who knows what kind of fucking karmic debt he's going to have to settle because of those things?"

"He was so torn and tormented by the whole thing," said Linda Johnson. "That's probably why he continued to have bad dreams for so long. He never had bad dreams before he went into the Army."

She thought her son despaired about his role as a medic—about how he went from helping people to injuring them. "But I also think there was maybe an anger at himself or the system or the situation," she said. Yet she didn't know how that anger would manifest itself.

I visited Roslyn Millantz at her house just outside of Greensburg, set against lush green hills. We sat in her kitchen as she shared many tender memories of her brother. She also remembered some of his "terrible, terrible nightmares and the violent behavior."

One day, Millantz had sat at the same table where we were seated while Roslyn prepared food in the kitchen. He was despondent and confessed how hopeless he felt. "He was talking about committing suicide," remembered Roslyn. "He talked about it all the time."

Roslyn wanted to be there for her brother and tried to support him whenever possible. But hearing his constant dejection also became exhausting at times. She lost patience and shouted at her brother.

"I've freakin' had it," she said, pointing her kitchen knife at him.

Millantz swiftly jerked the knife from Roslyn's hand and held it up to her throat. "I'm a trained killer," he said. "Don't ever do that again."

Roslyn never expected her younger brother to turn on her like that.

"I learned my lesson, whoa baby," she said. "Right then and there I [saw] a dramatic change. He went from being this sweet kid I knew to this twenty-four-, twenty-five-year-old trained killer."

It reminded me of the episode that Cindy Chavez recalled about her son Adam, when he, too, snapped and held a knife to the throat of a fellow soldier at Fort Wainwright, Alaska. It turned out that Jonathan Millantz and Adam Gray shared other post-war experiences as well.

During one summer day in 2007, Roslyn got a call from her brother. She "couldn't understand one flippin' word he said." Finally he managed to tell her, "There's an officer here who wants to talk to you." She was puzzled and waited for him to pass the phone to the police officer.

"Miss Millantz, do you have a valid Pennsylvania driver's license?" he asked.

Yes, she answered.

"Your brother was pulled over, just sitting here with his head ducked over in his lap ... He was unconscious."

Roslyn jotted down the address where her brother had been parked and drove there to pick him up. When she arrived, Millantz was unconscious and had saliva running down the side of his face. An empty pill bottle for Xanax lay beside him.

"I think there were thirty in there," she said later.

"Jonathan! Jonathan!" she shouted, shaking her brother. "What is with you? Talk to me or I'm taking you to the hospital!" Roslyn feared he had overdosed, and with the help of her mother she rushed him to the nearest emergency room.

"He had attempted suicide—he had admitted to that," said Roslyn. She pressed him about why he tried to take his life.

"Because life sucks," he said. "You don't know what went on in Iraq."

"I don't. But whenever you want to tell me I'm here to listen."

Millantz was in and out of consciousness as he lay in his hospital bed, and often mumbled incoherently. Roslyn bent over him to better understand what he kept repeating.

"I tried ..."

She bent closer.

"I tried so hard, Roslyn, to fix what I did."

"What are you talking about, Jonathan?"

"The tortures, the jails ..."

Roslyn was familiar with damaged veterans grappling with substance abuse: her father was a Vietnam veteran who battled alcoholism and his own personal demons. Roslyn and her mother disagreed about whether he saw any combat and if that fueled his addiction. But both of them conceded that alcohol consumption led to his death. Millantz was a small child when his father died, and he often referenced his death as a harbinger that loomed over him. Friends and family told me that Millantz discussed dreams in which his father warned him that the two would meet in heaven if he wasn't careful about substance abuse.

"You know, mom, I dreamed about daddy and he said, 'Son, if you're not careful you're going to join me,' " Millantz told his mother.

But those who knew Millantz thought he was determined to avoid that fate. Even I thought he had been making steady progress.

"He more than wanted to get life back on track, go to school, and become a psychologist and help the world," said his mother.

Yet some feared he would never rebound.

"I'm lonely. I can't handle it anymore. Life's too hard," Millantz told his sister during one conversation. He didn't call her for days afterward, which was unusual. Then Roslyn's mother phoned her, and she already had a sense of what she was going to say.

"Roslyn ..."

"Mom, I already know," she answered. "Jonathan is dead."

Just one week after my last conversation with Millantz, on April 3, 2009, Millantz's mother discovered her son dead in his bed. His death was chillingly similar to Adam Gray's in some regards. Millantz's mother said he had taken heavy doses of painkillers the night before. His death was ruled accidental, just like Adam Gray's. He was twenty-seven years old—three years older than Adam Gray when he died.[1]

After receiving the news about her brother Roslyn sped over to her mother's house. It was already filled with police and forensic workers who didn't want her to disrupt any of their investigative work. Roslyn insisted that they allow her inside to see her brother. They finally relented, and she marched upstairs and into his room. She remembered a putrid smell of death filling the air, and her brother lying in his bed.

She lay down and nudged him over so that she could fit on the bed beside him.

"Move over," she said.

Roslyn touched his body.

"You're so cold," she said, tugging a blanket over her brother. She pretended that they were still young kids who used to watch movies together in bed. Roslyn stroked him and tried to console him as they lay side by side.

"Jonathan, you don't have to worry anymore," she said. "You're in peace now. You're with daddy. Nobody can hurt you anymore. And there's no more pain ... no more pain."

I met Linda Johnson at St. Claire's Cemetery in Greensburg on a sunny day in March 2009. A winding tree-lined road divided the landscape, and clusters of stone markers lay on either side of the road. Some gravesites were separated into small groups, one of which was set aside for veterans. There, on freshly tamped brown soil, identified only by a small temporary marker, was Jonathan Wesley Millantz's grave.

Millantz's mother and I sat on a black granite bench a few feet away from where her son was buried. We talked about the scenery, the songbirds, the trees, and the deer that would come out to graze on the lawn. Millantz's father was buried there, and the family placed his son beside him.

"You know his body is there and that his father's body is there and as I said before, I believe that their souls are not here, that they are both in heaven," she said. "That's my greatest consolation."

I asked if it was painful for her to visit her son's grave.

No, she answered.

"I don't see the bodies," she answered. "Jonathan is not here. Jonathan's body that had given him so much trouble is here."

"Is there anything else you do to commemorate him?"

"Right now I am writing my memories of him, and I'm writing my memories of his last days. But then I am going to start from the beginning, as a little kid and things I remember about him growing up and what a delight he was ... Jonathan was a delight. He made me laugh from the day he was born. He either touched my heart or made me laugh. On occasion he made me sad when he did stupid things ... Jonathan's heart was pretty much always in the right place. He had a few lapses but for the most part he was a really good person who loved very deeply."

She paused to collect her thoughts.

"Had he been able to overcome everything, he would have made a wonderful contribution to the world. But maybe it was asking him to overcome too many things. There were so many things. There was so much ... His health was destroyed, his finances were destroyed, his social life was destroyed. His driving privileges had been taken away. His ability to develop a relationship with a girl was diminished because he had nothing to offer. It was just too much."

What about his last days?

"I remember Jonathan telling me that if he ever died, for me not to feel bad because he had a wonderful life. And he told me how much he loved me and appreciated me."

"It sounds like he was trying to say goodbye."

"I know, I know. And I didn't realize it at the time. I was constantly trying to tell him, 'Look, we'll get this straightened out and then we'll do this and do that.' He had been listening to that for three and a half years. I think he began to doubt that it was ever going to happen."

Johnson told me about the memorial service they held for Millantz. After a tearful ceremony, they commemorated him with raucous music and dancing. Johnson flipped through the pages of the guestbook, pointing out how each page was crammed with signatures. But she despaired that so few people had realized how sick and depressed her son had been, and how she, too, had difficulty coming to grips with it.

"That's the problem with so much of what was wrong with him. People couldn't see it," she said. "It's not like he lost a leg or an arm. They didn't really realize how sick he was. So many people were so upset that they hadn't helped him or come around or done more for him.

"I'm really angry at the VA. I'm also angry at Jonathan for not being more honest with me and telling me just how thoroughly disgusted he was. If I had known how much he was despairing I would have demanded that the VA put him into a program of some sort."

Shortly after Millantz died, his mother bumped into her next-door neighbor. They were always friendly and polite with each other but hadn't exchanged many words. The neighbor only knew Millantz in passing but could sense that he was an unhappy soul.

"He knew that Jonathan was ... troubled," said Johnson.

It was the very same word that Cindy Chavez used to describe her son, Adam Gray.

"I'm sure that Adam Gray and a lot of these soldiers were a lot like that," said Roslyn. "They were human."

Adam Gray and Jonathan Millantz, who had little in common in terms of background or political views, were both traumatized by their involvement in the abuse of prisoners at FOB Lion's jail. When they returned home, they experienced violent outbursts and depression, turned to drugs and alcohol, and attempted suicide. In the end, they took their own lives, regardless of whether it was intentional or not. Nonetheless, the military formally marked their deaths and honored their service.

Millantz had a military ceremony at his funeral, complete with a twenty-one-gun salute and a folded flag. Local members of Veterans of Foreign Wars (VFW) attended, along with throngs of mourners. Johnson appreciated the official commemoration for her son and the way it honored his service. His sister was less grateful. She described the military fanfare as "awkward" for her brother, given his antiwar activism and how the Iraq war affected him.

Some of Millantz's antiwar friends also felt uneasy with the military service he received. Eli Wright went through combat medic training with Millantz and likewise joined IVAW after he returned from Iraq. According to Wright, "Johnny put a lot more weight into his service as a medic than a soldier," and so he felt uncomfortable with having his friend commemorated with military honors.

"I don't think it's there to honor the dead—I think it's there to patronize the living. Honestly," said Wright. "I've been to quite a few funerals and military services, and I know for a fact that not all the guys who had died and were being honored at those services were fully in belief of what they had done.

"We lost more guys in my unit after we got back from Iraq than we lost in Iraq as a result of suicide, reckless behavior, ODs, whatever else. And those guys didn't die in honor of their service. They didn't die as patriots and defenders of freedom. Those guys died because they were trying to drown out and hide from the reality that that war had dug into their hearts."

Roslyn agreed. She thought about turning to the older VFW attendees at the funeral and saying, "You've got eighty years of your life, and my brother was robbed. Why was that?"

She told me, "I really wanted to scream 'Iraq Veterans Against the War!' " But she refrained, knowing that such an outburst would only upset her mother.

"It is traumatic for her ... because that's her only son," said Roslyn. "You want to look at your son or daughter as a hero, not as someone who went out there and tortured people."

"I do think of him as a hero," said Johnson. "He felt powerless to stop it."

While pundits and reporters pondered how US forces turned to torture, it seemed that the mothers who looked after their damaged sons and daughters sometimes had a clearer, unvarnished understanding of what had occurred.

"Their rage and the fact that they were given too much power, and the detainees were powerless, and the fact that there was no one protecting them ... that's how the abuses occurred," said Millantz's mother. "People might think, 'Oh, I would never do anything like that.' Wrong. It takes a very, very mature, moral, strong person to not abuse power ... They are very young and they make very unwise choices, which they regret.

"And it is all for naught."

Acknowledgements

THIS BOOK TOOK OVER five years to produce, and could not have come to fruition without the tremendous help and support of friends, family, and colleagues. I would first like to thank the researchers whose incredible work undergirds this book, especially Marilyn Souders, Anja Tranovich, Alex DiBranco, and Michael Gorup. Peter Miller and Shazia Ahmad also provided important research assistance.

I am eternally grateful to those who provided assistance to me overseas (sometimes while incurring great risks), including Wahidullah Amani, Laila Tomeh, Noorrahman Rahmani, Ragheed Ameen, and Salim Abraham.

I want to give special thanks to Gail Bensinger and Catherine Winter for their amazing eleventh-hour editing assistance. And I am very grateful to Esther Kaplan and the Nation Institute for their support. I also thank the Henry Demarest Lloyd Investigative Fund at the Center for Investigative Reporting for their support.

I am very thankful for the many dear friends and colleagues who helped me navigate the publishing industry and find a home for this book, including Brando Skyhorse, Lauren Wein, Robert Mank, Daphne Benedis-Grab, A. C. Thompson, Esther Kaplan and Ruth Baldwin. I want to thank Andrew Hsiao for accepting this book, and for his help shaping it. I am very grateful for the support of my agent, Robert E. Guinsler, who helped me weather many rough storms.

I had the privilege of working on parts of this project with the wonderful staff from American Public Media. I would especially like to thank my co-producer Michael Montgomery, as well as Catherine Winter, Ellen Guettler, Stephen Smith, Suzanne Pekow, and Nancy Rosenbaum.

Many other dear friends and colleagues helped me at many important intervals, including: Arun Venugopal, Nghia Nguyen, Liz Cook, Rhonda Roumani, Juan Pablo Ordonez, Daphne Eviatar, Bela Kapur, Arlene Getz, Keith Bunin, Clark Gard, Michael Shaikh, Katherine Zoepf, Richard Rodriguez, Shaheen Rassoul, Rabab Rifai, Ruhullah Khapalwak, Elisabeth Garber-Paul, Jean Maria Arrigo, Emad Mekay, Belquis Ahmadi, Dan Scheffey, Diana Fuller, David Danzig, Tim Bakken, Sheila Provencher, Max Fraser, and many others.

Many of my sources for this book have been of great assistance in helping me piece together difficult stories, especially Mark Fallon and Tony Sandoval.

I want to thank Darius Rejali for his enduring support and mentorship. I am forever grateful for the wonderful editing and guidance of Gail Bensinger.

I am indebted to Verso Books for publishing this book, and to all the staff who lent their help.

I am especially grateful to Rose Liebman for her love, support, and above all patience—she has been a truly indispensable ally and beloved partner. Likewise, I would like to thank my parents, Matt and Sandra Phillips, for their enduring love and encouragement.

I want thank all of the former detainees, soldiers, and members of the military who courageously shared their stories with me. I express my deepest gratitude to the families of Adam Gray and Jonathan Millantz for entrusting me with their sons' stories—especially Roy and Cindy Chavez, Linda Johnson, and Roslyn Millantz. I hope I have succeeded in representing them truthfully and respectfully, as I hope I have done with regard to all of the other souls in this book whose lives have been permanently shaped by the American legacy of torture.

Joshua E. S. Phillips
March 2010

Notes

Foreword

1 Charles J. Dunlap, Jr., *Learning from Abu Ghraib: The Joint Commander and Force Discipline*, Proceedings of the US Naval Institute, September 2005, 34–8.
2 Colonel Bernard gave me permission to quote from this email prior to his death.
3 For example, Lieutenant General Paul Van Riper, USMC, personal communication, October 2, 1996, Amphibious Warfare School, Quantico and reaffirmed in an April 2, 1998, email, giving permission to quote. At the time of the first communication, Lieutenant General Van Riper was commander of the entire Marine Corps training establishment as the MCCDC, the equivalent of the Army G-3.
4 B. T. Litz, et al., "Moral Injury and Moral Repair in War Veterans: A Preliminary Model And Intervention Strategy," *Clinical Psychology Review*, Vol. 29, Issue 8, December 2009, 695–706.
5 The Law of Land Warfare is the American armed forces' official summary of the binding "rules of war." This legal code is distilled from US statute, customary law, and treaty sources, such as the Geneva Conventions.
6 Francis Lieber, quoted by Telford Taylor, in Malham Wakin, ed., "War Crimes," *War, Morality, and the Military Profession*, 2nd ed., Boulder: Westview, 1986, 378.

Introduction

1 Darius Rejali and Paul Gronke, "US Public Opinion on Torture, 2001–2009," Reed College, PS Symposium: "Torture and the War on Terror," May 2, 2009, http://people.reed. edu/~gronkep/TortureWhitePaperV2.pdf.
2 Dafna Linzer, "Dozens of Prisoners Held by CIA Still Missing, Fates Unknown," *ProPublica*, April 22, 2009; and Karen J. Greenberg, "Detention Nation," *The National Interest*, May/June 2009.

3 Martha Huggins, Mika Haritos-Fatouros, and Philip Zimbardo, *Violence Workers*, Berkeley: University of California Press, 2002, xx: "Our own case study ... postulates that a search for the cause of atrocity—whether in military authoritarian states or in emerging or consolidated democracies—must go beyond simplistic personalistic 'bad apples' and vague 'unique' societywide 'culture of violence' perspectives: neither the psycho-biological or the general determinist perspective accounts for the effects of the bureaucratized systems that permit or encourage the social-psychological and cultural mechanisms that can engender [state violence] and grant impunity to perpetrators and facilitators alike."

4 "Of the hundreds of thousands of service members who are or have been deployed in Afghanistan and Iraq, there have been approximately 800 investigations into allegations of mistreatment, including approximately 600 criminal investigations"; see "The United States' Response to the Questions Asked by the Committee Against Torture," Geneva, Switzerland, May 8, 2006, http://www.state.gov/g/drl/rls/68562.htm. As of early 2010, the military had not publicly released updated figures for detainee abuse cases since 2006 (nor had any human rights organizations); Joshua E.S. Phillips, "Inside the Detainee Abuse Task Force," *Nation*, May 13, 2011; "Review of DOD-Directed Investigation of Detainee Abuse," Office of the Inspector General of the Department of Defense, report no. 06-INTEL-10, August 25, 2006.

5 David Dishneau, "Military High Court to Hear Abu Ghraib Appeals," Associated Press, September 14, 2009.

6 See films *Taxi to the Dark Side* (Dir. Alex Gibney) and *Ghosts of Abu Ghraib* (Dir. Rory Kennedy), and John Conroy, *Unspeakable Acts, Ordinary People*, New York: Alfred A. Knopf, 2000, 96–101.

7 Huggins, Haritos-Fatouros, and Zimbardo, *Violence Workers*, 253–4: "The failure of psychiatrists to predict accurately the outcome of Milgram's powerful demonstrations is an example of the fundamental attribution error ... Individualistic cultures typically focus on the actor and disregard the behavioral features of the setting: effects are thus attributed to the actor's personal characteristics. The training of psychiatrists, like that of many other medical-model professionals, focuses their scientific and clinical gaze on problems within individual psyches and away from environmental determinants of behavior."

8 Christina Lamb, "Five Years Ago the Americans Had the World's Most Wanted Man in their Sights but Failed to Pull the Trigger," *Sunday Times Magazine* (London), March 18, 2007, 46.

9 That is, importing the severe discipline and harsh interrogation techniques used in Guantanamo.

1. Searching for Answers

1 Bill Hanna, "12,000 Soldiers in Fort Hood, Texas, 'Digital Division' Deploy to Persian Gulf," *Fort Worth Star-Telegram*, January 21, 2003.

2 "Bush: Don't Wait for Mushroom Cloud," CNN, October 8, 2002.

3 Kimberly Hefling, "Iraq, Afghan Vets at Risk for Suicides," Associated Press, October 31, 2007; Jason Leopold and Mary Susan Littlepage, "Obama Administration Struggling to Tackle Mental Health Crisis Plaguing Military," *Truthout*, December 1, 2009; Kimberly Hefling, "Suicide Is Rising Among Young Male War Veterans," Associated Press, January 12, 2010.

4 Leopold and Littlepage, "Obama Administration Struggling"; and Tomas Dinges, "Study: More Soldiers Diagnosed with Problems at VA Hospitals," *The Star-Ledger*, July 17, 2009.

5 Steven L. Sayers, PhD, Victoria A. Farrow, B.S., Jennifer Ross, M.S., and David W. Oslin, M.D., "Family Problems Among Recently Returned Military Veterans Referred for a Mental Health Evaluation," *The Journal of Clinical Psychiatry* 70:2, 2009, 163–170; and Richard A. Kulka et al., *Trauma and the Vietnam War Generation: Report of Findings from the National Vietnam Veterans Readjustment Study*, New York: Brunner/Mazel, 1990, 923: "Data from both the veteran and his s/p [spouse/partner] indicate strongly that there are many severe problems in the families of male Vietnam veterans with PTSD."

2. The Story Begins in Afghanistan

1 Julian Borger, "Report Implicates Top Brass in Bagram Scandal," *Guardian*, May 21, 2005.

2 Reporter Carlotta Gall tracked down witnesses from Khost, and Tim Golden excerpted accounts contained in a leaked military report in "Threats and Responses: Prisoners; US Military Investigating Death of Afghan in Custody," *New York Times*, March 4, 2003. The story that fully detailed the abuses was Tim Golden, "In US Report, Brutal Details of 2 Afghan Inmates' Deaths," *New York Times*, May 20, 2005.

3 "Taleban Kill Afghanistan Reporter," *BBC News*, April 8, 2007.

4 Gregory Warner, "The Italian Lived; the Afghan Died," *Slate.com*, April 9, 2007.

5 "Barely visible in the distance is the Soviet air base at Khost, an important Red Army strongpoint and one of the few towns in which communism has attracted some grassroots support among Afghans—hence its nickname, 'Little Moscow.' " From David Ross, "Impasse in Afghanistan Mujahedeen Holding Out Against Soviets," *Globe and Mail*, December 27, 1986, A1.

6 Andrew North, "US Sorry for Holding BBC Reporter," *BBC News*, September 10, 2004.

7 United Nations Assistance Mission in Afghanistan, "Suicide Attacks in Afghanistan (2001–2007)," September 2007, 14. According to an ANSO report, a suicide attack also occurred on April 22, 2007, killing six people including the bomber.

8 "A number of US and Afghan forces are stationed in Sarabagh and the airport aims to carry out anti-Taleban and anti-Al-Qa'idah operations in Khost. These forces are known as campaign forces." From "Pressure Mounts on US–Afghan Coalition Base as Attackers Change Tactics," BBC Monitoring Central Asia Unit / Afghan Islamic Press News Agency, October 19, 2003. See also Ilene R. Prusher, "Two Top Al Qaeda Leaders Spotted," *Christian Science Monitor*, March 26, 2002: "... special troops who are called 'campaign forces' and were trained by the US to focus on the hunt for Al Qaeda and Taliban fugitives."

9 "The graves of Arab fighters who helped sweep the Taliban to power in the 1990s ... are clearly marked and neatly built with white stones covering them and green flags fluttering on bamboo poles." From Dawood Azami, "Kandahar's cemetery of 'miracles,' " *BBC News*, January 17, 2008.

10 See Physicians for Human Rights, *Broken Laws, Broken Lives: Medical Evidence of Torture by US Personnel and Its Impact*, 2008, 77. In assessing the effects of "forced standing" on select former US detainees, the report found: "Medical evaluation, while not conclusively confirming these accounts, was consistent with them. All of the former detainees reported that they continue to suffer from diffuse musculoskeletal pain, and pain in limbs, joints, muscles, and ligaments that they did not experience prior to detention. For example, one detainee reported arm numbness and weakness following being suspended by his arms ('free suspension'), which is highly consistent with a brachial plexus injury that often results from this type of suspension. Since his release from Abu Ghraib prison, this individual has been suffering from chronic pain in his neck, legs, right shoulder, and feet, all of which he attributed to injuries sustained during his incarceration (from beatings and being suspended in stress positions). Another former detainee described experiencing daily lower back pain and numbness in his legs, which began while he was in Guantánamo, and is exacerbated by lifting heavy objects and walking. This type of injury corroborates the allegation of being subjected to shackling and handcuffing for extended periods of time. Additionally, the thinning of the skin and decreased hair on this individual and another former detainee's wrists were attributable to handcuffs having rubbed against their skin."

11 "I remember he was healthier; he was a bit heavier than most Afghanis. He was well groomed, he came in with a group of other people and they were all in Isolation. He had an air of someone who was not a dirt farmer or a poor person. He seemed different than even the Afghanis we had working from day to day on the base." Statement of Thomas V. Curtis, taken

at Embassy Suites Hotel, Cincinnati, OH, February 4, 2004 (0134-02-CID369-23533/0137-02-CID369-23534), 4.

12 "[E]ven the interpreters had trouble understanding [Dilawar's] Pashto dialect." From Golden, "In US Report, Brutal Details."

13 "The twenty-one-year-old lead interrogator, Specialist Glendale C. Walls II, later contended that Mr. Dilawar was evasive. 'Some holes came up, and we wanted him to answer us truthfully,' he said. The other interrogator, Sergeant Salcedo, complained that the prisoner was smiling, not answering questions, and refusing to stay kneeling on the ground or sitting against the wall." From Golden, "In US Report, Brutal Details."

14 "The military police at Bagram had guidelines, Army Regulation 190-47, telling them they couldn't chain prisoners to doors or to the ceiling. They also had Army Regulation 190-8, which said that humiliating detainees wasn't allowed. Neither was applicable at Bagram, however, said [Maj. Jeff] Bovarnick, the former senior legal officer for the installation. The military police rulebook saying that enemy prisoners of war should be treated humanely didn't apply, he said, because the detainees weren't prisoners of war, according to the Bush administration's decision to withhold Geneva Convention protections from suspected Taliban and al Qaida detainees." From Tom Lasseter, "US Abuse of Detainees Was Routine at Afghanistan Bases," McClatchy Newspapers, June 16, 2008.

15 See the Church and Schlesinger reports.

16 Darius Rejali, *Torture and Democracy*, Princeton: Princeton University Press, 2007, 412. Rejali continues, "Examples of [this] include police torture in various American cities in the 1920s, police torture in Area 2 in Chicago in the 1970s and 1980s, and American torture in Vietnam in the 1960s."

17 Chris Mackey and Greg Miller, *The Interrogators: Inside the Secret War Against al Qaeda*, New York: Little, Brown and Company, 2004. Despite repeated requests for interviews over four years, Chris Mackey declined to speak with the author.

18 Ibid., 231.

19 Ibid., 248.

20 Ibid., 286–7.

21 Ibid., 287–8.

22 Ibid., 287.

23 Ibid., 287.

24 Emily Bazelon, "From Bagram to Abu Ghraib," *Mother Jones*, March/April 2005.

25 Ibid.

26 "Global War on Terrorism—Operation Enduring Freedom," Defense Manpower Data Center, Analysis and Programs Division, October 7, 2001 through February 6, 2010, http://siadapp.dmdc.osd.mil/personnel/CASUALTY/oefmonth.pdf.

27 Ibid.

28 Ibid.

29 Ibid.

30 Tom Lasseter, "US Abuse of Detainees Was Routine at Afghanistan Bases," McClatchy Newspapers, June 16, 2008.

31 Ibid.

32 Ibid.

33 Statement of Sergeant Jennifer N. Higginbotham, taken at Fort Bragg, NC, August 1, 2004, 9–10.

34 Statement of Thomas V. Curtis, 3.

35 Golden, "In US Report, Brutal Details."

36 Statement of Higginbotham, 9–10.

37 Statement of Curtis, 3.

38 Ibid.

39 Q: After the first death, [were] you given instructions about changes in policy for delivering strikes or recording them?
    A: Just to record them, not to stop doing it. There was also no requirement to get permission nor any limit placed on the number of strikes you could give.
    Statement of SPC Willie V. Brand, taken at Embassy Suites Hotel, Cincinnati, OH, February 3, 2004 (0137-02-CID369-23534), 3.

40 Elise Ackerman, "Blows That Led to Detainee's Death Were Common Practice, Reservist Says," Knight Ridder, March 25, 2005. See also Qader Khandan's account, and the following testimony:
    Q: Do you remember any other times you struck Dilawar (PUC 421)?
    A: There was a time when I was in the Isolation Cell with SFT Thomas Curtis trying to put Dilawar's hood back on and Dilawar was not cooperating, so I gave him a couple of knee strikes ...
    Q: How was Dilawar being non-compliant? What behavior was Dilawar engaged in that provoked a response from you?
    A: Not putting his hood back on, mule-kicking the door, pulling his hood off.
    Statement of Brand, 2.

41 "I do recall walking into the room, everyone was standing, Josh, the detainee, everyone. I was supposed to receive information about what they wanted done with the detainee after the interview, standing restraint, how compliant he had been, sleep deprivation, etc. Josh (SPC Claus whom I identified by a photograph) said he was 'being an ass' and I observed Josh force-feeding Dilawar water. He took a small [1/2 liter] bottle of water and shoved it in the detainee's mouth and squeezed water into his mouth, whatever water didn't squirt out, the detainee spit back out. I don't recall much else, we took him back and I think he still had his long and short cuffs on. I don't remember cuffing him again. I remember walking him, not having to

carry him. We usually give the Isolation Guard the number of the returning PUC and he goes back into the same cell. After reviewing my earlier statement, I recall that Josh said to 'leave him up,' meaning put him back in standing restraint. We re-shackled his arms to the ceiling and he gave us no trouble." Statement of James P. Boland, Jr., taken at US Army Reserve Center, Cincinnati, OH, January 23, 2004 (0134-02-CID369-23533), 12.

42 Statement of Boland, 12.

43 Statement of Brand, 2.

44 Ibid.

45 "[I]ncluding some 30 times in the flesh around the knees during one session in an isolation cell." From Lasseter, "US Abuse of Detainees Was Routine."

> Q: How many times at the most did you strike Dilawar (PUC 421) and under what circumstances?
>
> A: Somewhere in the area of thirty times, less than forty for sure. There was one time, which I did not remember before, where I told Dilawar that 'That's it', implying I was fed up with him. And I said I was going to give him 'fourteen pronial [sic] strikes in each leg'. Then I delivered the blows. When I recounted the story later, that is the way I told it. I told people that I had to switch knees because my leg got tired. I'm not absolutely certain I delivered thirty strikes at the time. That was the number I said, but it may have been a few more or less than that. There were also another five to seven times I struck him with knee strikes, during times when he was being non-compliant.
>
> Statement of Brand, 1.

46 Statement of Curtis, 6.

47   Q: How did you learn of Dilawar's death?

> A: Almost at the end of my shift, around 0530 or so, we were taking a guy to the bathroom from the end of the Isolation Cells where PUC 42 (Dilawar) was confined. I had to walk by his cell on the way, to observe the escort guards take the other guy to the bathroom. Dilawar was hanging limp in the chains, I thought he was sleeping, so I kicked the door and I could have sworn I got a response, a slight move of the head. I walked up and watched them shackle up a detainee. When I returned, Dilawar was still hanging there. I looked real close at him and called Morden. We stood outside the cell and I asked Morden, 'does he look all right to you?' Morden said he didn't look too good, so [we] went in to check him. We took the hood off and uncuffed him and he was dead weight. He just dropped. Morden started CPR, mouth to mouth and I called SOG (SSG Berkley). They carried him out on a stretcher and that was the last time I saw him.
>
> Statement of Curtis, 7.

48 "According to an Army investigation, Habibullah was so badly hurt by repeated knee strikes that 'even if he survived, both legs would have had to

be amputated.' " From Elise Ackerman, "Blows That Led to Detainee's Death Were Common Practice, Reservist Says," Knight Ridder, March 25, 2005.

49 Statement of Curtis, 8–9.

50 R. Jeffrey Smith, "General Cites Problems at US Jails in Afghanistan," *Washington Post*, December 3, 2004, A01.

51 See also John Sifton, "The Bush Administration Homicides," *thedailybeast.com*, May 5, 2009.

52 Human Rights Watch, "US: Failure To Provide Justice For Afghan Victims," *US Fed News*, February 16, 2007. See also "No US military officer above the rank of captain has been called to account for what happened at Bagram." From Lasseter, "US Abuse of Detainees Was Routine." "Capt. Christopher M. Beiring, 39, had been charged with lying to investigators and being derelict in his duties, in part by neglecting after the first death to order his soldiers to stop chaining up prisoners by the arms at the behest of military interrogators who wanted to deprive them of sleep before questioning … 'They certainly had a case to investigate—two guys died,' Captain Beiring said yesterday in an interview. 'And, obviously, some soldiers did some stuff wrong and needed to be punished. But I think it got blown out of proportion. At some point, they were just playing politics.' " From Tim Golden, "Case Dropped Against US Officer in Beating Deaths of Afghan Inmates," *New York Times*, January 8, 2006. Beiring did receive a letter of reprimand that said his "command failures enabled an environment of abuse," according to Daniel Schorn, "The Court-Martial Of Willie Brand—Tells Scott Pelley 'I Am Not A Violent Person,' " *60 Minutes*, CBS, March 5, 2006.

53 This figure includes thirty-six named detainees and sixty-four unnamed but documented accounts. It does not include cases of CIA abuse and torture. There were seven incidents of stress positions; six of sleep deprivation; five that included chaining; four that included chaining from the ceiling; three of temperature manipulation; two detainees sodomized; two threatened with dogs. This research was produced by Alex DiBranco during 2009.

54 See Damien M. Corsetti's interview in the film *Taxi to the Dark Side*.

55 See Department of Defense, *Review of DoD Detention Operations and Detainee Interrogation Techniques* (a.k.a., the "Church Report"), Executive Summary, March 2005. See also Department of the Army, *The Inspector General Detainee Operations Inspection* (a.k.a., the "Mikolashek Report"), July 21, 2004: "As documented in previous reports (including MG Fay's and MG Taguba's investigations), stronger leadership and greater oversight would have lessened the likelihood of abuse" (19); "In at least 15 of the 125 incidents reviewed by the DAIG Team, immediate corrective action was not taken by the chain of command. The reasons for this leadership failure included either a

lack of fundamental unit discipline, ambiguous command and control over the facility or individuals involved, ambiguous guidance from command on the treatment of detainees, no control processes in place to provide oversight and notify the command of the incident or, in very few cases, leader complicity at the Lieutenant Colonel level and below in the actions. This led to the second category of detainee abuse, referred to as progressive abuse because these usually develop from an isolated incident into a more progressive abuse" and "although many of the guard personnel were aware of the techniques being used, the abusive behavior was not reported" (36).

56 Rejali, *Torture and Democracy*, 412. Rejali states: "Examples of [this] include police torture in various American cities in the 1920s, police torture in Area 2 in Chicago in the 1970s and 1980s, and American torture in Vietnam in the 1960s."

57 R. Jeffrey Smith, "General Cites Problems at US Jails in Afghanistan," *Washington Post*, December 3, 2004, A1.

58 Lasseter, "US Abuse of Detainees Was Routine."

3. *"We weren't in the CIA—we were soldiers"*

1 http://www.globalsecurity.org/military/world/iraq/balad-ab.htm.

2 For examples of how other US forces faced similar problems with the shift in conventional warfare to counterinsurgency fighting, see Thomas E. Ricks, *Fiasco: The American Military Adventure in Iraq*, New York: Penguin Press, 2006, 272.

3 US officials employed the very same reasoning at Guantanamo and elsewhere when they formulated a regimen of harsh interrogations. "The Chief of the Interrogation Control Element [at Guantanamo] recalled a meeting with [Army Lieutenant Colonel Diane] Beaver [the staff judge advocate at Guantanamo] on the maximum length of an interrogation session, no more than twenty hours in a twenty-four-hour period. 'We came to that number after reading about the United States Army Ranger Course,' he explained, in which 'our soldiers are subjected to twenty-hour days and are apparently only required to have four hours of sleep.' If that was okay, he explained, 'then in our minds it was okay to subject the terrorist to twenty-hour interrogations,' although keeping a detainee awake for five days straight 'would be sleep deprivation,' which was prohibited." From Summarized [REDACTED] Witness Statement of the Intelligence Control Element (ICE) Chief for JTF-170, given to Schmidt-Furlow Investigation on March 3, 2005, 3. Philippe Sands, *Torture Team: Rumsfeld's Memo and the Betrayal of American Values*, New York: Palgrave MacMillan, 2008, 62.

4 Other troops also used a battery of physical exercises and other kinds of force. See Ricks, *Fiasco*, 271: "Prisoners were also made to exercise until they

couldn't stand, and then they were doused in cold water. Some were made to wear sandbags on their heads on which were written 'IED,' signifying to soldiers—incorrectly in most cases, it appears—that their wearer had been caught trying to bomb US troops."

5 This reaction was shared by other troops as well. See Ricks, *Fiasco*, 270: "after the 101st had suffered its worst month ever of casualties while in Iraq, losing twenty-five soldiers in November ... soldiers wanted payback. 'Guys get pissed when they see their buddies blown away,' he said."

6 Such reactions occurred elsewhere with other US troops in Iraq. See Ricks, *Fiasco*, 278: "These attacks weren't inflicted to collect intelligence but simply to blow off steam. 'Everyone in camp knew if you wanted to work out your frustration you show up at the PUC ['persons under control,' pronounced 'puck'] tent. In a way it was a sport.' " [Statement from an infantry fire team leader from the 82nd Airborne.]

4. Shock the Conscience

1 From Interrogation Log Detainee 063: "2050: Doctor returns and performs EKG. Heartbeat is regular but very slow—35 bpm. Doctor consults with another doctor."

2 "Securing Our Borders, Protecting Our Nation," *Customs and Border Protection Today*, January/February 2005. http://www.customs.gov/xp/CustomsToday/2005/JanFeb/other/ecawards.xml.

3 Philip Shenon, "Panel Says a Deported Saudi Was Likely '20th Hijacker,' " *New York Times*, January 27, 2004.

4 Paisley Dodds, "FBI Letter Complains of Aggressive Interrogation at Guantanamo in 2002," Associated Press, December 7, 2004; and Adam Zagorin and Michael Duffy, "Inside the Interrogation of Detainee 063," *Time*, June 20, 2005.

5 Donna Miles, "Al Qaeda Manual Drives Detainee Behavior at Guantánamo Bay," American Forces Press Service, June 29, 2005. The FBI translated the manual into English, and it is readily available on the Department of Justice website and elsewhere. See thesmokinggun.com/archive/jihadmanual.html.

6 According to General Richard Myers, Guantanamo detainees were so dangerous that they would "gnaw hydraulic lines in the back of a C-17 [aircraft] to bring it down." From DoD News Briefing—Secretary Rumsfeld and Gen. Myers, January 11, 2002, 2:10 PM EST.

7 Gerry J. Gilmore, "Rumsfeld Visits, Thanks US Troops at Camp X-Ray in Cuba," American Forces Press Service, January 27, 2002.

8 Mark Denbeaux et al., "Report on Guantanamo Detainees—A Profile of 517 Detainees through Analysis of Department of Defense Data," Seton Hall University, February 8, 2006, 2–3.

9 Seymour Hersh, *Chain of Command: The Road from 9/11 to Abu Ghraib*, New York: HarperCollins, 2004, 2–3.

10 Lawrence Wilkerson, "Some Truths about Guantánamo Bay," *The Washington Note*, March 17 2009.

11 Ibid. For more information about the way in which detainees were picked up in Afghanistan (prior to their subsequent transfer to Guantanamo), see Mark Denbeaux, "Report on Guantánamo Detainees." The study found the following: "Bounty hunters or reward-seekers handed people over to American or Northern Alliance soldiers in the field, often soon after disappearing; as a result, there was little opportunity on the field to verify the story of an individual who presented the detainee in response to the bounty award. Where that story constitutes the sole basis for an individual's detention in Guantanamo, there would be little ability either for the Government to corroborate or a detainee to refute such an allegation." In addition, "Examples of evidence that the government cited as proof that the detainees were enemy combatants include the following:
   • Associations with unnamed and unidentified individuals and/or organizations;
   • Associations with organizations, the members of which would be allowed into the United States by the Department of Homeland Security;
   • Possession of rifles;
   • Use of a guest house;
   • Possession of Casio watches; and
   • Wearing of olive drab clothing"
   The report also states: "The evidence against 39% of the detainees rests in part upon the possession of a Kalashnikov rifle."

12 Deputy Inspector General for Intelligence, "Review of DoD-Directed Investigations of Detainee Abuse," August 25, 2006.

13 Ibid., 25–6.

14 Matthew Rosine, "Getting SERE-ious," *Airman*, Fall 2007, 43.

15 Hearing of the Constitution, Civil Rights and Civil Liberties Subcommittee of the House Judiciary Committee; Subject: Torture and the Cruel, Inhuman, and Degrading Treatment of Detainees: The Effectiveness and Consequences of "Enhanced" Interrogation, Federal News Service, June 1, 2007. See also Amy Goodman, *Democracy Now!*, "Program Subject: Declassification of a Department of Defense Inspector General Report On Interrogation," June 1, 2007, 8:00 A.M.; and Jane Mayer, "The Experiment," *The New Yorker*, July 11, 2005.

16 Mayer, "The Experiment."

17 "Numerous experiments aimed at documenting trainees' stress levels have been conducted by SERE-affiliated scientists. By analyzing blood and saliva, they have charted fluctuations in trainees' level of cortisol, a stress

hormone, and these data have been used to understand what inspires maximum anxiety in the trainees." From Mayer, "The Experiment."

18 Intelligence Science Board, *Educing Information Interrogation: Science And Art—Foundations For The Future*, National Defense Intelligence College, Washington, DC, December 2006, 22. According to the report, "Most training materials and guides on law enforcement interrogation emphasize the need for one or more interrogators to develop a rapport with the subject. Indeed, rapport is widely regarded as an essential foundation for most successful [law enforcement] interrogations," 22.

19 This research was produced by Anja Tramovich and Alix DiBranco during 2007–9.

20 Mary Anne Case, "Gender Performance Requirements of the US Military in the War on Islamic Terrorism as Violence by and against Women," paper presented at the American Society of International Law Proceedings, 2008.

21 For insight into discussions that helped shape the Rumsfeld memo of December 2, 2002, see "Counter Resistance Strategy Meeting Minutes," October 2, 2002. The minutes reveal the following exchange:

COL CUMMINGS: We can't do sleep deprivation.

LTC BEAVER: Yes, we can—with approval.

[Note added to memo] Disrupting the normal camp operations is vital. We need to create an environment of "controlled chaos."

LTC BEAVER: We may need to curb the harsher operations while ICRC [International Committee of the Red Cross] is around. It is better not to expose them to any controversial techniques. We must have the support of the DOD.

BECKER: We have had many reports from Bagram about sleep deprivation being used.

LTC BEAVER: True, but officially it is not happening. It is not being reported officially.

22 Kenneth Anderson and Elisa Massimino, "The Cost of Confusion: Resolving Ambiguities in Detainee Treatment," WCL Research Paper No. 2008-77, The Stanley Foundation, American University Bridging the Foreign Policy Divide Project, March 2007.

23 Chris Mackey and Greg Miller, *The Interrogators: Inside the Secret War Against al Qaeda*, New York: Little, Brown and Company, 2004, 477.

24 See "Counter Resistance Strategy Meeting Minutes." According to CIA lawyer Jonathan Fredman, "It is very effective to identify phobias and use them (i.e., insects, snakes, claustrophobia). The level of resistance is directly related to the person's experience." For Fredman's response, see Sheri Fink, "Tortured Profession: Psychologists Warned of Abusive Interrogations, Then Helped Craft Them," *ProPublica*, May 5, 2009—updated May 7, 2009: "Jonathan Fredman, former chief legal counsel for the CIA Counterterrorist Center, has disputed the accuracy of the October 2, 2002, minutes of a

meeting held at Guantánamo Bay to discuss interrogation techniques. Through a Freedom of Information Act request, *ProPublica* obtained a letter written by Fredman and sent to leaders of the Senate Committee on Armed Services on November 17, 2008. In it, Fredman says that comments he made at the meeting were 'paraphrased sloppily and poorly.' While he did not dispute in particular the quote used in this story, which was attributed to him in the meeting's minutes, Fredman wrote that at the meeting he 'emphasized that all interrogation practices and legal guidance must not be based upon anyone's subjective perception; rather, they must be based upon definitive and binding legal analysis from the Department of Justice; that DoD must ensure that its treatment of detainees is fully lawful and authorized by the military chain of command; that the legal analysis and specific authorizations be fully documented, just as the interrogations themselves must be; and that comprehensive investigations must be conducted should a detainee pass away.' "

25 Interview with John Sifton on May 2, 2008.

26 This research was conducted by the author and researchers, and involved repeated inquiries to Human Rights Watch, Human Rights First, Physicians for Human Rights, New York University's Center for Human Rights and Global Justice and various think tanks during 2007–2009.

27 Neil A. Lewis, "Interrogators Cite Doctors' Aid at Guantanamo Prison Camp," *New York Times*, June 24, 2005; and Jamie Wilson, "Cheney's Resort Comment Rebuked," *Guardian*, June 25, 2005. The spider story is told in Michael Isikoff and Evan Thomas, "The Lawyer and the Caterpillar," *Newsweek*, April 27, 2009.

28 Katherine Eban, "Rorschach and Awe," *Vanity Fair*, July 17, 2007.

29 In 2009, researcher Alex DiBranco found 128 cases of detainee abuse at US bases in Afghanistan during 2002, and at least 23 cases of detainee abuse that occurred at Guantanamo before Secretary of Defense Donald Rumsfeld signed the "Counter-Resistance Techniques" memo on December 2, 2002. Most of these abuses occurred before SERE instructors trained Guantanamo interrogators in "harsh techniques."

30 Josh White, "Documents Tell of Brutal Improvisation by GIs," *Washington Post*, August 3, 2005.

31 Seymour Hersh, "The Gray Zone—How a Secret Pentagon Program Came to Abu Ghraib," *The New Yorker*, May 24, 2004: "The notion that Arabs are particularly vulnerable to sexual humiliation became a talking point among pro-war Washington conservatives in the months before the March 2003 invasion of Iraq. One book that was frequently cited was *The Arab Mind*, a study of Arab culture and psychology, first published in 1973, by Raphael Patai, a cultural anthropologist who taught at, among other universities, Columbia and Princeton, and who died in 1996. The book includes a twenty-five-page chapter on Arabs and sex, depicting sex as a taboo vested with shame and repression ... The Patai book, an academic

told me, was 'the bible of the neocons on Arab behavior.' In their discussions, he said, two themes emerged—'one, that Arabs only understand force and, two, that the biggest weakness of Arabs is shame and humiliation.' The government consultant said that there may have been a serious goal, in the beginning, behind the sexual humiliation and the posed photographs. It was thought that some prisoners would do anything—including spying on their associates—to avoid dissemination of the shameful photos to family and friends. The government consultant said, 'I was told that the purpose of the photographs was to create an army of informants, people you could insert back in the population.' The idea was that they would be motivated by fear of exposure, and gather information about pending insurgency action, the consultant said. If so, it wasn't effective; the insurgency continued to grow."

32 "The use of such [coercive] techniques appears motivated by a folk psychology that is demonstrably incorrect." Shane O'Mara, "Torturing the Brain: On the folk psychology and folk neurobiology motivating 'enhanced and coercive interrogation techniques," *Trends in Cognitive Science: Science and Society*, Trinity College Institute of Neuroscience, 2009.

33 For recent examples, see ibid. O'Mara explains, "Solid scientific evidence on how repeated and extreme stress and pain affect memory and executive functions (such as planning or forming intentions) suggests these techniques are unlikely to do anything other than the opposite of that intended by coercive or enhanced interrogation."

34 Lawrence Hinkle, Jr. "The Physiological State of the Interrogation Subject As It Affects Brain Function," in *The Manipulation of Human Behavior*, Albert Biderman and Herbert Zimmer, eds, New York: John Wiley and Sons, 1961, 20. See also "High Stress Hormone Levels Impair Memory," *Science-Daily*, http://www.sciencedaily.com/releases/1999/06/990617072302.htm, June 17, 1999.

35 Central Intelligence Agency, *Human Resources Exploitation Training Manual*, 1983, K10.

36 For greater detail on the way these ideas developed and the myriad actors involved in turning them into policy, see Philippe Sands, *Torture Team: Rumsfeld's Memo and the Betrayal of American Values*. According to Sands, "In September 2002 there were a series of brainstorming meetings, some which were led by [Army Lieutenant Colonel] Diane Beaver [the staff judge advocate at Guantánamo] … The aim of these sessions was to gather possible new interrogation techniques … Where were the ideas coming from? All over the place, [Beaver] said. Discussion was wide-ranging. Some ideas came from people's own training experiences: several people had been in SERE courses, but no one in the group was a SERE expert. Some colleagues then went off to Fort Bragg, SERE's home, including a Gitmo psychologist and psychiatrist. Others had experience in the Joint Personnel

Recovery Agency, which was charged with recovery of detained US personnel and oversaw SERE training for the services."

37 Joby Warrick and Dan Eggen, "Waterboarding Recounted," *Washington Post*, December 11, 2007; and Mark Thompson and Bobby Ghosh, "Did Waterboarding Prevent Terrorism Attacks?" *Time*, April 21, 2009.

38 See Peter Finn and Joby Warrick, "Detainee's Harsh Treatment Foiled No Plots: Waterboarding, Rough Interrogation of Abu Zubaida Produced False Leads, Officials Say," *Washington Post*, March 29, 2009, A01: "In the end, though, not a single significant plot was foiled as a result of Abu Zubaida's tortured confessions, according to former senior government officials who closely followed the interrogations. Nearly all of the leads attained through the harsh measures quickly evaporated, while most of the useful information from Abu Zubaida—chiefly names of al Qaeda members and associates—was obtained before waterboarding was introduced, they said. Moreover, within weeks of his capture, US officials had gained evidence that made clear they had misjudged Abu Zubaida. President George W. Bush had publicly described him as 'al Qaeda's chief of operations,' and other top officials called him a 'trusted associate' of al Qaeda leader Osama bin Laden and a major figure in the planning of the Sept. 11, 2001, terrorist attacks. None of that was accurate, the new evidence showed."

5. Rumors, Myths, and Ticking Bomb Stories

1 High-ranking officers lodged similar complaints about the fallibility of these tests—a year after Lagouranis was in Mosul. See Michael Moss, "Iraq's Legal System Staggers Beneath the Weight of War," *New York Times*, December 17, 2006. See also Nikki Prodromos, "Coalition Forces Convoy Hits IED, Captures Perpetrators," *NewsBlaze.com*, June 17, 2006. In 2005, "Maj. Gen. William H. Brandenburg, then the task force commander, became concerned about a swipe test that soldiers used on suspects to detect gunpowder. The test was so unreliable that cigarette lighter residue and even a common hand lotion would register as gunpowder."

2 Black Opels were identified in many instances where there were attacks and engagements with insurgents. See "Kidnapped American's interpreters found dead: reports," AFP, January 6, 2007; Yasser Salihee, "8 Officers Die in Suicide Bombing," Knight Ridder, November 30, 2004; "Inquiry into US leak on spying," *Sunday Telegraph*, January 1, 2006; "Inside The Firefight With Fort Drum Soldiers: Looking For Trouble, Meaning No Harm," *Post-Standard*, October 26, 2005.

3 Cell phones have, in fact, been used to trigger IEDs in Iraq, though it appears to be unclear how prevalent they've been compared to other devices. "Insurgents building IEDs first started out using a wide selection of consumer

electronics devices as wireless triggers, ranging from garage door openers to cordless phones. US and Coalition forces deployed multifrequency jammers to cover the frequencies used for the IED triggers, but the devices quickly ended up interfering with a broad range of gear, including convoy communications nets and even the links to unmanned aerial vehicles." From Doug Mohney, "Army's Jamming Strategy Blows Up," *Mobile Radio Technology*, March 1, 2008. See also "Iraqi Informants Lead US Soldiers to Weapons, IED Caches," *US Fed News*, July 19, 2007; and Rowan Scarborough, "Cell-phone technology an explosive tool for insurgents," *Washington Times*, March 7, 2005, A1.

4 For more incidents of US forces arresting Iraqis under similar suspicions, see Thomas E. Ricks, *Fiasco*, 279: " 'Few of the raids and detentions executed by Task Force Iron Gunner have resulted in the capture of any anti-coalition members or the seizure of illegal weapons,' [a member of a psychological operations team attached to the 4th Infantry Division] wrote. He placed the blame squarely with the artillery unit's commander, Col. Kevin Stramara. 'This team has witnessed the colonel initiate these events.' He charged that detention practices were capricious, sometimes based on the whim of the commander or because more than one hundred dollars in Iraqi dinars had been found in someone's possession."

5 See "Operations In Mosul, Iraq—Stryker Brigade Combat Team 1 3rd Brigade, 2nd Infantry," in "Army Stryker Brigade Initial Impressions Report on Operations in Mosul, Iraq," Center for Army Lessons Learned, December 21, 2004, 79: "The tribal, multi-ethnic and historical alliances and allegiances have made it difficult for HUMINT and SIGINT collection. Communications channels, linguistic dialects and slang terms and cultural customs and courtesies make collection even more challenging. These barriers also affect the analysis of intelligence."

6 Bob Drogin, "Most 'Arrested by Mistake': Coalition Intelligence Put Numbers at 70% to 90% of Iraq Prisoners, Says a February Red Cross Report, Which Details Further Abuses," *Los Angeles Times*, May 11, 2004.

7 Taken from a sworn statement of the sergeant assigned to the Detainee Assessment Board, May 18, 2004. See also Ricks, *Fiasco*, 280: "One of the sworn statements filed by a civilian employee of the Defense Department working at the brigade's jail—apparently as an interpreter, although he didn't say so—seemed to back up that conclusion. 'I think 80 percent of the people we bring in are "at the wrong place at the wrong time" [and] have no intelligence value,' he said."

8 According to "Army Stryker Brigade Initial Impressions Report," soldiers' lack of knowledge concerning cultural differences is one of the most conspicuous challenges of the US occupation in Iraq (see note 5 above). A DoD memorandum issued in 2007 raised the question of cultural knowledge and

experience among interrogators specifically, stating that "as the demand for HUMINT personnel has risen, the standards we use to select applicants to the HUMINT field have dropped, yielding a higher percentage of young and *inexperienced personnel.*" *See also* Oliver Burkeman, *"Al-Qaida Inmates* 'Outwitting Interrogators,' " *Guardian,* April 22, 2002; Julian Borger, "Interrogators 'Botched Hunt for WMDs,' " *Guardian,* April 27, 2005; and John Mintz, "Al Qaeda Interrogations Fall Short of the Mark," *Washington Post,* April 21, 2002.

9 According to Jameel Jaffer and Amrit Singh, Sanchez's directive "formally authoriz[ed] interrogators to use techniques beyond those listed in the [US Army] Field Manual. The directive, issued on September 14, 2003, was informed by the working group report that had been commissioned by Rumsfeld for Guantanamo, but purported to be 'modified for applicability to a theater of war in which the Geneva Conventions apply.' " Jaffer and Singh, *The Administration of Torture: A Documentary Record from Washington to Abu Ghraib and Beyond,* New York: Columbia University Press, 2007, 25. Rumsfeld's "Counter-Resistance Techniques" memo even informed other interrogators early in Afghanistan. See Senator Carl Levin, "Committee Inquiry into the Treatment of Detainees in US Custody, Executive Summary and Conclusions": "Shortly after Secretary Rumsfeld's December 2, 2002 approval of his General Counsel's recommendation to authorize aggressive interrogation techniques, the techniques—and the fact the Secretary had authorized them—became known to interrogators in Afghanistan," xxii.

10 Jaffer and Singh, *The Administration of Torture,* 26.

11 Based on an interview with the ACLU's Jameel Jaffer conducted on September 23, 2008.

12 R. Jeffrey Smith, "Documents Helped Sow Abuse, Army Report Finds—Top Officials Did Not Make Interrogation Policies Clear," *Washington Post,* August 30, 2004. The fact that at least three "confusing and inconsistent" interrogation directives were approved within a month-long period "contributed to the belief" that illegal interrogation techniques were condoned, the Army report stated. An absence of leadership and oversight also left room for what the Army report described as "word of mouth" techniques to be passed around and followed by interrogators deployed to Iraq.

13 For real-world examples where military anecdotes were exchanged during discussions about applying coercive interrogation techniques, see Senator Levin's report to the Senate Armed Services Committee on December 11, 2008, which shows how JPRA personnel involved with SERE training believed that "disruption of sleep and biorhythms ... may be very effective in inducing learned helplessness and breaking the [Afghan] detainees' willingness to resist," 27–28.

14 Philippe Sands, *Torture Team: Rumsfeld's Memo and the Betrayal of American Values*, 62.

15 http://www.rushlimbaugh.com/home/rush_photos_main/panel_ discussion___24__and_america_s_image_in_fighting_terrorism.guest.html.

16 *The 9/11 Commission Report*, 77.

17 Ibid., 80.

18 Ibid., 77.

19 'Scenes of Torture of Primetime Network TV, 1995–2005,' no longer available online.

20 David Bauder, "US Rights Group Says Torture Seen on Television Influences Interrogators in Iraq," Associated Press, February 12, 2007.

21 Deborah Sontag, "The Struggle for Iraq: Interrogations; How Colonel Risked His Career by Menacing Detainee and Lost," *New York Times*, May 27, 2004.

22 Ibid.

23 Ricks, *Fiasco*, 281.

24 Ibid.

25 Jean Lartéguy, *The Centurions*, trans. Xan Fielding, New York: Avon Books, 1961.

6. Crimes of Omission

1 Agent's Investigation Report, Department of the Army, United States Army Criminal Investigation Command, 3rd Military Police Group (CID) 78th Military Police Detachment (CD) (FWD) Baghdad, IZ, July 28, 2004, DOD-DOACID001248, July 28, 2004, 2, http://www.aclu.org/ torturefoia/released/1248_1288.pdf.

2 Other US units elsewhere in Iraq also broke detainees' bones. See Thomas E. Ricks, *Fiasco: The American Military Adventure in Iraq*, 278: "One day in the fall of 2003, a cook came by [at a PUC tent at Forward Operating Base Mercury], ordered a prisoner to hold a metal pole, and 'broke the [detainee's] leg with a mini Louisville Slugger that was a metal bat.' Broken bones from beatings occurred 'maybe every other week,' said the sergeant. 'I think the officers knew about it but didn't want to hear about it.' "

3 Ricks, *Fiasco*, 278. For similar maltreatment, see ibid., 271: " 'I saw the chief throw them down, put his knee in his neck and back, and grind them into the floor,' one witness stated. 'He would use a bullhorn and yell at them in Arabic and play heavy metal music extremely loud; they got so scared they would urinate on themselves. He was very aggressive and rough with detainees.' "

4 For a related example, see Justine Sharrock, "Am I a Torturer?" *Mother Jones*, March/April 2008: "[Prison guard] Ben [Allbright] made a verbal complaint to his platoon leader and later to his platoon leader's boss, asking for an investigation [into detainee abuse]. The officers seemed surprised. 'They said

they'd look into it and tell their superiors,' Ben recalls. 'But it didn't seem like a priority.' Nothing happened."

5 Richard Lardner, "Study: DoD IG Rarely Sides with Whistleblowers," Associated Press, October 31, 2008.

6 Horton's report continues: "He then asked if anyone had observed any incidents they wished to discuss with him. The result of such a process is entirely predictable. MG Fay worked hard to limit the number of accounts of abuse in order to sustain a preconceived theory that the abuse at Abu Ghraib was the result of a handful of 'rotten apples' rather than systematic instructions rendered through the chain of command. The soldiers with whom I spoke all felt that anyone providing evidence of abuse would be the target of certain retaliation in the form of (i) criminal charges; (ii) hazing and harassment; or (iii) potential exposure and 'friendly fire' death on the field of battle in Iraq. One specifically inquired about the possibility of securing political asylum in Germany, and I arranged for this soldier to obtain US and German legal counsel on that issue."

7 Sgt. Samuel J. Provance, Prepared Statement before the National Security Subcommittee of the House Committee on Government Reform, February 13, 2006, http://www.humanrightsfirst.info/pdf/06214-usls-provance-statment.pdf.

8 Richard A. Serrano, "Soldier 'Bewildered' Over Abuse," *Los Angeles Times*, August 7, 2004.

9 Linda Jeleniewski, "Reserve Soldier Wins JFK Library Profile in Courage Award," *US Army Reserve* Magazine, September 22, 2005; and Joe Darby (as told to Wil S. Hylton), "Prisoner of Conscience," *GQ Magazine*, September 2006.

10 Letter to Senator John McCain, published in the *Washington Post*, September 28, 2005.

11 Thomas Ricks reinforces this point in *Fiasco*, 272: "It wasn't that soldiers were ordered to be cruel, it is that acts of cruelty were tolerated in some units, to the point that one officer in the 82nd Airborne, Capt. Ian Fishback, would later charge it was systemic."

12 Letter to McCain, *Washington Post*.

13 Eric Schmitt, "Officer Criticizes Detainee Abuse Inquiry," *New York Times*, September 28, 2009.

14 John Conroy, "Confessions of a Torturer—An Army Interrogator's Story," *Chicago Reader*, March 1, 2007.

15 "UN Report to urge end to torture by US," *New York Times*, May 19, 2006.

16 There were other cases of misconduct and abuse that weren't fully completed because military investigators couldn't locate witnesses. See Ricks, *Fiasco*, 275–6: "[T]he Army itself would conclude that some other 3rd ACR [Armored Cavalry Regiment] soldiers had indeed acted like

criminals. Nine soldiers from a howitzer platoon in the 3rd ACR's 2nd squadron, who were assigned to checkpoint duty in western Iraq, allegedly stole thousands of dollars from Iraqis, but they weren't prosecuted because investigators couldn't locate the alleged victims, according to an internal Army document obtained by the ACLU."

17 Based on an interview with CID's Chief of Public Affairs Christopher Grey conducted on May 9, 2006. CID did not respond to requests for comment regarding Susan Burke's attempts to provide military investigators access to her clients for their investigations into detainee abuse.

18 Jameel Jaffer and Amrit Singh, *Administration of Torture: A Documentary Record from Washington to Abu Ghraib and Beyond*, 37: "The failure of investigators to seriously investigate abuses seems to have been a particularly common problem with respect to abuses alleged to have been perpetrated by special forces."

19 "Official response to abuse allegations," *Hardball with Chris Matthews*, http:// www.msnbc.com, January 17, 2006.

7. Silent Suffering

1 Frantz Fanon, *The Wretched of the Earth*, trans. Constance Farrington, New York: Grove Press, 1968, 269; Martha Huggins, Mika Haritos-Fatouros, and Philip Zimbardo, *Violence Workers*, Berkeley, CA: University of California Press, 2002.

2 Richard A. Kulka et al., *Trauma and the Vietnam War Generation: Report of Findings from the National Vietnam Veterans Readjustment Study*, New York: Brunner/Mazel, 1990; and based on an interview with Kulka. The authors of the NVVRS took ninety-seven war experiences and clustered them into five categories: Exposure to Combat; Exposure to Abusive Violence and Related Conflicts; Deprivation (general discomfort during war); Loss of Meaning and Control; and Prisoner of War. Exposure to Abusive Violence and Related Conflicts included this criteria (for men): "degree of involvement in torturing, wounding or killing hostages or POWs; involvement in mutilation of bodies of enemy or civilians; witnessed or involved in situation where women, children, or old people were injured or killed by Americans or South Vietnamese soldiers."

3 See Richard McNally, *Remembering Trauma*, Cambridge, MA: Belknap Press, 2003.

4 See Jane Mayer, *The Dark Side: The Inside Story of How the War on Terror Turned Into a War on American Ideals*, New York: Doubleday, 2008, 151: "On August 1, 2002, in an infamous memo written largely by [former deputy assistant attorney general in the Office of Legal Counsel, John] Yoo but signed by Assistant Attorney General Jay S. Bybee, the OLC re-defined

the crime of torture to make it all but impossible to commit. They argued that torture required the intent to inflict suffering 'equivalent in intensity to the pain accompanying serious physical injury such as organ failure, impairment of bodily function, or even death.' Mental suffering, they wrote, had to 'result in significant duration, e.g., last for months or years.' "

5   Matthew McAllester, "Recovering from Saddam; Iraqis Find Salve in Their Faith," *Newsday*, July 4, 2004, A3.

6   Physicians for Human Rights, *Broken Laws, Broken Lives: Medical Evidence of Torture by US Personnel and Its Impact,* 2008

7   Unlike Qaissi, Marouji said he received an electric shock when a US soldier dropped a live wire into a puddle of water.

8   Scott Wilson, "Iraqi Refugees Overwhelm Syria; Migrants Who Fled Violence Put Stress on Housing Market, Schools," *Washington Post*, February 2, 2005. UNHRC statistics confirm 700,000 Iraqi refugees residing in Syria by 2006, see "Iraq: Displacements Upset Religious, Ethnic Communities," Radio Free Europe, March 1, 2007.

9   Ian Black, " 'Chemical Ali' on Trial for Brutal Crushing of Shia Uprising," *Guardian*, August 22, 2007. According to a Human Rights Watch report, "The number of arrests, like that of casualties, will undoubtedly remain forever unknown, and Karbala will remain one of the blackest pages in the annals of the repression of Iraq's Shi'a." See "Endless Torment—The 1991 Uprising in Iraq and Its Aftermath," Human Rights Watch, June 1992.

10 Rebecca Leung, "Operation Iraqi Freedom—Kroft Finds a Baathist Police Chief in Karbala Whose Residents Saddam Persecuted," CBS News December 4, 2003.

11 According to polling data, Americans disapprove of techniques that involve sexual humiliation and forced nakedness. While there is no data on this question in Middle Eastern societies, one can expect that the American level of disapproval is comparatively lower (i.e., we expect Middle Eastern attitudes on such techniques to be equal or greater than American disapproval) because of the long-standing social taboos against sexual humiliation and forced nakedness in Middle Eastern societies, taboos that such techniques exploited. See also Darius Rejali and Paul Gronke, "US Public Opinion on Torture, 2001–2009," Reed College, PS Symposium, May 2, 2009, http:// people. reed.edu/~gronkep/TortureWhitePaperV2.pdf.

12 George Packer, "Betrayed—The Iraqis Who Trusted the Americans the Most," *The New Yorker*, March 26, 2007.

13 Ibid. See also Katherine Zoepf, "Iraqi Ex-Employees of US Face Death Threats or Exile," *New York Times*, June 5, 2005.

14 According to the following polling data from "Public Opinion in Iraq— First Poll Following Abu Ghraib Revelations," Independent Institute for Administration and Civil Society Studies, June 16, 2004: "You said you were surprised by the abuses at Abu Ghraib; why?—It humiliates Iraqis:

48+ percent. You said you were NOT surprised by the abuses at Abu Ghraib; why?—I expect the worst from Americans: 64+ percent. Do you believe that the abuse of prisoners at Abu Ghraib represents fewer than 100 people or that all Americans behave this way?—All Americans are like this: 54 percent."

15 Darius Rejali, *Torture and Democracy*, Princeton: Princeton University Press, 2007, 459: "Nothing illustrates the power of public cooperation more clearly than the way the British police caught five men alleged to have planted bombs on London buses and trains on July 21, 2005. Police captured the 21 July bombers using accurate public information, and they did this within ten days." According to Rejali, the Gestapo, as well as the French paramilitary in Algeria, got most of their breaks from informers and public cooperation, see 460, 482–5, 493–4, and 515. See also David Bayley, *Forces of Order*, Berkeley: University of California Press, 1976, 10: "unless the public specifically identifies suspects to the police, the chances that a crime will be solved falls to about 10 percent." In Rod Morgan and Tim Newburn, *The Future of Policing*, Oxford: Clarendon Press, 1997, 117–18, the authors make the claim that about 5 percent of crimes in England are solved by surveillance, fingerprinting, DNA sampling, forensic tests, house-to-house inquiries, and offender profiling. For more information on the extent to which police rely on public cooperation for crime detection and resolution, see Peter W. Greenwood and Joan Petersilia, "The Criminal Investigation Process: Volume I: Summary and Policy Recommendations," in David Bayley, ed., *What Works in Policing*, New York: Oxford University Press, 1998, 75–107.

16 For further information about how abuse can undermine public cooperation, see Martha Finnemore and Kathryn Sikkink, "International Norm Dynamics and Political Change," *International Organization*, Vol. 52, No. 4, Autumn 1998; Kalevi J. Holsti, "Political Causes of Humanitarian Emergencies," *War, Hunger and Displacement: The Origins of Humanitarian Emergencies*, Wayne Nafziger, Frances Stewart and Raimo Vayrynen, eds, Oxford: Oxford University Press, 2000, 239–81; Andreas Wimmer, "Who Owns the State? Understanding Ethnic Conflict in Post-Colonial Societies," *Nations and Nationalism*, Vol. 3, 1997; Stathis Kalyvas, "The Paradox of Terrorism in Civil War," *The Journal of Ethics*, Vol. 8, No. 1, 2004, 97–138.

17 Martin Weil and Michael Alison Chandler, "Virginian Taken Hostage in Iraq Is Found Dead," *Washington Post*, March 11, 2006, A1.

18 "Military Operation Frees 2 Canadian Hostages in Iraq," CBC News, March 23, 2006.

19 Emad Mekay, "Abu Ghraib Tactics Inspire Torture in Neighbor Egypt," Inter Press Service, June 22, 2004.

20 Amany Radwan, "Fighting for Their Rights," *Time Europe*, October 11, 2004.

21 Tom Nicholson, "Police Filmed Abusing Roma Children—Nine Officers Face Criminal Charges After Forcing Teens to Strip and Slap Each Other," *The Slovak Spectator*, April 13, 2009.

22 Ibid. According to the report, "In one shot, six young Roma boys standing in a tiny room begin pulling their clothes off. A voice from above shouts at them to be quick, that the last to disrobe will be punished. One thin boy hesitates to pull off his white underwear. 'Take it all off!' a voice shouts. 'Hands behind your heads!' The camera that is filming this humiliating scene closes in on the boys' genitals and then pans out to capture one of them looking up at his tormentors."

23 Sandra Laville, "Met Officers Accused of Waterboarding Suspects," *Guardian*, June 10, 2009.

24 See Rejali, *Torture and Democracy*, 312, "The Brazilians even invented an electrotorture dubbed 'the Vietnam'"; and 536, "Attaching electric wires to force the victim to keep his balance was known only in Brazil ('the Vietnam')."

8. Confronting Torture's Legacy

1 Abdul Waheed Wafa, "Cheney Unhurt After Bombing in Afghanistan," *New York Times*, February 27, 2007.

2 Raymond F. Toliver, *The Interrogator: The Story of Hanns Joachim Scharff, Master Interrogator of the Luftwaffe*, Atglen, PA: Schiffer Books, 1997, 71–2.

3 Philippe Sands, *Torture Team: Rumsfeld's Memo and the Betrayal of American Values*, 108.

4 Ibid.

5 David Rose, *Guantanamo: The War on Human Rights*, New York: New Press, 2004, 81.

6 Jason Vest, "Haunted by Abu Ghraib," *Government Executive*, http:// www.govexec.com, April 1, 2006.

7 Asha Rangappa, "Torture Makes the FBI's Job Harder—Goodwill Toward the United States Is an Agent's Best Tool, at Home and Abroad," *Slate.com*, posted September 2, 2009: "Policies like the use of torture make it more difficult for the FBI to develop relationships based on trust. Even when torture is used on a few people and in another country, and by a different agency, it casts doubts on the US government's overall willingness to act in good faith. Targets often project the skepticism about the United States that torture fosters onto individual FBI agents, who are often the only face of the government they see." See also Patrick Cockburn, "Torture? It Probably Killed More Americans than 9/11," *Independent*, April 26, 2009: "The use of torture by the US has proved so counter-productive that it may have led to the death of as many US soldiers as civilians killed in 9/11, says the leader of a crack US

interrogation team in Iraq. 'The reason why foreign fighters joined al-Qa'ida in Iraq was overwhelmingly because of abuses at Guantánamo and Abu Ghraib and not Islamic ideology,' says Major Matthew Alexander, who personally conducted 300 interrogations of prisoners in Iraq. 'In the case of foreign fighters—recruited mostly from Saudi Arabia, Egypt, Syria, Yemen and North Africa—the reason cited by the great majority for going to Iraq was what they had heard of the torture in Guantánamo and Abu Ghraib.' "

9. Homecoming

1 www.pittsburghlive.com/x/pittsburghtrib/obituaries/?mode=view&obit _id=170037

Index

Fictional characters alphabetized by first name when full name used.